ROUTLEDGE
PHILOSOPHY OF MIND

Volume 4

BRAIN AND MIND

BRAIN AND MIND

Modern Concepts of the Nature of Mind

Edited by
J. R. SMYTHIES

Routledge
Taylor & Francis Group

LONDON AND NEW YORK

First published in 1965

This edition first published in 2015
by Routledge
2 Park Square, Milton Park, Abingdon, Oxon, OX14 4RN

and by Routledge
711 Third Avenue, New York, NY 10017

Routledge is an imprint of the Taylor & Francis Group, an informa business

British Library Cataloguing in Publication Data
A catalogue record for this book is available from the British Library

ISBN: 978-1-138-82464-5 (Set)
eISBN: 978-1-315-74048-5 (Set)
ISBN: 978-1-138-82494-2 (Volume 4)
eISBN: 978-1-315-74027-0 (Volume 4)
Pb ISBN: 978-1-138-82514-7 (Volume 4)

Publisher's Note
The publisher has gone to great lengths to ensure the quality of this book but points out that some imperfections from the original may be apparent.

Disclaimer
The publisher has made every effort to trace copyright holders and would welcome correspondence from those they have been unable to trace.

BRAIN AND MIND

Modern Concepts
of the Nature of Mind

by

Hartwig Kuhlenbeck   Anthony Quinton

D. M. MacKay   J. R. Smythies

Antony Flew   C. J. Ducasse

Lord Brain   H. H. Price

J. Beloff

Edited by

J. R. Smythies

LONDON

ROUTLEDGE & KEGAN PAUL

NEW YORK : THE HUMANITIES PRESS

First published 1965
by Routledge & Kegan Paul Ltd
Broadway House, 68–74 Carter Lane
London, E.C.4

Printed in Great Britain
by Richard Clay (The Chaucer Press), Ltd
Bungay, Suffolk

CONTENTS

v

PREFACE

THE problem of the nature of the mind and its relationship to the brain is one that naturally concerns a number of different disciplines—philosophy, psychology, psychiatry, neurology and neurobiology. This book presents some modern views on this subject and the contributors, drawn from these various disciplines, consist of four philosophers, one neuroanatomist, one neurologist, one psychiatrist, one psychologist and a cybernetician. The central thesis to all these essays is the nature of mind. The contributors are divided not only on a basis of discipline, but also on their philosophical outlook. We have Professor Price putting the case for the new theory of non-Cartesian dualism. This is developed and supported by myself, and closely similar accounts are put forward by Professor Kuhlenbeck and Dr. Beloff. The currently orthodox monistic account is expounded by Professor Flew, Lord Brain, and with variations by Professor MacKay. Professor Ducasse and Anthony Quinton sit on the side lines, as it were, with regard to both sides of this debate.

The development of our thought on this problem has seen over the years the waxing and waning of several approaches, 'solutions', attitudes, theories and counterclaims. The vast complex of western thought has flowed tumultuously forward throughout the centuries. At times it favours one main channel, at other times another. Swirls and eddies of intense argument, interest and conflict form, develop, and die away. The theory of mind–brain relationship is surely vital to human interest and touches on questions of deep religious significance. The traditional theory for centuries was derived from Christian doctrine and was stated in terms consonant with seventeenth century thought by Descartes. It is a dualist theory. In the last hundred years the monistic theory has gradually gained the ascendant. This is based on the decay of the authority of religion and the fact that the basic working plan of a materialistic science has passed into common usage and forms the 'commonsense' of most educated people today. The advances of a behavioural psychology, of our increasing knowledge of brain function in health and disease, the linguistic strategies in philosophy have all led to a situation where few philosophers, psychologists or scientists today would regard themselves as dualists in any sense. However, as is often the case in philosophy, there are signs of a swing of the pendulum. In July 1952 Professor Price delivered a lecture to the Society for Psychical Research entitled 'Survival and the idea of "another world" '. In this he put forward the first clear formulation of the theory of non-Cartesian dualism. As is often the case of radical new ideas a similar theory had been put forward many years before by C. D. Broad, and at much the same time by H. D. Lewis and myself. We are reprinting parts of this original paper by Professor Price by kind permission of the Society for Psychical Research. The theory has a wide impact on philosophy, psychology, religion, and cosmology and should stir up some lively interest and debate.

The limits of what the mind–brain problem really consists of are continually being narrowed by the rigorous disciplines of cybernetics and neurology, and Professor MacKay and Lord Brain present here an account of some of these limits of discourse. Advances of computor theory and design have rendered empty all attempts to distinguish between men (with 'minds') and ('mindless') machines on a basis of any intellectual or specifiable 'mind-like' operation. Likewise the role of the brain in the control of thinking, emotion, sensation and behaviour is daily becoming more clearly understood. Advocates of dualism have to take cognisance of these points. However, it will be clear that the new 'dualism-monism' antithesis presented here rests on a quite different basis from the old one and that no preconceptions should be carried over from the one to the other. The situation is now certainly more interesting. The match is no longer a walk-over for the 'monistic' side. The concept of the mind as an entity in its own right—even if it is not at all like Descartes' original idea of the matter—is making a vigorous come-back. A debate between two more or less equal opponents is always more interesting than a rout. For, in intellectual affrays, the latter tends to leave the victor, lacking a vigorous opposition party, prey to degeneration into shadow boxing with imaginary opponents. If all philosophers agreed with each other, that would surely be the end of philosophy.

We are grateful to the Editor of the *Proceedings of the Society for Psychical Research* for permission to reprint Professor Price's article, and to the Editors of the *Proceedings of the Aristotelian Society* and the transactions of the Victoria Institute for permission to republish material in Professor MacKay's article.

J. R. SMYTHIES

SURVIVAL AND THE IDEA
OF 'ANOTHER WORLD'
H. H. Price

IN this essay I am only concerned with the conception of Survival; with the *meaning* of the Survival Hypothesis, and not with its truth or falsity, nor with any evaluation of the alleged evidence for survival. When we consider the Survival Hypothesis, whether we believe it or disbelieve it, what is it that we have in mind? Can we form any idea, even a rough and provisional one, of what a disembodied human life might be like? Supposing we cannot, it will follow that what is called the Survival Hypothesis is a mere set of words and not a hypothesis at all. The evidence adduced in favour of it might still be evidence for something, and perhaps for something important, but we should no longer have the right to claim that it is evidence for Survival. There cannot be evidence for something which is completely unintelligible to us.

Now let us consider the situation in which we find ourselves after seventy years of psychical research. A very great deal of work has been done on the problem of Survival, and much of the best work by members of the Society for Psychical Research. Yet there are the widest differences of opinion about the results. A number of intelligent persons would maintain that we now have a very large mass of evidence in favour of Survival; that some of it is of very good quality indeed, and cannot be explained away unless we suppose that the supernormal cognitive powers of some embodied human minds are vastly more extensive and more accurate than we can easily believe them to be; in short, that on the evidence available the Survival Hypothesis is more probable than not. Some people —and not all of them are silly or credulous—

would even maintain that the Survival Hypothesis is proved, or as near to being so as any empirical hypothesis can be. On the other hand, there are also many intelligent persons who entirely reject these conclusions. Some of them, no doubt, have not taken the trouble to examine the evidence. But others of them have; they may even have given years of study to it. They would agree that the evidence is evidence of *something*, and very likely of something important. But, they would say, it cannot be evidence of Survival; there *must* be some alternative explanation of it, however difficult it may be to find one. Why do they take this line? I think it is because they find the very conception of Survival unintelligible. The very idea of a 'discarnate human personality' seems to them a muddled or absurd one; indeed not an idea at all, but just a phrase—an emotionally exciting one, no doubt—to which no clear meaning can be given.

Moreover, we cannot just ignore the people who have not examined the evidence. Some of our most intelligent and most highly educated contemporaries are among them. These men are well aware, by this time, that the evidence does exist, even if their predecessors fifty years ago were not. If you asked them why they do not trouble to examine it in detail, they would be able to offer reasons for their attitude. And one of their reasons, and not the least weighty in their eyes, is the contention I mentioned just now, that the very idea of Survival is a muddled or absurd one. To borrow an example from Whately Carington, we know pretty well what we mean by asking whether Jones has survived a shipwreck. We are asking whether he continues to live after the shipwreck has occurred. Similarly it makes sense to ask whether he survived a railway accident, or the bombing of London. But if we substitute 'his own death' for 'a shipwreck', and ask whether he has survived it, our question (it will be urged) becomes unintelligible. Indeed, it *looks* self-contradictory, as if we were asking whether Jones is still alive at a time when he is no longer alive—whether Jones is both alive and not alive at the same time. We may try to escape from this logical absurdity by using phrases like 'discarnate existence', 'alive, but disembodied'. But such phrases, it will be said, have no clear meaning. No amount of facts, however well established, can have the slightest tendency to support a meaningless hypothesis, or to answer an unintelligible question. It would therefore be a waste of time to examine such facts in detail. There are other and more important things to do.

If I am right so far, questions about the meaning of the word 'survival' or of the phrase 'life after death' are not quite so arid and academic as they may appear. Anyone who wants to maintain that there is empirical evidence for Survival ought to consider these questions, whether he thinks the evidence strong or weak. Indeed, anyone who thinks there is a *problem* of Survival at all should ask himself what his conception of Survival is.

Now why should it be thought that the very idea of life after death is unintelligible? Surely it is easy enough to conceive (whether or not it is true) that experiences might occur after Jones's death which are linked with experiences which he had before his death, in such a way that his personal identity is preserved? But, it will be said, the idea of after-death *experiences* is just the difficulty. What kind of experiences could they conceivably be? In a disembodied state, the supply of sensory stimuli is perforce cut off, because the supposed experient has no sense organs and no nervous system. There can therefore be no sense-perception. One has no means of being aware of material objects any longer; and if one has not, it is hard to see how one could have any emotions or wishes either. For all the emotions and wishes we have in this present life are concerned directly or indirectly with material objects, including of course our own organisms and other organisms, especially other human ones. In short, one could only be said to have experiences at all, if one is aware of some sort of a *world*. In this way, the idea of Survival is bound up with the idea of 'another world' or a 'next world'. Anyone who maintains that the idea of Survival is after all intelligible must also be claiming that we can form some conception, however rough and provisional, of what 'the next world' or 'the other world' might be like. The sceptics I have in mind would say that we can form no such conception at all; and this, I think, is one of the main reasons why they hold that the conception of Survival itself is unintelligible. I wish to suggest, on the contrary, that we *can* form some conception, in outline at any rate, of what a 'next world' or 'another world' might be like, and consequently of the kind of experiences which disembodied minds, if indeed there are such, might be supposed to have.

3

The thoughts which I wish to put before you on this subject are not at all original. Something very like them is to be found in the chapter on Survival in Whately Carington's book *Telepathy*, and in the concluding chapter of Professor C. J. Ducasse's book *Nature, Mind and Death*.[1] Moreover, if I am not mistaken, the Hindu conception of *Kama Loka* (literally 'the world of desire') is essentially the same as the one which I wish to discuss; and something very similar is to be found in Mahayana Buddhism. In these two religions, of course, there is not just one 'other world' but several different 'other worlds', which we are supposed to experience in succession; not merely the Next World, but the next but one, and another after that. But I think it will be quite enough for us to consider just the Next World, without troubling ourselves about any additional Other Worlds which there might be. It is a sufficiently difficult task, for us Western people, to convince ourselves that it makes sense to speak of any sort of after-death world at all. Accordingly, with your permission, I shall use the expressions 'next world' and 'other world' interchangeably. If anyone thinks this an over-simplification, it will be easy for him to make the necessary corrections.

The Next World, I think, might be conceived as a kind of dream-world. When we are asleep, sensory stimuli are cut off, or at any rate are prevented from having their normal effects upon our brain-centres. But we still manage to have experiences. It is true that sense-perception no longer occurs, but something sufficiently like it does. In sleep, our image-producing powers, which are more or less inhibited in waking life by a continuous bombardment of sensory stimuli, are released from this inhibition. And then we are provided with a multitude of objects of awareness, about which we employ our thoughts and towards which we have desires and emotions. Those objects which we are aware of behave in a way which seems very queer to us when we wake up. The laws of their behaviour are not the laws of physics. But however queer their behaviour is, it does not at all disconcert us at the time, and our personal identity is not broken.

In other words, my suggestion is that the Next World, if there is one, might be a world of mental images. Nor need such a world be so 'thin and unsubstantial' as you might think. Paradoxical

[1] C. J. Ducasse, *Nature, Mind and Death* (La Salle, Illinois, Open Court Publishing Co., 1951).

as it may sound, there is nothing imaginary about a mental image. It is an actual entity, as real as anything can be. The seeming paradox arises from the ambiguity of the verb 'to imagine'. It does sometimes mean 'to have mental images'. But more usually it means 'to entertain propositions without believing them'; and very often they are false propositions, and moreover we *dis*believe them in the act of entertaining them. This is what happens, for example, when we read Shakespeare's play *The Tempest*, and that is why we say that Prospero and Ariel are 'imaginary characters'. Mental images are not in this sense imaginary at all. We do actually experience them, and they are no more imaginary than sensations. To avoid the paradox, though at the cost of some pedantry, it would be well to distinguish between *imagining* and *imaging*, and to have two different adjectives 'imaginary' and 'imagy'. In this terminology, it is imaging, and not imagining, that I wish to talk about; and the Next World, as I am trying to conceive of it, is an *imagy* world, but not on that account an imaginary one.

Indeed, to those who experienced it an image-world would be just as 'real' as this present world is; and perhaps so like it that they would have considerable difficulty in realizing that they were dead. We are, of course, sometimes told in mediumistic communications that quite a lot of people do find it difficult to realize that they are dead; and this is just what we should expect if the Next World is an image-world. Lord Russell and other philosophers have maintained that a material object in this present physical world is nothing more nor less than a complicated system of *appearances*. So far as I can see, there might be a set of visual images related to each other perspectively, with front views and side views and back views all fitting neatly together in the way that ordinary visual appearances do now. Such a group of images might contain tactual images too. Similarly it might contain auditory images and smell images. Such a family of inter-related images would make a pretty good object. It would be quite a satisfactory substitute for the material objects which we perceive in this present life. And a whole world composed of such families of mental images would make a perfectly good world.

Let us now put our question in another way, and ask what kind of experience a disembodied human mind might be supposed to have. We can then answer that it might be an experience in which *imaging* replaces sense-perception; 'replaces' it, in the sense that imaging would perform much the same function as sense-perception performs now, by providing us with objects about which we could have thoughts, emotions and wishes. There is no reason why we should not be 'as much alive', or at any rate *feel* as much alive, in an image-world as we do now in this present material world, which we perceive by means of our sense-organs and nervous systems. And so the use of the word 'survival' ('life after death') would be perfectly justifiable.

It will be objected, perhaps, that one cannot be said to be alive unless one has a body. But what is meant here by 'alive'? It is surely conceivable (whether or not it is true) that *experiences* should occur which are not causally connected with a physical organism. If they did, should we or should we not say that 'life' was occurring? I do not think it matters much whether we answer Yes or No. It is purely a question of definition. If you define 'life' in terms of certain very complicated physico-chemical processes, as some people would, then of course life after death is by definition impossible, because there is no longer anything to be alive. In that case, the problem of survival (*life* after bodily death) is misnamed. Instead, it ought to be called the problem of after-death *experiences*. And this is in fact the problem with which all investigators of the subject have been concerned. After all, what people want to know, when they ask whether we survive death, is simply whether experiences occur after death, or what likelihood, if any, there is that they do; and whether such experiences, if they do occur, are linked with each other and with *ante mortem* ones in such a way that personal identity is preserved. It is not physico-chemical processes which interest us, when we ask such questions. But there is another sense of the words 'life' and 'alive' which may be called the psychological sense; and in this sense 'being alive' just *means* 'having experiences of certain sorts'. In this psychological sense of the word 'life', it is perfectly intelligible to ask whether there is life after death, even though life in the physiological sense does *ex hypothesi* come to an end when someone dies. Or, if you like, the question is whether one could *feel* alive after bodily death, even though (by hypothesis) one would not *be* alive at that time. It will be quite enough to satisfy most of us if the *feeling* of being alive continues after death. It will not make a halfpennyworth of difference that one will not then *be* alive in the physiological or biochemical sense of the word.

6

It may be said, however, that 'feeling alive' (life in the psychological sense) cannot just be equated with having experiences in general. Feeling alive, surely, consists in having experiences of a special sort, namely *organic sensations*—bodily feelings of various sorts. In our present experience, these bodily feelings are not as a rule separately attended to unless they are unusually intense or unusually painful. They are a kind of undifferentiated mass in the background of consciousness. All the same, it would be said, they constitute our feeling of being alive; and if they were absent (as surely they must be when the body is dead) the feeling of being alive could not be there.

I am not at all sure that this argument is as strong as it looks. I think we should still feel alive—or alive enough—provided we experienced emotions and wishes, even if no organic sensations accompanied these experiences, as they do now. But in case I am wrong here, I would suggest that *images* of organic sensations could perfectly well provide what it needed. We can quite well image to ourselves what it feels like to be in a warm bath, even when we are not actually in one; and a person who has been crippled can image what it felt like to climb a mountain. Moreover, I would ask whether we do not feel alive when we are dreaming. It seems to me that we obviously do—or at any rate quite alive enough to go on with.

This is not all. In an image-world, a dream-like world such as I am trying to describe, there is no reason at all why there should not be *visual* images resembling the body which one had in this present world. In this present life (for all who are not blind) visual percepts of one's own body form as it were the constant centre of one's perceptual world. It is perfectly possible that visual images of one's own body might perform the same function in the next. They might form the continuing centre or nucleus of one's image world, remaining more or less constant while other images altered. If this were so, we should have an additional reason for expecting that recently dead people would find it difficult to realize that they were dead, that is, disembodied. To all appearances they *would* have bodies just as they had before, and pretty much the same ones. But, of course, they might discover in time that these image-bodies were subject to rather peculiar causal laws. For example, it might be found that in an image-world our wishes tend *ipso facto* to fulfil themselves in a way they do not now. A wish to go to Oxford might be immediately followed by the occurrence of a vivid and detailed set of Oxford-like images; even though, at the moment before, one's images had resembled Piccadilly Circus or the palace of the Dalai Lama in Tibet. In that case, one would realize that 'going somewhere'—transferring one's body from one place to another—was a rather different process from what it had been in the physical world. Reflecting on such experiences, one might come to the conclusion that one's body was not after all the same as the physical body one had before death. One might conclude perhaps that it must be a 'spiritual' or 'psychical' body, closely resembling the old body in appearance, but possessed of rather different causal properties. It has been said, of course, that phrases like 'spiritual body' or 'psychical body' are utterly unintelligible, and that no conceivable empirical meaning could be given to such expressions. But I would suggest that they might be a way (rather a misleading way perhaps) of referring to a set of body-like images. If our supposed dead empiricist continued his investigations, he might discover that his whole world—not only his own body, but everything else he was aware of—had different causal properties from the physical world, even though everything in it had shape, size, colour and other qualities which material objects have now. And so eventually, by the exercise of ordinary inductive good sense, he could draw the conclusion that he was in 'the next world' or 'the other world' and no longer in this one. If, however, he were a very dogmatic philosopher, who distrusted inductive good sense and preferred *a priori* reasoning, I do not know what condition he would be in. Probably he would never discover that he was dead at all. Being persuaded, on *a priori* grounds, that life after death was impossible, he might insist on thinking that he must still be in this world, and refuse to pay any attention to the new and strange causal laws which more empirical thinkers would notice.

I think, then, that there is no difficulty in conceiving that the experience of feeling alive could occur in the absence of a physical organism; or, if you prefer to put it so, a disembodied personality could *be* alive in the psychological sense, even though by definition it would not be alive in the physiological or biochemical sense.

Moreover, I do not see why disembodiment need involve the destruction of personal identity. It is, of course, sometimes supposed that personal identity depends on the continuance of a back-ground of organic sensation—the 'mass of bodily feeling' mentioned before. (This may be called the Somato-centric Analysis of personal identity.) We must notice, however, that this background of organic sensation is not literally the same from one period of time to another. The very most that can happen is that the organic sensations which form the background of my experience now should be *exactly similar* to those which were the background of my experience a minute ago, and as a matter of fact the present ones need not *all* be exactly similar to the previous ones. I might have a twinge of toothache now which I did not have then. I may even have an overall feeling of lassitude now which I did not have a minute ago, so that the whole mass of bodily feeling, and not merely one part of it, is rather different; and this would not interrupt my personal identity at all. The most that is required is only that the majority (not all) of my organic sensations should be closely (not exactly) similar to those I previously had. And even this is only needed if the two occasions are close together in my private time series; the organic sensations I have now might well be very unlike those I used to have when I was one year old. I say 'in my private time series'. For when I wake up after eight hours of dreamless sleep my personal identity is not broken, though in the physical or public time series there has been a long interval between the last organic sensations I experienced before falling asleep, and the first ones I experience when I wake up. But if similarity, and not literal sameness, is all that is required of this 'continuing organic background', it seems to me that the continuity of it could be perfectly well preserved if there were organic *images* after death very like the organic *sensations* which occurred before death.

As a matter of fact, this whole 'somato-centric' analysis of personal identity appears to me highly disputable. I should have thought that Locke was much nearer the truth when he said that personal identity depends on memory. But I have tried to show that even if the 'somato-centric' theory of personal identity is right, there is no reason why personal identity need be broken by bodily death, provided there are images after death which sufficiently resemble the organic sensations one had before; and this is very like what happens when one falls asleep and begins dreaming.

There is, however, another argument against the conceivability of a disembodied person, to which some present-day Linguistic Philosophers would attach great weight. It is neatly expressed by Professor Flew when he says, 'People are what you meet.'[2] By 'a person' we are supposed to mean a human organism which behaves in certain ways, and especially one which speaks and can be spoken to. And when we say, 'This is the same person whom I saw yesterday', we are supposed to mean just that it is the same human organism which I saw yesterday, and also that it behaves in a recognizably similar way.

'People are what you meet.' With all due respect to Flew, I would suggest that he does not in this sense 'meet' *himself*. He might indeed have had one of those curious out-of-body experiences which are occasionally mentioned in our records, and he might have seen his own body from outside (if he has, I heartily congratulate him); but I do not think we should call this 'meeting'. And surely the important question is, what constitutes my personal identity *for myself*. It certainly does not consist in the fact that other people can 'meet' me. It might be that I was for myself the same person as before, even at a time when it was quite impossible for others to meet me. No one can 'meet' me when I am dreaming. They can, of course, come and look at my body lying in bed; but this is not 'meeting', because no sort of social relations are then possible between them and me. Yet, although temporarily 'unmeetable', during my dreams I am still, for myself, the same person that I was. And if I went on dreaming *in perpetuum*, and could never be 'met' again, this need not prevent me from continuing to be, for myself, the same person.

As a matter of fact, however, we can quite easily conceive that 'meeting' of a kind might still be possible between discarnate experients. And therefore, even if we do make it part of the definition of a 'a person', that he is capable of being met by others, it will still make sense to speak of 'discarnate persons', provided we allow that telepathy is possible between them. It is true that

---

[2] *University*, Vol. II, no. 2, p. 38; in a symposium on 'Death' with Professor D. M. Mackinnon. Mr. Flew obviously uses 'people' as the plural of 'person'; but if we are to be linguistic, I am inclined to think that the *nuances* of 'people' are not quite the same as those of 'person'. When we use the word 'person', in the singular or the plural, the notion of consciousness is more prominently before our minds than it is when we use the word 'people'.

a special sort of telepathy would be needed; the sort which in this life produces *telepathic apparitions*. It would not be sufficient that A's thoughts or emotions should be telepathically affected by B's. If such telepathy were sufficiently prolonged and continuous, and especially if it were reciprocal, it would indeed have some of the characteristics of social intercourse; but I do not think we should call it 'meeting', at any rate in Flew's sense of the word. It would be necessary, in addition, that A should be aware of something which could be called 'B's body', or should have an experience not too unlike the experience of *seeing* another person in this life. This additional condition would be satisfied if A experienced a telepathic apparition of B. It would be necessary, further, that the telepathic apparition by means of which B 'announces himself' (if one may put it so) should be recognizably similar on different occasions. And if it were a case of meeting some person *again* whom one had previously known in this world, the telepathic apparition would have to be recognizably similar to the physical body which that person had when he was still alive.

There is no reason why an image-world should not contain a number of images which are telepathic apparitions; and if it did, one could quite intelligently speak of 'meeting other persons' in such a world. All the experiences I have when I meet another person in this present life could still occur, with only this difference, that percepts would be replaced by images. It would also be possible for another person to 'meet' me in the same manner, if I, as telepathic agent, could cause him to experience a suitable telepathic apparition, sufficiently resembling the body I used to have when he formerly 'met' me in this life.

I now turn to another problem which may have troubled some of you. If there be a next world, *where* is it? Surely it must be somewhere. But there does not seem to be any room or it. We can hardly suppose that it is up in the sky (i.e. outside the earth's atmosphere) or under the surface of the earth, as Homer and Vergil seemed to think. Such suggestions may have contented our ancestors, and the Ptolemaic astronomy may have made them acceptable, for some ages, even to the learned; but they will hardly content us. Surely the next world, if it exists, must be somewhere; and yet, it seems, there is nowhere for it to be.

The answer to this difficulty is easy if we conceive of the Next World in the way I have suggested, as a dream-like world of mental images. Mental images, including dream images, are in a space of their own. They do have spatial properties. Visual images, for instance, have extension and shape, and they have spatial relations to one another. But they have no spatial relation to objects in the physical world. If I dream of a tiger, my tiger-image has extension and shape. The dark stripes have spatial relations to the yellow parts, and to each other; the nose has a spatial relation to the tail. Again, the tiger image as a whole may have spatial relations to another image in my dream, for example to an image resembling a palm tree. But suppose we were to ask how far it is from the foot of my bed, whether it is three inches long, or longer, or shorter; is it not obvious that these questions are absurd ones? We cannot answer them, not because we lack the necessary information or find it impracticable to make the necessary measurements, but because the questions themselves have no meaning. In the space of the physical world these images are nowhere at all. But in relation to other images of mine, each of them is somewhere. Each of them is extended, and its parts are in spatial relations to one another. There is no *a priori* reason why all extended entities must be in physical space.

If we now apply these considerations to the Next World, as I am conceiving of it, we see that the question 'where is it?' simply does not arise. An image-world would have a space of its own. We could not find it anywhere in the space of the physical world, but this would not in the least prevent it from being a spatial world all the same. If you like, it would be its own 'where'.[3]

It follows that when we speak of 'passing' from this world to the next, this passage is not to be thought of as any sort of movement in space. It should rather be thought of as a change of consciousness, analogous to the change which occurs when we 'pass' from waking experience to dreaming. It would be a change from the perceptual type of consciousness to another type of consciousness in which perception ceases and imaging replaces it, but unlike the change from waking consciousness to dreaming

---

[3] Conceivably its geometrical structure might also be different from the geometrical structure of the physical world. In that case the space of the Next World would not only be other than the space of the physical world, but would also be a different *sort* of space.

in being irreversible. I suppose that nearly everyone nowadays who talks of 'passing' from this world to the other does think of the transition in this way, as some kind of irreversible change of consciousness, and not as a literal spatial transition in which one goes from one place to another place.

So much for the question 'where the next world is', if there be one. I have tried to show that if the next world is conceived as a world of mental images, the question simply does not arise. I now turn to another difficulty. It may be felt that an image-world is somehow a deception and a sham, not a *real* world at all. I have said that it would be a kind of dream-world. Now when one has a dream in this life, surely the things one is aware of in the dream are not *real* things. No doubt the dreamer really does have various mental images. These images do actually occur. But this is not all that happens. As a result of having these images, the dreamer believes, or takes for granted, that various material objects exist and various physical events occur; and these beliefs are mistaken. For example, he believes that there is a wall in front of him and that by a mere effort of will he succeeds in flying over the top of it. But the wall did not really exist, and he did not really fly over the top of it. He was in a state of delusion. Because of the images which he did really have, there *seemed* to him to be various objects and events which did not really exist at all. Similarly, you may argue, it may *seem* to discarnate minds (if indeed there are such) that there is a world in which they live, and a world not unlike this one. If they have mental images of the appropriate sort, it may even *seem* to them that they have bodies not unlike the ones they had in this life. But surely they will be mistaken? It is all very well to say, with the poet, that 'dreams are real while they last'—that dream-objects are only called 'unreal' when one wakes up, and normal sense perceptions begin to occur with which the dream experiences can be contrasted. And it is all very well to conclude from this that if one did *not* wake up, if the change from sense-perception to imaging were irreversible, one would not call one's dream objects unreal, because there would then be nothing with which to contrast them. But would they not still *be* unreal for all that? Surely discarnate minds, according to my account of them, would be in a state of permanent delusion; whereas a dreamer in this life (fortunately for him) is only in a temporary one. And the fact that a delusion goes on for a long time, even for ever and ever, does not make it any the less delusive. Delusions do not turn themselves into realities just by going on and on. Nor are they turned into realities by the fact that their victim is deprived of the power of detecting their delusiveness.

Now, of course, if it were true that the next life (supposing there is one) is a condition of permanent delusion, we should just have to put up with it. We might not like it; we might think that a state of permanent delusion is a bad state to be in. But our likes and dislikes are irrelevant to the question. I would suggest, however, that this argument about the 'delusiveness' or 'unreality' of an image-world is based on a confusion.

One may doubt whether there is any clear meaning in using the words 'real' and 'unreal' *tout court*, in this perfectly general and unspecified way. One may properly say, 'this is real silver, and that is not', 'this is a real pearl and that is not', or again 'this is a real pool of water, and that is only a mirage'. The point here is that something X is mistakenly believed to be something else Y, because it does resemble Y in some respects. It makes perfectly good sense, then, to say that X is not really Y. This piece of plated brass is not real silver, true enough. It only looks like silver. But for all that, it cannot be called 'unreal' in the unqualified sense, in the sense of not existing at all. Even the mirage is something, though it is not the pool of water you took it to be. It is a perfectly good set of visual appearances, though it is not related to other appearances in the way you thought it was; for example, it does not have the relations to tactual appearances, or to visual appearances from other places, which you expected it to have. You may properly say that the mirage is not a real pool of water, or even that it is not a real physical object, and that anyone who thinks it is must be in a state of delusion. But there is no clear meaning in saying that it is just 'unreal' *tout court*, without any further specification or explanation. In short, when the word 'unreal' is applied to something, one means that it is different from something else, with which it might be mistakenly identified; what that something else is may not be explicitly stated, but it can be gathered from the context.

What, then, could people mean by saying that a next world such as I have described would be 'unreal'? If they are saying anything intelligible, they must mean that it is different from something else, something else which it does resemble in some respects, and might therefore be confused with. And what is that something else? It is this present physical world in which we now live. An image-world, then, is only 'unreal' in the sense that it is not really physical, though it might be mistakenly thought to be physical by some of those who experience it. But this only amounts to saying that the world I am describing would be an *other* world, other than this present physical world, which is just what it ought to be; other than this present physical world, and yet sufficiently like it to be possibly confused with it, because images do resemble percepts. And what would this otherness consist in? First, in the fact that it is in a *space* which is other than physical space; secondly, and still more important, in the fact that the *causal laws* of an image-world would be different from the laws of physics. And this is also our ground for saying that the events we experience in dreams are 'unreal', that is, not really physical, though mistakenly believed by the dreamer to be so. They do in some ways closely resemble physical events, and that is why the mistake is possible. But the causal laws of their occurrence are quite different, as we recognize when we wake up; and just occasionally we recognize it even while we are still asleep.

Now let us consider the argument that the inhabitants of the Other World, as I have described it, would be in a state of delusion. I admit that some of them might be. That would be the condition of the people described in the mediumistic communications already referred to—the people who 'do not realize that they are dead'. Because their images are so like the normal percepts they were accustomed to in this life, they believe mistakenly that they are still living in the physical world. But, as I have already tried to explain, their state of delusion need not be permanent and irremediable. By attending to the relations between one image and another, and applying the ordinary inductive methods by which we ourselves have discovered the causal laws of this present world in which *we* live, they too could discover in time what the causal laws of *their* world are. These laws, we may suppose, would be more like the laws of Freudian psychology than the laws of physics. And once the discovery was made, they would be cured of their delusion. They would find out, perhaps with surprise, that the world they were experiencing was *other* than the physical world which they experienced before, even though in some respects like it.

Let us now try to explore the conception of a world of mental images a little more fully. Would it not be a '*subjective*' world? And surely there would be many *different* next worlds, not just one; and each of them would be private. Indeed, would there not be as many next worlds as there are discarnate minds, and each of them wholly private to the mind which experiences it? In short, it may seem that each of us, when dead, would have his own dream world, and there would be no common or public Next World at all.

'Subjective', perhaps, is rather a slippery word. Certainly, an image world would have to be subjective in the sense of being mind-dependent, dependent for its existence upon mental processes of one sort or another; images, after all, are mental entities. But I do not think that such a world need be completely private, if telepathy occurs in the next life. I have already mentioned the part which telepathic apparitions might play in it, in connection with Flew's contention that 'people are what you meet'. But there is more to be said. It is reasonable to suppose that in a disembodied state telepathy would occur more frequently than it does now. It seems likely that in this present life our telepathic powers are constantly being inhibited by our need to adjust ourselves to our physical environment. It even seems likely that many telepathic 'impressions' which we receive at the unconscious level are shut out from consciousness by a kind of biologically-motivated censorship. Once the pressure of biological needs is removed, we might expect that telepathy would occur continually, and manifest itself in consciousness by modifying and adding to the images which one experiences. (Even in this life, after all, some dreams are telepathic.)

If this is right, an image-world such as I am describing would not be the product of one single mind only, nor would it be purely private. It would be the joint-product of a group of telepathically-interacting minds and public to all of them. Nevertheless, one would not expect it to have unrestricted publicity. It is likely that there would still be *many* next worlds, a different one for each group of like-minded personalities. I admit I am not quite sure what might be meant by 'like-minded' and 'unlike-minded' in this connection. Perhaps we could say that two personalities are like-minded if their memories or their characters are sufficiently similar. It might be that Nero and Marcus Aurelius do not have a world in common, but Socrates and Marcus Aurelius do.

So far, we have a picture of many 'semi-public' next worlds, if one may put it so; each of them composed of mental images, and yet not not wholly private for all that, but public to a limited group of telepathically-interacting minds. Or, if you like, after death everyone does have his own dream, but there is still some overlap between one person's dream and another's, because of telepathy.

I have said that such a world would be mind-dependent, even though dependent on a group of minds rather than a single mind. In what way would it be mind-dependent? Presumably in the same way as dreams are now. It would be dependent on the *memories* and the *desires* of the persons who experienced it. Their memories and their desires would determine what sort of images they had. If I may put it so, the 'stuff' or 'material' of such a world would come in the end from one's memories, and the 'form' of it from one's desires. To use another analogy, memory would provide the pigments, and desire would paint the picture. One might expect, I think, that desires which had been unsatisfied in one's earthly life would play a specially important part in the process. That may seem an agreeable prospect. But there is another which is less agreeable. Desires which had been *repressed* in one's earthly life, because it was too painful or too disgraceful to admit that one had them, might also play a part, and perhaps an important part, in determining what images one would have in the next. And the same might be true of repressed memories. It may be suggested that what Freud (in one stage of his thought) called 'the censor'—the force or barrier or mechanism which keeps some of our desires and memories out of consciousness, or only lets them in when they disguise themselves in symbolic and distorted forms—operates only in this present life and not in the next. However we conceive of 'the censor', it does seem to be a device for enabling us to adapt ourselves to our environment. And when we no longer have an environment, one would expect that the barrier would come down.

We can now see that an after-death world of mental images can also be quite reasonably described in the terminology of the Hindu thinkers as 'a world of desire' (*Kama Loka*). Indeed, this is just what we should expect if we assume that dreams, in this present life, are the best available clue to what the next life might be like. Such a world could also be described as 'a world of memories'; because imaging, in the end, is a function of memory, one of the ways in which our memory-dispositions manifest themselves. But this description would be less apt, even though correct as far as it goes. To use the same rather inadequate language as before, the 'materials' out of which an image-world is composed would have to come from the memories of the mind or group of minds whose world it is. But it would be their desires (including those repressed in earthly life) which determined the ways in which these memories were used, the precise kind of dream which was built up out of them or on the basis of them.

It will, of course, be objected that memories cannot exist in the absence of a physical brain, nor yet desires, nor images either. But this proposition, however plausible, is after all just an empirical hypothesis, not a necessary truth. Certainly there is empirical evidence in favour of it. But there is also empirical evidence against it. Broadly speaking one might say, perhaps, that the 'normal' evidence tends to support this Materialistic or Epiphenomenalist theory of memories, images and desires, whereas the 'supernormal' evidence on the whole tends to weaken the Materialist or Epiphenomenalist theory of human personality (of which this hypothesis about the brain-dependent character of memories, images and desires is a part). Moreover, any evidence which directly supports the Survival Hypothesis (and there is quite a lot of evidence which does, provided we are prepared to admit that the Survival Hypothesis is intelligible at all) is *pro tanto* evidence against the Materialistic conception of human personality.

In this essay, I am not of course trying to argue in favour of the Survival Hypothesis. I am only concerned with the more modest task of trying to make it intelligible. All I want to maintain, then, is that there is nothing self-contradictory or logically absurd in the hypothesis that memories, desires and images can exist in the absence of a physical brain. The hypothesis may, of course, be false. My point is only that it is not absurd; or, if you like, that it is at any rate intelligible, whether true or not. To put the question in another way, when we are trying to work out for ourselves what sort of thing a discarnate life might conceivably

18

be (if there is one) we have to ask what kind of *equipment*, so to speak, a discarnate mind might be supposed to have. It cannot have the power of sense-perception, nor the power of acting on the physical world by means of efferent nerves, muscles and limbs. What would it have left? What could we take out with us, as it were, when we pass from this life to the next? What we take out with us, I suggest, can only be our memories and desires, and the power of constructing out of them an image world to suit us. Obviously we cannot take our material possessions out with us; but I do not think this is any great loss, for if we remember them well enough and are sufficiently attached to them, we shall be able to construct image-replicas of them which will be just as good, and perhaps better.

In this connection I should like to mention a point which has been made several times before. Both Whately Carington and Professor Ducasse have referred to it, and no doubt other writers have. But I believe it is of some importance and worth repeating. Ecclesiastically-minded critics sometimes speak rather scathingly of the 'materialistic' character of mediumistic communications. They are not at all edified by these descriptions of agreeable houses, beautiful landscapes, gardens and the rest. And then, of course, there is Raymond Lodge's notorious cigar. These critics complain that the Next World as described in these communications is no more than a reproduction of this one, slightly improved perhaps. And the argument apparently is that the 'materialistic' character of the communications is evidence against their genuineness. On the contrary, as far as it goes, it is evidence *for* their genuineness. Most people in this life do like material objects and are deeply interested in them. This may be deplorable, but there it is. If so, the image-world they would create for themselves in the next life might be expected to have just the 'materialistic' character of which these critics complain. If one had been fond of nice houses and pleasant gardens in this life, the image-world one would create for oneself in the next might be expected to contain image-replicas of such objects, and one would make these replicas as like 'the real thing' as one's memories permitted; with the help, perhaps, of telepathic influences from other minds whose tastes were similar. This would be all the more likely to happen if one had not been able to enjoy such things in this present life as much as one could wish.

But possibly I have misunderstood the objection which these ecclesiastical critics are making. Perhaps they are saying that if the Next World is like this, life after death is not worth having. Well and good. If they would prefer a different sort of Next World, and find the one described in these communications insipid or unsatisfying to their aspirations, then they can expect to get a different one—in fact, just the sort of next world they want. They have overlooked a crucial point which seems almost obvious; that if there is an after-death life at all, there must surely be many next worlds, separate from and as it were impenetrable to one another, corresponding to the *different* desires which different groups of discarnate personalities have.

The belief in life after death is often dismissed as 'mere wish-fulfilment'. Now it will be noticed that the Next World as I have been trying to conceive of it is precisely a wish-fulfilment world, in much the same sense in which some dreams are described as wish-fulfilments. Should not this make a rational man very suspicious of the ideas I am putting before you? Surely this account of the Other World is 'too good to be true'? I think not. Here we must distinguish two different questions. The question whether human personality continues to exist after death is a question of fact, and wishes have nothing to do with it one way or the other. But *if* the answer to this factual question were 'Yes' (and I emphasize the 'if'), wishes might have a very great deal to do with the kind of world which discarnate beings would live in. Perhaps it may be helpful to consider a parallel case. It is a question of fact whether dreams occur in this present life. It has to be settled by empirical investigation, and the wishes of the investigators have nothing to do with it. It is just a question of what the empirical facts are, whether one likes them or not. Nevertheless, granting that dreams do occur, a man's wishes might well have a very great deal to do with determining what the content of his dreams is to be; especially unconscious wishes on the one hand, and on the other, conscious wishes which are not satisfied in waking life. Of course the parallel is not exact. There is one very important difference between the two cases. With dreams, the question of fact is settled. It is quite certain that many people do have dreams. But in the case of Survival, the question of fact is not settled, or not at present. It is still true, however, that though wishes have nothing to do with it, they might have a very great deal to do with the kind of world we should live in after death, *if* we survive death at all.

Every adult person has what we call 'a character'; a set of more or less settled and permanent desires, with the corresponding emotional dispositions, expressing themselves in a more or less predictable pattern of thoughts, feelings and actions. But it is perfectly possible to desire that one's character should be different, perhaps very different, from what it is at present. This is what philosophers call a 'second-order' desire, a desire that some of one's own desires should be altered. Such second-order desires are not necessarily ineffective, as New Year resolutions are supposed to be. People can within limits alter their own characters, and sometimes do; and if they succeed in doing so, it is in the end because they *want* to. But these 'second-order' desires—desires to alter one's own character—are seldom effective immediately; and even when they appear to be, as in some cases of religious conversion, there has probably been a long period of subconscious or unconscious preparation first. To be effective, desires of this sort must occur again and again. I must go on wishing to be more generous or less timid, and not just wish it on New Year's day; I must train myself to act habitually—and think too—in the way that I should act and think if I possessed the altered character for which I wish. From the point of view of the present moment, however, one's character is something fixed and given. The wish I have at half-past twelve today will do nothing, or almost nothing, to alter it.

These remarks may seem very remote from the topic I am supposed to be discussing. But they have a direct bearing on a question which has been mentioned before: whether, or in what sense, the Next World as I am conceiving of it should be called a 'subjective' world. As I have said already, a Next World such as I have described *would* be subjective, in the sense of mind-dependent. The minds which experience it would also have created it. It would just be the manifestation of their own memories and desires, even though it might be the joint creation of a number of telepathically interacting minds, and therefore not wholly private. But there is a sense in which it might have a certain objectivity all the same. One thing we mean by calling something 'objective' is that it is so whether we like it or not, and even if we dislike it. This is also what we mean by talking about 'hard facts' or 'stubborn facts'.

At first sight it may seem that in an image-world such as I have described there could be no hard facts or stubborn facts, and nothing objective in this sense of the word 'objective'. How could there be, if the world we experience is itself a wish-fulfilment world? But a man's character *is* in this sense 'objective'; objective in the sense that he has it whether he likes it or not. And facts about his character are as 'hard' or 'stubborn' as any. Whether I like it or not, and even though I dislike it, it is a hard fact about me that I am timid or spiteful, that I am fond of eating oysters or averse from talking French. I may wish sometimes that these habitual desires and aversions of mine were different, but at any particular moment this wish will do little or nothing to alter them. In the short run, a man's permanent and habitual desires are something 'given', which he must accept and put up with as best he can, even though in the very long run they are alterable.

Now in the next life, according to my picture of it, it would be these permanent and habitual desires which would determine the nature of the world in which a person has to live. His world would be, so to speak, the outgrowth of his character; it would be his own character represented to him in the form of dream-like images. There is therefore a sense in which he gets exactly the sort of world he wants, whatever internal conflicts there may be between one of these wants and another. Yet he may very well dislike having the sort of character he does have. In the short run, as I have said, his character is something fixed and given, and objective in the sense that he has that character whether he likes it or not. Accordingly his image-world is also objective in the same sense. It is objective in the sense that it insists on presenting itself to him whether he likes it or not.

To look at the same point in another way: the Next World as I am picturing it may be a very queer sort of world, but still it would be subject to causal laws. The laws would not, of course, be the laws of physics. As I have suggested already, they might be expected to be more like the laws of Freudian psychology. But they would be laws all the same, and objective in the sense that they hold good whether one liked it or not. And if we do dislike the image-world which our desires and memories create for us— if, when we get what we want, we are horrified to discover what things they were which we wanted—we shall have to set about altering our characters, which might be a very long and painful process.

Some people tell us, of course, that all desires, even the most permanent and habitual ones, will wear themselves out in time by the mere process of being satisfied. It may be so, and perhaps there is some comfort in the thought. In that case the dream-like image world of which I have been speaking would only be temporary, and we should have to ask whether after the Next World there is a next but one. The problem of Survival would then arise again in a new form. We should have to ask whether personal identity could still be preserved when we were no longer even dreaming. It could, I think, be preserved through the transition from this present perceptible world to a dream-like image world of the kind I have been describing. But if even imaging were to cease, would there be anything left of human personality at all? Or would the state of existence—if any—which followed be one to which the notion of personality, at any rate our present notion, no longer had any application? I think that these are questions upon which it is unprofitable and perhaps impossible to speculate. (If anyone wishes to make the attempt, I can only advise him to consult the writings of the mystics, both Western and Oriental.) It is quite enough for us to consider what the *next* world might conceivably be like, and some of you may think that even this is too much.

Before I end, I should like to make one concluding remark. You may have noticed that the Next World, according to my account of it, is not at all unlike what some metaphysicians say *this* world is. In the philosophy of Schopenhauer, this present world itself, in which we now live, is a world of 'will and idea'. And so it is in Berkeley's philosophy too; material objects are just collections of 'ideas', though according to Berkeley the will which presents these ideas to us is the will of God, acting directly upon us in a way which is in effect telepathic. Could it be that these Idealist metaphysicians have given us a substantially correct picture of the next world, though a mistaken picture of this one? The study of metaphysical theories is out of fashion nowadays. But perhaps students of psychical research would do well to pay some attention to them. *If* there are other worlds than this (again I emphasize the 'if') who knows whether with some stratum of our personalities we are not living in them now, as well as in this present one which conscious sense-perception discloses? Such a repressed and unconscious awareness of a world different from this one might be expected to break through into consciousness occasionally in the course of human history, very likely in a distorted form, and this might be the source of those very queer ideas which we read of with so much incredulity and astonishment in the writings of some speculative metaphysicians. Not knowing their source, they mistakenly applied these ideas to this world in which we now live, embellishing them sometimes with an elaborate façade of deductive reasoning. Viewed in cold blood and with a sceptical eye, their attempts may appear extremely unconvincing, and their deductive reasoning fallacious. But perhaps, without knowing it, they may have valuable hints to give us if we are trying to form some conception, however tentative, of 'another world'. And this is something we must try to do if we take the problem of Survival seriously.

COMMENTS BY ANTONY FLEW: SOME OBJECTIONS TO CARTESIAN VIEWS OF MAN

It is possible, and sometimes useful, to distinguish two fundamentally different sorts of conception of the nature of man. The one sort, while allowing of course that we are always or usually in fact associated in some peculiar and peculiarly intimate way with our bodies, takes us to be ultimately and essentially incorporeal. The other sort of view insists that we just are organisms, albeit rather special organisms: special, for instance, in our capacities for rationality and irrationality, for thinking and doing, for suffering and enjoying, for action and passion. Views of the first sort can be seen as falling within a Cartesian, and ultimately Platonic, tradition. Those of the second sort may, perhaps with some slight strain, claim Aristotle as their eponymous first great forefather.[4] My various comments here are united by a concern to defend a conception of man which is, in this limited sense, Aristotelian against the powerful Cartesian advocacy of some fellow contributors.

[4] For a development and defence of this perspective see Antony Flew, *Body, Mind, and Death* (New York, Collier Books, 1964); and compare Gilbert Ryle, *A Rational Animal* (London, Athlone Press, 1962) and William Kneale, *On Having a Mind* (Cambridge, Cambridge University Press, 1962).

It was a great pleasure to have this occasion to reread once again Professor H. H. Price's fascinating exploration 'Survival and the Idea of "Another World" '; and it is good to think that this will now be seen by a wider and different public from the unfortunately small membership of the Society for Psychical Research. Immediately after the original publication Price and I had some discussion in the correspondence columns of the *Journal* of that Society.[5] But now in this second round I want to approach from a different angle. Price addresses himself to the question: 'why should it be thought that the very idea of life after death is unintelligible?' (p. 3). 'Surely,' he continues, 'it is easy enough to conceive (whether or not it is true) that experiences might occur after Jones's death which are linked with experiences which he had before his death, in such a way that his personal identity is preserved?' (p. 3). The objection which Price goes on to consider is this: 'But, it will be said, the idea of after-death *experiences* is just the difficulty. What kind of experiences could they conceivably be?' (p. 3: italics in original).

Now, quite certainly, the crucial question is the one about the possibility of after-death experiences: it is indeed the hope or fear of having such experiences, and of their being of this sort or of that, which gives the question of a future life all its point. It is just this which makes it an issue of such urgent human concern. But prior to the difficulty to which Price mainly devotes himself there is another and more fundamental. Before any question can arise about the object or content of experiences there has to be some subject to which these experiences can be attributed. It would make no more sense to speak of experiences without anyone to have them than it would to discourse about grins totally detached from faces. Of course Price himself does not actually speak of experiences in this way. What he does is first to take it for granted that persons are essentially incorporeal; and then afterwards these persons,[6] thought of as incorporeal subjects, are envisaged as making do with whatever experiences might still remain available to them since the loss of their bodies. In making this assumption Price is setting himself within a great tradition. Nevertheless it is a tradition which starts from the wrong place, and stands every issue it touches upon its head. For, as I had urged in the note to which Price refers,[7] people or perhaps better (as he suggests) persons, are in fact corporeal. Person words are quite manifestly and undeniably taught and learnt and used by and

---

[5] *Journal of the Society for Psychical Research*, Vol. XXXVII (1953).

[6] Or 'minds': but compare my comments on Ducasse in Chapter 4.

[7] This has since been reprinted, more accessibly, in Antony Flew and Alasdair MacIntyre (Editors), *New Essays in Philosophical Theology* (London, S.C.M. Press, 1955).

for reference to a certain sort of corporeal object. We do meet people, not just the containers in which they are kept. They do see us, and not just what we happen to inhabit. This was the point which I tried to epitomize in the possibly misleading slogan: 'People are what you meet.'

Wherever we may end quite certainly this is where we have to begin. Perhaps it will prove to be possible to construct a sense for the expression *incorporeal person* such that there would be sufficient resemblance between persons and incorporeal persons to justify us in using the same word to denominate both; and someone might then even be able to suggest some process of continuous change by which a person could be said to develop into an incorporeal person. Perhaps at the same time we might show how, and how many of, the innumerable words which are now applied only or distinctively to persons—and the meanings of which are at present taught and learnt with reference to the doings and sufferings of these familiar beings—could be predicated, either unequivocally or analogously, of such putative incorporeal persons. But it is at least not obvious that these intellectual projects could be brought to a successful issue. For it is as members of a class of material objects, albeit a very special class, that persons are identified and individuated. The problem of identification for an incorporeal person is one: not merely of showing how your incorporeal person can be picked out as an object of thought; but also of establishing that such objects would be ones which could significantly be spoken of as existing in their own right and not, like grins, merely as attributes of something else. The difficulties of the problem of individuation here are best seen by considering the troubles encountered by Locke and Hume in their efforts to give an account of personal identity: troubles which are made relevant and instructive for us by the fact that they surely sprang in large part from their shared Cartesian assumption that persons simply are incorporeal. No doubt this is at least part of what lies behind Wittgenstein's gnomic apothegm: 'The human body is the best picture of the human soul.'[8]

It also explains why I coined that slogan: 'People are what you meet.' Price replies to me:

> I would suggest that he does not in this sense 'meet' *himself*. He might indeed have one of those curious out-of-body experiences which are occasionally mentioned in our records . . .; but I do not think that we should call this 'meeting'. And surely the important question is, that constitutes my personal identity *for myself*. . . . No one can 'meet' me

[8] *Philosophical Investigations* (Oxford, Blackwell, 1963), p. 178. Compare here S. Shoemaker, *Self-Knowledge and Self-Identity* (Ithaca, N.Y., Cornell University Press, 1963), *passim*; also P. T. Geach, *Mental Acts* (London, Routledge & Kegan Paul, undated), Sections 25 ff.

when I am dreaming. They can, of course, come and look at my body [*sic*] lying in bed; but this is not 'meeting', because no sort of social relations are then possible between them and me. Yet, although temporarily 'unmeetable' during my dreams I am still, for myself, the same person that I was. And if I went on dreaming *in perpetuum*, and could never be 'met' again, this need not prevent me from continuing to be, for myself, the same person (p. 10: italics and punctuation as in original).

Now to the extent that Price's criticism latches on to the ineptness of applying the social concept of meeting either to myself alone or to an encounter with a person asleep, I hope I have already allowed sufficiently for its force, and taken adequate steps to remove its occasion. However, although Price puts a deal of emphasis on this point about meeting, he must surely consider that the implications of his reply are more widely damaging to my objections. The clue perhaps lies in his concern about the identity of persons, *for themselves*. This is presumably not to be construed as implying that a person at one time can be the same as another person at another time for himself, but not for other people; or the other way about. I take it rather that what Price is wanting to underline is the undoubted fact that a person is very often, as a matter of fact, the best or even the only authority about his own doings and sufferings. But if this interpretation is correct then the fact being urged has no tendency to support the desired conclusion. Discounting for the moment recent advances in the investigation of the physiology of dreams, we could well allow that some person presently asleep would, when and if he wakes up, be in an uniquely strong position to give us an account of his dreams. But this is no sort of reason for suggesting that the dreamer is other than the person we can now see in his bed asleep.

Price's mention of 'out-of-body experiences' is perhaps especially significant. Certainly there have been a fair number of what seem to be reliable claims to have had such experiences, usually at a critical stage in a serious illness. It has seemed to the subjects as if they were observing themselves from a point of view outside themselves. But whatever explanation is to be offered for these curious experiences, they surely have no tendency to show that a person word must be used to refer to an incorporeal entity which might significantly be said to detach itself from the person in question. It is well worth noting here that one major source of the temptation to believe that persons are essentially incorporeal lies in a beguiling misinterpretation of some of the mental imagery which is sometimes involved in certain exercises of the imagination.[9] The temptation is to think that, because you are

[9] See Annis Flew, 'Images, Supposing, and Imagining' in *Philosophy*, Vol. XXVIII (1953).

able, for instance, to image a pretty passable mental representation of your own future funeral, you are thereby imagining—and hence showing that there is no logical absurdity in the notion of—yourself witnessing your own funeral after you are dead.[10]

I would of course fully accept Professor Price's theory and indeed extend it from images to sense-data as well. His further speculations on what may happen to us after death envisage that we may enter some sort of 'dream world'. This development devolves on two separate considerations that we should perhaps keep distinct. The first is that if images are in a space of their own it becomes certainly possible that after the destruction of the physical body, that an individual consciousness could continue, with images, or even hallucinatory sense-data, as its content. But whether these images would behave as they do in dreams or not seems another question. The recent work on the physiology of dreaming seems to suggest that certain aspects of dreaming are closely correlated with particular brain states.[11] Visual imagery may even be abolished by brain lesions.[12] There is also good evidence that wishes and desires depend on a normal brain function.

It is of course possible that a record of mental events may be laid down in some part of the mind—in the image world—that is not normally accessible during life (e.g. it cannot come to our rescue when we lose our memories following some brain disease). This store in some way might only become manifest to the Ego after death and possibly in such a way that we are forced to undergo the just consequences of our acts during life—as Price suggests. On the other hand, it is also possible that the image could possess its own manner of existence. This is normally kept inhibited by the brain—for we cannot live in two worlds at once. We may be able to catch glimpses of this 'other world' when this inhibitory power of the brain is momentarily released, as in certain visionary states or by the action of hallucinogenic drugs. This theory suggests that heaven, purgatory and hell may after all be very poignant realities. After death we may be cast into a world determined by our own wishes, etc., as Price describes, and that is

[10] See Antony Flew, 'Can a Man Witness his own Funeral?' in *Hibbert Journal*, Vol. LIV (1956). I leave it to the reader to consider how much weight Descartes himself places on this sort of argument: see, for instance, *Discourse*, IV and *Meditations*, II.

[11] Ian Oswald, *Sleeping and Waking*, Elsevier, 1962.

[12] M. E. Humphrey and O. L. Zangwill, 'Cessation of dreaming after brain injury'. *J. Neurol. Neurosurg. Psychiat.*, **14**, 322, 1951.

salutory enough. It is also possible that we may be cast into the strange and terrible world revealed by the so-called hallucinogenic or psychodelic drugs. Any student of the novels of Charles Williams will be familiar with the latter notion. In fact non-Cartesian dualism suggests that Charles Williams, particularly in *All Hallows Eve*, may be giving an almost factual account of what events after death may be like—a sort of mixture of Price's and my suggestions. In any event, what these theories do suggest is that the current widespread ideas that science has somehow disposed of the soul and of heaven and hell, are based on a naïve limitation of thought about the nature of this world—i.e. that there can be only one space in the world.

REPLY TO ANTONY FLEW BY H. H. PRICE: 'PEOPLE ARE
WHAT YOU MEET'

Instead of discussing Professor Flew's comments point by point, I shall offer some reflections on his dictum 'People are what you meet'. I hope that this will throw light on the issues about which we differ, and may also suggest that some of the differences between us are not quite so radical as they appear to be.

I think we are greatly indebted to Flew for this thought-provoking remark of his. It is someting like the 'mind-twisting' apothegms which the Zen mystical teachers are said to prescribe to their pupils for meditation. I myself have meditated on it often, as others no doubt have, and I have often changed my mind about it. But at present what it suggests to me is something like this: Traditional discussions of the mind–body problem have gone wrong because they have neglected the 'social dimension' of human personality.

After all, the most important and the most obvious thing about 'meeting' is that meeting is a social relation, or the bringing about of a social relation. To say 'people are what you meet' amounts to saying that persons are entities with which one may have social relations: or rather, not 'with which', but 'with whom'. For we must not forget the peculiarities of personal pronouns, especially if we approach philosophical problems from the linguistic point of view, as Flew himself does. A person is not just 'it' and Flew's phrase on page 26 'a certain sort of corporeal object' is therefore inappropriate. (For the same reason the relative pronoun 'what' is inappropriate, and so is the asymmetry between 'what' and 'you'.) The meeting of two persons is not like the meeting of two billiard balls. However corporeal I am, I am not just a corporeal object: I am a conscious, and moreover a self-conscious being, and the same is true of my neighbour whom I meet, however corporeal he is. Otherwise it would be permissible for me to treat him merely as a means, which clearly it is not.

Nevertheless, it may well seem that unless both of us are corporeal entities (though not corporeal objects) we cannot meet at all: in which case being embodied—and moreover perceptibly embodied—would be at any rate a necessary condition for having social relations. And if this is true, it is a very important point indeed. For the capacity of having social relations seems to be an essential part of what we mean by 'being a person', and not only the capacity for having them but the actualization of them. Persons are who you meet. But unless you actually did meet them (at least sometimes) you would not be a person yourself.

Let us now take the Platonic standpoint for a moment, and ask why 'a mind' or 'a soul' *needs* to have a body. The answer seems to be that the function of the body is to be the outward and perceptible manifestation of inward mental states: its function, one might say, is an expressive one. Is this a possible interpretation of Wittgenstein's 'gnomic epigram' given by Flew on page 26 of his Comments ('The human body is the best picture of the human soul')? There must be something to perform this 'expressive' function if social relations are to be possible, and without such relations personality could not exist. It is true that 'souls' or 'minds' might still exist in an unembodied state (if we take the Platonic view) but they could not be *personal* souls unless they were somehow embodied. To put the point in an extravagant way, a person needs to have a face, or some equivalent for a face, in order to be a person: or at least a finite person needs one, and we are not here concerned with the Infinite Personality of God.

It is true that according to the Platonic Socrates the soul does not need a body at all, and would be better off without one. He seems to have thought of the body as a prison (cf. Flew's word 'container'), and surely one would rather be out of prison than in it? But we may note that this view is not characteristic of the Platonic tradition as a whole. The Neoplatonists seem to have thought that a physically-disembodied 'soul' still has to have a body of some kind, and that the only completely unembodied spiritual entity is the supreme 'One' itself. It was the Neoplatonists who invented the concept of the *augoeides* or 'radiant body' which the soul in its highest stage of *post mortem* spiritual development is supposed to have.

Now if we think of the body in this sort of way, as the means for making social relations possible, what consequences are we committed to when we try to speculate about life after death? As Professor C. D. Broad has recently reminded us,[13] the overwhelming majority of

---

[13] *Lectures on Psychical Research* (Routledge & Kegan Paul, 1962), p. 408.

believers in a life after death have thought of it as an embodied state. It would seem that they had some grounds for thinking so, if life after death is a *personal* life, and if a personal life has to be in some degree a social one.

I think that the view suggested in my paper does fulfil those conditions, though in rather a complicated way. What I did was to start from the analogy of dreaming, and then to 'stretch' this analogy a little. The image-world which I described is not a purely solipsistic one. It is supposed to have some degree of publicity, though not the unrestricted publicity which our familiar physical world has. In my image-world, each person is supposed to have an 'image-body' and he can make this image body perceptible to other persons with whom he is in telepathic *rapport*. This is something like what happens in this present life when one person experiences a telepathic apparition of another person. So far as I can see, such a 'telepathically-transmissible' image could perform all the social functions for which a body is needed. In that case, the social dimension of personality—which is indispensable for the very existence of personality, if the preceeding argument is right—would still be preserved in the life after death.

Of course, this is not the only way of securing the desired result. Instead, we may conceive of *post mortem* embodiment in a quasi-physical manner, as the Occultists and the Spiritualists do. For instance, we may suppose that there are image bodies which are objective entities, located (presumably) in a non-physical space and endowed with causal properties different from those which 'this-wordly' physics, chemistry, anatomy and physiology attribute to our present material organisms. Most believers in a life after death probably have thought of *post mortem* embodiment in this way. They may be right too. At any rate I do not know how to prove that they are mistaken. The only advantage of an 'image' theory of the *post mortem* body (and of the other world in general) is that it is more economical, since we do know that mental images exist, and we have strong evidence for believing that telepathy exists and that telepathic apparitions sometimes occur.

REPLY TO J. R. SMYTHIES BY H. H. PRICE

In the first paragraph of his Comments Dr. Smythies points out that certain aspects of dreaming are closely correlated with particular brain states; at any rate, recent work on the physiology of dreaming suggests this. In my paper, however, it was the phenomenology of dreaming, rather than the physiology of it, which I mainly had in mind. I wanted to suggest that from the phenomenological point of view *post mortem* experience might be dream-like. No doubt hallucinatory experience would also have been a suitable analogy for my purpose, provided that we consider cases where the whole visual field (not merely a part of it) is hallucinatory. The only trouble is that such totally hallucinatory experiences are quite unfamiliar to nearly everyone, whereas dream-images, on the contrary, are quite familiar to nearly everyone. Not quite to everyone, perhaps. Some time after writing my paper I was dismayed to hear from two philosophical colleagues that their dreams were entirely verbal. They just told improbable stories to themselves, presumably by means of auditory images of words—stories which they believed at the time and disbelieved when they woke up again. Confronted with these too-intellectual persons, I have no way of conveying to them the kind of 'other world' which I was trying to describe. I can only tell them how much I pity them for the miserably empty lives they must lead in this present world. Even when they are asleep they cannot escape from the domination of words.

Nevertheless, the physiological considerations mentioned by Smythies are relevant to my argument in another way. They suggest, I think, that there can be no survival at all unless a Bergsonian theory of memory is correct. For whatever mental images we have, and however bizarre some of them may be, it is memory, in the end, which provides the materials for all of them. According to Bergson the function of the brain is primarily an inhibitory one, so far as memory is concerned. It prevents us from recollecting too much, or limits our recollections to those which are biologically relevant at any particular time. There are, however, conditions (sleep is one of them) in which these inhibitory activities are relaxed or suspended, and of course, they cease altogether when we are dead. Thereafter we are freed from biological exigencies and the whole of our past is open to our recollection, presumably in the form of mental imagery.

I am not sure whether Smythies himself accepts a Bergsonian theory of memory. But when he says, at the beginning of paragraph 2 of his Comments: 'It is possible that a record of mental events may be laid down in some part of the mind, in the image-world that is not normally accessible during life' it looks as if he was at any rate prepared to consider a Bergsonian theory. This part of the mind would be what Bergson calls 'Pure Memory'.

In the second paragraph of his Comments he distinguishes two alternative views, and the difference between them is further elaborated later. The first view is the one I have just mentioned about 'a record of mental events'. But according to the second view 'the image world would possess its own manner of existance. This (i.e our awareness of it?) is normally kept inhibited by the brain—for we cannot live in two worlds at once'. I am not quite sure that we cannot. I think it depends on the span of our consciousness, which varies greatly at different times and between different persons (what is 'beyond the margins of consciousness' for A may be 'just within the margin' for B). Moreover, I am inclined to think that the span of consciousness can be very considerably increased by repeated voluntary effort, and probably also by the meditative practices which religious people in all ages have recommended. Sometimes it has seemed to me that a continuous dream-life goes on all through our waking hours, and that just occasionally we may catch a glimpse of it, as if there were two different but concurrent 'streams of consciousness'. On the view stated in my paper, this would amount to saying that we *can* live in two worlds at once, and occasionally we do. Indeed, Smythies himself admits that this can happen 'in certain visionary states or by the action of hallucinogenic drugs' (page 28) I suggest that it might also happen in other circumstances and without such aids; and it does not seem to me impossible that some exceptional persons may live consciously 'in two worlds' all the time.

Finally, what are we to say of 'the strange and terrible world revealed by so-called hallucinogenic or psychodelic drugs' (page 29)? I should think that the most promising way of dealing with it, if we follow the line of thought suggested in my paper, would be to distinguish between the personal and the impersonal unconscious. The 'locus', so to speak, of the image-world described in my paper was the personal unconscious of the discarnate person, modified and enriched in some degree by the mutual telepathic influence of one discarnate person upon another. But the impersonal unconscious might have its image contents too, and it might be that at death the barrier between the personal and the impersonal unconscious is removed.

It may be remembered, however, that in my paper I did distinguish between the 'next world' and the 'next but one', about which I did not venture to speculate. Perhaps this strange and terrible world referred to by Dr. Smythies might be the next but one?

THE IDENTITY HYPOTHESIS:
A CRITIQUE
John Beloff

IN this paper I shall examine a certain ingenious and elegant solution of the mind–body problem that has been forcefully canvassed in the past few years by a number of distinguished philosophers. Although it parades under various names and takes various forms I shall, for convenience, refer to it simply as the 'Identity Hypothesis'. My paper falls into three parts: in Part 1 I shall give a short exposition of the doctrine itself, both in its official form and in its principal variant. In Part 2 I shall argue that the doctrine is (*a*) important, in the sense that either its acceptance or its rejection has far-reaching philosophical consequences, and (*b*) valid, in the sense that there are no logical or *a priori* reasons for supposing that it *could* not be true. In Part 3 I shall state my reasons for doubting whether it is in fact true and, finally, I shall indicate very briefly in what direction we might look for a positive alternative.

1. The doctrine takes, as its starting-point, the familiar and undeniable fact that there is a prima facie duality in all knowledge between what I shall hereafter refer to as the 'phenomenal' and the 'physical', between, that is to say, whatever can be known by inspection, by direct acquaintance, by introspection and whatever can be known only indirectly or conceptually by description and inference. The phenomenal objects or entities thus include everything that Empiricist philosophers have, at various times, referred to as ideas, sensations, secondary qualities, sensory qualities, sense-data, sensa, qualia or, if they were American,

35

'raw-feels'. The physical objects or entities include everything that realist philosophers regard as existing independently of experience and yet as being capable of being brought into a causal relationship with experience, whether it be part of the furniture of the commonsense world or the constructs of theoretical physics. The mind–body problem, as it concerns us here, is simply the question as to how the entities of the one class are related to the entities of the other class.

Now, traditionally, there have been two main answers given to this question, the phenomenalist and the materialist. The phenomenalist answer was to treat only the entities of the former class as having ontological status in reality and to regard the members of the latter class as no more than convenient hypothetical abstractions whose relationship with the members of the former class was therefore of an essentially logical type. This was philosophically a neat solution but, while it was sparing with its ontology, it was very costly in the demand it made on one's credulity and, as a result, it was generally repudiated, if not derided, as an affront alike to commonsense and to the logic of science. The materialist answer, on the other hand, though it could not categorically deny the existence of phenomenal entities laid all the emphasis on physical entities. In its *epiphenomenalist* form, which came into its own in the late nineteenth century, it held that the relationship of the physical and the phenomenal was one of cause and effect; only physical events, it insisted, could be causally efficacious, mental events being no more than the epiphenomena of brain-events. But while epiphenomenalism satisfied the scientists, who were chiefly concerned about being able to treat the world as a physically closed system, it was looked upon by the philosophers as an unsatisfactory solution inasmuch as it left the relationship between the physical and phenomenal looking altogether too arbitrary and contingent. The Identity Hypothesis will, I suggest, be best appreciated if it is understood as, in the first instance, an attempt to retain the scientific advantages of epiphenomenalism while satisfying the philosophical demand for parsimony and elegance.

The solution that it proposes may be expressed as follows: the world consists exclusively of physical entities and physical space–time events. What, all this while, we have been calling the phenomenal facts are, it transpires, merely particular physical facts, i.e. brain-states and brain-processes, that happen to become known to us in a very special way, namely by direct acquaintance. This, in a nutshell, is the whole hypothesis.[1] Now, it must be clearly understood that what is being asserted here is not a *logical* identity between the phenomenological account of a particular experience and the physical description of its corresponding brain processes, obviously the two will differ radically from one another in form, in content and in meaning, it is rather an empirical identity, in other words, it is with respect to what is being denoted in either case that we are asked to identify the two. And, of course, there is nothing paradoxical in two radically different descriptions referring to one and the same object: 'the present Queen of England' and 'the successor to George VI' *mean* two quite distinct things but they happen to have the same referent.

One common misunderstanding, however, must be cleared up before we can proceed. Commonsense, being irredeemably naïve-realist in its epistemology, imagines that if a surgeon were to open up a patient's skull and peer in at his brain he would be getting *direct* knowledge of what was going on inside the patient's head, and it is then puzzled because what the surgeon would see there, namely a certain mass of spongy grey tissues, bears no conceivable resemblance to anything that is mentioned by the patient himself when he talks about what he feels and experiences. The fallacy, here, is the pictorial fallacy of confusing the brain as a phenomenal object with the brain as a physical object. The patient's experiences are, according to the Identity Hypothesis, *located* in the patient's physical brain; at the same time the patient's

---

[1] For an account of the Identity Hypothesis, in whatever is the opposite of a nutshell, see Herbert Feigl, 'The "Mental" and the "Physical"' in H. Feigl, M. Scriven & G. Maxwell (Eds.), *Minnesota Studies in the Philosophy of Science*, Vol. II (Univ. of Minnesota Press. Minneapolis, 1958), pp. 370–497. This huge article with its 359 listed items of bibliography constitutes the main source of what I am here calling the Official Version. Bertrand Russell put forward this solution of the mind–body problem in 'Mind and Matter' in *Portraits from Memory* (George Allen & Unwin, 1956) and in 'My Present View of the World', Chap. 2 of *My Philosophical Development* (George Allen & Unwin, 1959). Other proponents of the doctrine include Stephen Pepper, see 'A Neural-Identity Theory of Mind' in S. Hook (Ed.), *Dimensions of Mind* (New York Univ. Press, 1960); R. J. Hirst, see *Problems of Perception* (George Allen & Unwin, 1959) pp. 191–6 and in G. M. Wyburn, R. W. Pickford and R. J. Hirst, *Human Senses and Perception* (Oliver & Boyd, 1964), Part III; and Anthony Quinton, see 'Mind and Matter' (this volume, q.v.).

physical brain is the *cause* of the surgeon's perceptual experience of seeing or touching 'a spongy grey mass' an experience which, in turn, is, of course, located in the surgeon's own physical brain. On the theory we are considering, which takes for granted a causal theory of perception, the physical brain can never be an object of direct acquaintance. It is not the surgeon, therefore, who has direct access to what goes on in the patient's head through his observations, it is rather the patient himself who has this direct knowledge through his introspections. The patient's knowledge is immediate, the surgeon's inferential. Most physical events, of course, are known only in the latter indirect sense. Why any events at all should be knowable in the former direct sense and why, in particular, only a certain class of brain-events should have this introspectible content is a point which the theory does not purport to explain. We presumably just have to accept it as an irreducible fact about the world.

The doctrine that I have expounded in the aforegoing is one that I have taken as the canonical version of the Identity Hypothesis. There is, however, another still more radical and tough-minded version, which has also attracted a following recently, which I must now mention. It would be tempting to call it the Australian Heresy, since its main support appears to be among Australian philosophers, but the name favoured by its principal spokesmen is 'Central-State Materialism'.[2] The crux of this version is that it does away entirely with phenomenal entities of any kind. It does this by making use of a number of well-known philosophical devices taken from Operationism and from Logical Behaviourism but its most original and effective manoeuvre is its daring assimilation of perception and of introspection to the concept of belief. Thus perception is simply an acquiring of beliefs about the external physical environment *as a result of* sensory stimu-

[2] My main source for Central State Materialism is J. J. C. Smart, see *Philosophy and Scientific Realism* (Routledge & Kegan Paul, 1963), also 'Sensations and Brain Processes' (*Phil. Review*, **68**. 1959. 141–56), 'Colours' (*Phil.*, **36**. 1961. 128–43) and 'Materialism' (*J. of Phil.*, **60**. 1963. 651–62). In his book Smart acknowledges his debt to U. T. Place for the latter's 'Is Consciousness a Brain Process?' (*Brit. J. of Psychol.*, **47**. 1956. 44–51). Another supporter of the theory is D. M. Armstrong, see esp. 'The Nature of Perception', Chap. 9 of *Perception and the Physical World* (Routledge & Kegan Paul, 1961) and *Bodily Sensations* (Routledge & Kegan Paul, 1962), although Armstrong's analysis does not tally at all points with that of Smart.

lation (beliefs which are true if the perception is veridical, false if the perception is illusory). Likewise introspection is an acquiring of beliefs about the internal physical environment, in particular the subject's own brain. Now, just as we do not need any existential entity to be the object of a belief, so we do not need one in the case of perception or introspection. The so-called 'secondary qualities'‚ of objects, such as colours, are not phenomenal entities, after all, they are simply properties of physical entities that 'evoke certain sorts of discriminatory responses in human beings'.[3] If, against this interpretation, it is pointed out that we can have a colour sensation, as in an after-image, when there is no physical colour-stimulus, this merely shows that sometimes we can have an experience that is exactly *like* the experience we have with the appropriate physical stimulus (the temptation to ask in what *respect* the two are alike must be resisted). Similarly, if I declare that I have a pain, this does not imply that a pain can be the object of immediate awareness, it is to be understood as meaning that something, whatever it may be, is going on inside me *like* what goes on when someone sticks a pin into me.[4] In short, the language of experience is always *topic-neutral*, it leaves quite open the nature of its referent. It is of course conceivable that this might be some sort of a psychic stuff, as dualists have maintained, but there is nothing to compel us to accept such a suggestion and it is much simpler to suppose that the referent is something physical, namely a state of the brain or nervous-system. Naturally, commonsense does not realize that when a person says he is happy he is actually talking about the *physical* condition of his nervous system, nature has made us in such a way that we neither know, nor do we need to know, what goes on inside our skin, but thanks to science and philosophical analysis we are now in a position to say that being happy refers not to a mental state at all but to a physical state, one, moreover, which has among its consequences that it causes a person to behave in a characteristically happy way.

If Central-State Materialism can be sustained there is no reason why it should not supersede entirely the official version of the Identity Hypothesis since it is clearly more parsimonious and more successfully physicalistic. I am, however, by no means con-

---

[3] Smart, 'Sensations and Brain Processes' (*op. cit.*) p. 149.
[4] *Idem*, pp. 153–4.

vinced as yet that the doctrine *is* a defensible one. The stumbling-block lies, I suspect, in its key concept of 'topic neutrality'. Now, in the usual way, a statement may be regarded as topic neutral if it is in some critical sense indeterminate (the example Smart himself offers is the sentence 'someone is coming through the garden'[5]). But a description in phenomenal terms can be as determinate as one pleases, that is the content of an experience could, in principle, be specified uniquely and exhaustively. It is hard to see, therefore, what room is left for reinterpreting such descriptions as really describing something quite different, namely certain electro-chemical processes. We may agree with Smart that there are good arguments for denying that introspective reports are ever indubitable or incorrigible in the strictest sense, but this is a very far cry from asserting that they are always and necessarily misleading. On the contrary, we still have every reason to believe that our own experiences constitute that domain of facts on which each of us remains perforce the best possible authority. For such reasons I am very doubtful if Central-State Materialism is a valid, let alone a plausible solution of the mind–body problem. By effectively denying any reality to consciousness it runs into all the old objections that bedevilled early mechanistic behaviourism, objections based on the privacy and epistemological priority of introspection, while forfeiting any of the commonsense appeal of Rylean behaviourism. For our present purposes, however, a verdict is scarcely necessary. Since it is, avowedly, the more audacious doctrine it is only proper that, in my capacity as critic, I should concentrate my attack on the more innocent-seeming double-aspect version of the Identity Hypothesis.

2. One reason why the Identity Hypothesis has acquired a certain topical interest is the now widely acknowledged failure of the linguistic *dissolution* of the mind–body problem. The idea that perhaps the facts of behaviour and the facts of experience were not, after all, two different kinds of facts, that somehow had to be related to one another, but rather represented two different ways of talking about the same set of facts, both equally admissible, was not a new idea. It had a precedent in Aristotle's distinction between the physical and the dialectical modes of discourse. But,

---

[5] *Philosophy and Scientific Realism* (op. cit.), p. 95.

those who took their cue from Wittgenstein made an all-out effort to attack the mind–body problem, especially the public/ private dichotomy, purely by the methods of linguistic analysis. The fatal weakness of a two-language theory, however, is that if the physical and the phenomenal are really just two different languages they ought to be mutually translatable. But in that case since the objective language has the wider field of application and is scientifically the more valuable the case for translating phenomenological accounts wherever possible into physical accounts would be unanswerable and so the demands of the Identity Hypothesis would in fact be met.

A similar weakness beset Ryle's attempt to interpret mental states in terms of dispositions. For, as soon as we stop to consider what *explains* the dispositions we are forced to recognize that it is nothing more than the structure of our nervous-system. The state of the brain explains, say, a person's beliefs precisely as the composition of glass explains its brittleness. Thus, the logical outcome of taking Ryle seriously can only be a Central-State Materialism. To write a complete defence of behaviourism, as Ryle did, and then in the final chapter of your book to disclaim with scorn the imputation of mechanism and materialism seems now, more than ever, a case of double-talk. If Ryle is right that mind is nothing beyond what can be exemplified in overt performance then, equally, Smart has every right to feel confident that 'even the behaviour of man himself will one day be explicable in mechanistic terms'.[6]

Merely to intone the old tautologies that man is man, an animal is an animal, a machine is a machine, while it may induce temporary complacency, can hardly be expected in the long run to carry conviction.

What, then, is the mind–body problem about? To say that it is not just about words does not imply of course that it is purely about facts. It is not a scientific controversy, if by that is meant that it might be settled by some crucial experiment or by some decisive new discovery but neither is it a purely metaphysical issue, if by that is meant that scientific knowledge has no bearing on the problem. Like most of the perennial problems of philosophy it is partly empirical and partly conceptual. There will always be a certain latitude as to how one is to interpret the facts but the

[6] 'Sensations and Brain Processes' (*op. cit.*), p. 42

interpretations gain or lose in credibility as the factual content of our knowledge changes.

The question which the mind–body problem poses may now be stated as follows: for the interpretation of human behaviour and experience do we, or do we not, need any concepts that cannot be analyzed in terms of the concepts used in the interpretation of physical events? If the answer is that we do, then we are clearly committed to some form of dualism, but if the answer is that we do not, then the Identity Hypothesis is vindicated. The view that I am taking in this paper is that while the case for an Identity Hypothesis is strong, and will probably become even stronger, it cannot be considered overwhelming; in other words those who, for one reason or another, find it repellent can still justify their opposition on rational grounds.

Why, one may ask, should anyone try to produce a completely physicalist theory of mind? It would, I think, be a great mistake to regard such a theory as just another philosophical *tour-de-force*; its justification is, I believe, implicit in the very nature of the scientific enterprise itself. Now, perhaps the primary aim of science, as an intellectual pursuit, is to expand indefinitely the explanatory power of its theories. This aim, however, involves two subsidiary aims: (*a*) to subsume as many phenomena as possible under one or another scientific law and (*b*) to derive as many of the laws as possible from the least number of basic laws. Determinism may be defined as the doctrine which holds that there is no limit in principle to the attainment of aim (*a*) and Reductionism as the doctrine which holds that there is no limit to the attainment of aim (*b*). Materialism, in its strongest form (which I shall denote by using a capital M) may then be defined as a doctrine that jointly affirms both Determinism and Reductionism. As such, incidentally, it reflects better perhaps than any other philosophical position the aspirations of science. In virtue of its deterministic principle it refuses to acknowledge that there can be any phenomena that must for ever remain outside what Feigl calls 'the nomological net', in virtue of its reductionist principle it refuses to acknowledge that there can be any irreducibly *emergent* laws. Thus, if Materialism is true there are no inherent limits to scientific progress but if Materialism is not true then the success of the scientific enterprise can never be more than partial. The Identity Hypothesis is simply the logical consequence of applying the Materialist standpoint to the mind–body problem.

In assessing the current strength of Materialism it is important to remember that even within the most basic and universal of the sciences, theoretical physics, neither of its two main objectives looks, at present, like being fulfilled. The deterministic principle has broken down in the face of quantum phenomena and it has not been found possible to reduce the laws governing the gravitational field, the electromagnetic field and the forces holding between nuclear particles to any common set of basic equations nor to resolve the duality of wave and particle. Nevertheless, it would, I think, be obscurantist to interpret this as a major defeat for Materialism. Determinism still holds at the macroscopic level even if it cannot (as certain unorthodox theorists still hope) be salvaged at the microscopic level. Likewise, even if Einstein spent thirty years of his life in a vain attempt to produce a unified field theory some new Einstein may yet come along to vindicate the reductionist principle.

But whatever the prospects for physics there can, to my mind, be no doubt that developments in biology have given Materialism a very considerable boost. The phenomena of life were, after all, one of the traditional testing grounds of materialist philosophy. Some philosophers even argued that the distinction between living and non-living things was even more fundamental than the distinction between the presence and absence of mind. Modern advances in biochemistry and biophysics has now virtually destroyed the case for Vitalism. There are, it is true, a few thinkers who still believe that we shall always need certain 'biotonic' laws in addition to our physical laws,[7] but the overwhelming weight of informed opinion is against them. This has become especially apparent since Crick and Watson unravelled the structure of the DNA molecule about ten years ago and thereby made possible a whole new science of molecular genetics. Since then there has been a general shift in the focus of biological research to molecular biology and many of the basic biological processes, cell-division and differentiation, morphogenesis, reproduction, etc., are now being tackled in molecular terms. Even the old

---

[7] Cf. W. Elsasser, *The Physical Foundations of Biology* (Pergamon Press, 1958) or, for a more full-blooded defence of Vitalism, R. O. Kapp, *Science versus Materialism* (Methuen, 1940).

problem of the origin of life has recently been a target for serious scientific investigation. As a result, even if we cannot as yet synthesize life *in vitro* we do, it seems, know enough about the chemical preconditions of life to be able to link Darwinian evolution with that much longer process of chemical evolution that preceded it and culminated in the macro-molecules out of which life developed.

It is against these new perspectives in science and evolutionary theory that the Identity Hypothesis must be seen. So long as epiphenomenalism was the only answer which Materialism could offer when confronted by the phenomena of mind, the position of these phenomena inside the nomological net could never be considered very secure, the possibility that there might be emergent laws of mind which would resist reductive analysis could never be completely eliminated. But once the Identity Hypothesis is accepted then, of course, it becomes theoretically impossible that mind should manifest any kind of autonomy, one cannot talk of an interaction between two aspects of one and the same thing; thunder and lightning cannot interact! Thus the Identity Hypothesis promises to remove the last important philosophical impediment to the unity of the sciences; the remaining difficulties would be of a technical nature only. It is true that this final hurdle may be surmounted only at the cost of transforming our preconceptions about the intrinsic properties of matter but, it would, as Smart has put it, 'vastly simplify our cosmological outlook'.[8]

There are, however, certain *a priori* objections to Materialism that must first be considered before we can be sure that the Identity Hypothesis is not based on some logical fallacy. The arguments I wish to consider in this context are those that seek to show that Reductionism is not a programme which can, even in principle, be fulfilled. Two arguments, in particular, are advanced in this connection which I shall call respectively the logical and the epistemological arguments.

The logical argument has been used extensively by philosophers in recent times to refute the claims both of Operationism and Positivism, both notoriously reductionist positions. It points out that except in purely formal disciplines like symbolic logic or pure mathematics, higher-level concepts never entail any set or disjunction of lower-level concepts and, conversely, no set or dis-

---

[8] 'Materialism' (*op. cit.*), p. 661.

junction of lower-level concepts can ever be made logically equivalent to a concept of higher-level. No matter in which direction we proceed at some point we have to jump a logical gap. Thus, if we take as an example some ordinary commonsense observable, say, a chair, we soon realize that the concept of the chair can never be unpacked, or logically explicated, either physically, as a particular molecular configuration or, phenomenally, as a specifiable sequence of actual or potential sense-data. And, of course, what applies to something as commonplace as a chair applies even more forcibly to the sophisticated concepts of science or philosophy which are always, in the very nature of the case, open-ended.

The epistemological argument is one that has recently been developed in great detail and with great skill by Polanyi.[9] Here the emphasis is upon the tacit or unspecifiable aspects of the act of knowing. When we grasp, what Polanyi calls, a 'comprehensive entity' (e.g. a concrete object, a machine, an organism, a person, a sentence, a work of art, a scientific theory) we are invariably doing so by relying on a tacit awareness of its particulars. For, the moment we focus attention on the particulars the comprehensive entity vanishes. One cannot, at one and the same time, perceive an object and attend to the sense-data on which perception of the object depends. One cannot understand a spoken phrase while attending to the speech-sounds of which it is comprised (words, in fact, are only meaningful so long as they remain transparent). Even a machine, according to Polanyi, cannot be understood wholly in terms of physics and chemistry, since to understand a machine is to understand the operational principles which govern the interconnection of its parts. Nor, for similar reasons, can the Universe itself be comprehended as a Laplacean machine of interacting particles because such a conception would rob the Universe of all meaning leaving it with no features that could be identified or explained. In particular, Polanyi singles out Behaviourism as an example of the reductionist fallacy because it attempts to identify minds with those behavioural particulars on which we tacitly rely for our knowledge of other minds.

Now I believe both these arguments are valid and important

[9] *Vide* M. Polanyi, 'Tacit Knowing': Its Bearing on some Problems of Philosophy' (*Reviews of Modern Physics*, **34**. 1962. 601–16), see also his book *Personal Knowledge* (Routledge & Kegan Paul, 1958).

but that they are valid only as refutations of, respectively, logical reductionism and epistemological reductionism. Materialism can, I believe, be formulated in such a way as to avoid these vicious sorts of reductionism. What it does involve is what I shall call 'Theoretical Reductionism' and not only is this legitimate, but science, as opposed to pure descriptive generalizations, would be inconceivable without it. Theoretical reduction can be illustrated quite easily by considering any of the familiar laws of elementary science. Take, for example, Boyle's Law. This gives us the relationship that holds between the temperature, pressure and volume in a given body of gas. But the theory of gases, as developed in the nineteenth century by Maxwell and Boltzmann, was able to show that this relationship, as well as many other properties of gases, was a necessary consequence of the kinetic energy of the individual particles of which the gas was composed. There is here no question of a logical reduction, properties such as temperature, pressure, volume, etc., still remain properties of the high-level concept 'gas', indeed they would make no sense applied to the low-level concept 'molecule'. Nor does it follow that we could arrive at the concept 'gas' if we concentrated solely on the concept 'molecule'. Nevertheless, theoretical reduction has been achieved. A similar reduction was achieved in the present century when Morgan was able to identify the Mendelian transmitters of heredity with the 'genes' located in the chromosomes of the germ-cells; a reduction which, as we have seen, was taken yet a stage further when the genes themselves were identified as DNA molecules. When the Materialist claims, therefore, that mental states can be identified with a specific circuitry of brain-cells we must not do him the injustice of supposing that he cannot tell the difference between the meaning of these two concepts or the way in which they come to be apprehended. All he asks us to do is to admit that psychology could be theoretically reduced to neurophysiology in exactly the same way as biology has been reduced to biochemistry and macrophysics to microphysics.

3. If I am right in thinking that Identity Hypothesis offers a genuine and coherent solution of the mind–body problem, then it remains only to consider whether the solution it offers is a plausible one. Now, there are many critics who, even if they could not say what exactly was wrong with it, would want to dismiss it

on the intuitive grounds that it 'felt wrong' to them. I shall not be concerned, however with this subjective sort of plausibility, I want to consider only how well the theory can stand up within the frame of reference in which it has been defended. Accordingly, my critique will deal with three points only: (*a*) the oddity of making consciousness a functionally redundant product of evolution, (*b*) the apparent lack of congruence between the phenomenal and physical domains, and (*c*) the difficulties of accounting, on this theory, for the empirical evidence for paranormal events.

(*a*) Since the implications of the Identity Hypothesis do not appear to differ materially from those of epiphenomenalism it has to meet one objection, at any rate, that was always levelled against the earlier doctrine, namely, that it makes it impossible to ask why (as opposed to when, or under what conditions) we should ever have to come to *feel* anything or *be aware of* anything whatsoever. That desire or pleasure should arise in connection with *adient* behaviour while fear and pain should be associated with *abient* behaviour remains simply a brute fact of nature but has no more bearing on the explanation of such behaviour than, say, the screeching of automobile brakes has on the explanation of their braking-action.

Feigl, it is true, denies that the Identity Hypothesis does have these embarrassing implications. He argues, on the contrary, that as against epiphenomenalism, where mental events are indeed no more than 'nomological danglers', the Identity Hypothesis restores to them their commonsense causal efficacy. 'This is so,' he writes 'because the raw-feel terms are then precisely in those loci of the nomological net where science puts (what dualistic parallelism regards as) their neural correlates.'[10] His plea is interesting and ingenious but, I fear, largely specious. What matters, surely, is the character of the nomological net. But since, on Feigl's analysis, physical determinism is in no way affected it follows that we could still, in principle, predict every item of behaviour given only the physical facts, disregarding completely any conscious concomitants. The analogy would be to the case in which one was presented with a clockwork mechanism where one would obviously ignore any optical properties or effects that one might observe as quite irrelevant to the dynamics of the situation.

[10] 'The "Mental" and the "Physical"' (*op. cit.*), p. 475.

That consciousness should have arisen at all becomes all the more puzzling when we consider how far adaptive behaviour can go without benefit of sentience. Thus, not only are all the internal vegetative processes of the organism unconscious but so, also, are those overt responses that we call reflex or habitual. Even in visual perception it is only the finished product, as it were, that enters into conscious awareness, all those reflex processes on which successful vision depends: lens-accommodation, pupillary contraction, binocular convergence, eye-movement, etc., all take place at an unconscious level. And, since consciousness confers no biological advantages, one may speculate that, given a slightly different twist at some earlier point of the phylogenetic sequence, evolution could just as well have culminated in a race of wholly insentient automata! Conceivably, these creatures would have been able to do all that we can do, they might even have looked like us, so that a human being introduced into their midst would never suspect that they were different. Conceivably, too, if, as now seems rather probable, evolution elsewhere in the Universe has produced rational intelligent creatures they may indeed *be* insentient automata; for consciousness being no more than a meaningless freak of nature might well depend on an organism being compounded of the right sort of terrestrial protein! These reflections, of course, do not dispose of the theory, nature may be even odder than we had supposed, but they do alert us to the possibility that there may be something queer about the assumptions on which the theory is based.

(*b*) It might, on first glance, seem as if the sheer variety of possible mental states would defeat any hope of establishing a one–one correspondence with brain-states. For, after all, one brain-cell, so far as we can tell, is structurally and functionally very much like any other brain-cell. Yet, when we reflect that the entire range of phenotypical variations in organisms can now be plausibly accounted for in terms of genes differing from one another only in minor details of chemical structure, it seems perhaps less extraordinary that all our mental states should be reducible to the arousal of different combinations of cell-assemblies.

There is, however, one respect in which the reduction of the phenomenal to the physical poses problems quite unlike that which occurs in any other field. For, elsewhere in science, however much the properties of the macro-object may differ from those of the micro-object both fit equally the universal conceptual framework of physical space. Phenomenal objects, on the other hand, cannot be thus anchored in physical space, nor, it would seem, is there any set of dimensions that would constitute a common phenomenal space for objects belonging to diverse sense-modalities. Such an apparent incommensurability between the phenomenal and physical domains did not matter much on an epiphenomenalist theory where the correspondence was any-how no more than a causal one, it might even be tolerated by a Gestaltist adherent of isomorphic parallelism, but for a theory which insists upon a numerical identity between the two domains this is a definite obstacle.

When next we consider what kind of a correspondence might obtain between the phenomenal particulars and their neural sub-strata we find from the empirical evidence that it is of an essentially topographical nature. In other words, we can, at last, after a cen-tury of psycho-physiological research on the localization of brain functions, affirm that the diverse sense-modalities correspond to different regions of the cerebral cortex while the gamut of intra-modal sensations correspond to different loci within those regions. That, roughly, is what is meant by the theory of cortical projection which, as a first approximation at any rate, is now an integral part of the standard theory of sensory physiology. Now the fact that mere variation of position on the brain surface should turn out to be identifiable with the manifold qualitative varia-tions of the phenomenal domain is itself remarkable enough but a peculiar difficulty arises when we inquire what constitutes the neural substratum of phenomenal space.

If, for example, we consider the spatial properties of the visual field we find that, thanks to the psychological laws of size and shape constancy, the geometry of visual space corresponds fairly closely with the geometry of the external physical environment (it is precisely because of this that naïve realism is psychologically so compelling). But, for this very reason, there can be no such correspondence with the projection of the visual scene on the irregular convoluted surface of the observer's brain. A circular stimulus-figure, viewed from the appropriate angle will produce a phenomenal circle in the observer's sense-field, but the cortical projection of this circle in the observer's occipital lobe will be very far from circular.[11] And this discrepancy becomes all the more striking when we consider the case of three-dimensional figures, let us suppose the observer is looking down a hollow tube. Here, a double projection at the cortical level has somehow to be fused to give a single depth-effect at the perceptual level.

Smythies even goes so far as to suggest that this breakdown in topological correspondence between the two domains argues decisively against an Identity Hypothesis.[12] But this is perhaps going too far. Whichever way we look at it the postulated identity is of such a unique kind that it is hard to say precisely what criteria it has to satisfy. Conceivably, therefore, the spatial properties of phenomenal objects might turn out to be identical with certain invariant properties of cell-assemblies that were not themselves spatial in any sense. At all events it would be premature to suggest that the theory could not be rescued by some more subtle analysis. In the meantime, however, such considerations undoubtedly increase one's misgivings. Admittedly, if you adopt the Central-State version of the theory such considerations will not worry you, for then there simply are no phenomenal objects of any kind spatial or non-spatial, only certain kinds of beliefs expressed in topic-neutral language, but it is not everyone who is prepared to pay the philosophical price for this immunity.

(c) I have left until last what I personally regard as the most damaging objection to any materialist theory of mind, namely, the parapsychological evidence. This, it seems to me, is the empirical reef on which the Identity Hypothesis is doomed to founder even if it can survive all other hazards. Most of its supporters do indeed recognize the danger but, like Feigl, pin their faith to the ability of science to explain the ESP phenomena eventually along more or less conventional lines (obscure brain-functions, unsuspected sources of energy, etc.). Such faith, though plausible enough twenty or thirty years ago, is now increasingly unrealistic. The choice that confronts us today, I submit, is a very drastic one: either we must blankly refuse to credit the evidence or we must be prepared to accept a radical

[11] Cf. W. Russell Brain, *Mind, Perception and Science* (Blackwell, Oxford, 1951), pp. 4–9.
[12] *Vide* 'The Representative Theory of Perception' (this volume, q.v.).

revision to the whole contemporary scientific world-picture on which materialism has taken its stand.[13]

Those who have opted for the former alternative can justify their scepticism by exploiting a peculiar dilemma of parapsychology which may be described as follows: Phenomena may be classified as either of the spontaneous type or of the laboratory type. The former, though often rich in psychological content, are bound, almost in the nature of the case, to be poor in evidential worth. The latter, though often impeccable from an evidential standpoint, are notoriously difficult to replicate and usually meagre in psychological meaning. Hence, the former can easily be attributed to the fallibility of human testimony while the latter can always be put down to miscellaneous experimental artifacts of an unspecified kind. It seems safe to say, therefore, that until such a time as the laboratory phenomena can be brought under full experimental control there is little likelihood of this deadlock being broken and so of overcoming the suspicion with which parapsychology is still regarded by the representatives of official science.

But while it is the prerogative of official science to suspend judgment in a case like this there can be no excuse for a philosopher to feign ignorance or act as if parapsychology were some sort of international conspiracy. The extent and quality of the literature,[14] its persisting rate of accumulation, the credentials of its authors, force us to reckon with the possibility that the facts are as they purport to be. This means that, on present showing, we must reckon with such intractable phenomena as telepathy (including long-distance telepathy), precognition, clairvoyance and, perhaps, psychokinesis.[15] The question arises then as to what exactly it would mean to say that these are merely physical

[13] I have defended this view more fully elsewhere, see my article 'Explaining the Paranormal' (*J. of the S.P.R.*, 42. 1963. 1–5), also 'The Paranormal', Chap. 7 of my book *The Existence of Mind* (MacGibbon & Kee, 1962).

[14] Cf. G. Zorab, *Bibliography of Parapsychology* (Parapsych. Foundation. New York, 1957), which gives a wide international coverage, also Helene Pleasants (Ed.), *Biographical Dictionary of Parapsychology* (Helix Press, Garrett Publications, New York, 1964).

[15] E. Girden, in his 'Review of Psychokinesis' (*Psychol. Bull.*, 59. 1962. 353–89) disputes the validity of this claim but see also the counter-attack by Gardner Murphy, myself and others in 'A Discussion of Psychokinesis' (*Internat. J. of Parapsych.* Winter 1964. 77–137).

phenomena of an unusual sort? Or, perhaps, the same question can be put more concretely if we ask: how, in principle, would one set about designing, equipping and programming a computer so that it would be capable of telepathic, clairvoyant or precognitive performances?

It is, I think, significant that those who bother to ask themselves this question at all do so, usually, only with reference to telepathy.[16] For, of all psi-phenomena, telepathy is clearly the one that most naturally invites a physical analogue. Yet, the fact remains that all attempts to substantiate a 'radio-communication' hypothesis have failed completely.[17] It is not surprising therefore that those who take the physicalist approach seriously are be-beginning to realize that the minimum requirement of a physics capable of incorporating telepathy is one that can allow for direct causal interaction across a spatio-temporal gap.[18] Now, such a physics is not by any means unthinkable, conceivably as matter becomes more and more highly organized in ever more complex wholes (and nothing in the Universe exceeds in complexity the human brain) new effects become observable that would not be detectable where matter exists in a less complex state, and that it is precisely these effects that we now call 'paranormal'. There are even several important precedents for such an extension of physics to cover extreme conditions. What is of course unthinkable is that such an extension could be accomplished without

[16] Thus, M. Scriven writes: 'The evidence for telepathy in humans is hard to dismiss fairly, but *there is no ground* for thinking that it cannot be regarded as a brain function of a new kind, analogous to the generation of the alpha- and beta-rhythms.' (my italics). 'The Compleat Robot', in *Dimensions of Mind* (*op cit.*), p. 138. Yet just how formidable *are* the grounds against such a supposition were clearly stated by W. Grey Walter in his *The Living Brain* (Penguin Books, 1961), pp. 214–5.

[17] It is significant in this connection that despite the obvious anxiety of Soviet scientists to find a respectable explanation of telepathy Russia's foremost parapsychologist, Prof. L. L. Vasiliev (head of the Department of Physiology at Leningrad University), was forced in the end to discard a 'radio' or electromagnetic hypothesis. One reason was that positive results were still forthcoming even when percipient and/or agent were encased inside a radiation-proof cabin! *vide Experiments in Mental Suggestion* (Leningrad Univ. press. 1962, transl. Gregory & Kohsen. Galley Hill Press. I.M.S.I., Church Crookham. Hants., 1963).

[18] Cf. N. Marshall 'ESP and Memory: A Physical Theory' (*Brit. J. for The Philosophy of Science.* **10**. 1959. 265–87).

radically changing our entire conception of matter and of the physical world. And, even then, one may wonder whether it would be enough to do the trick. After all, in the case of clairvoyance the *real* puzzle is not just the absence of the normal channels of sensory communication but the fact that some specific stimulus can be singled out from among all the stimuli from the environment for recognition.

If, on the strength of any or all the arguments I have advanced in this paper, we decide to reject the Identity Hypothesis what should be our next step? Certainly there is little to be said for reverting to the now discredited doctrine of epiphenomenalism. In the circumstances, and despite the inevitable antagonism which such a move must arouse from those who see themselves as the defenders of the scientific faith, the most promising opening seems to me to lie in some form of avowed interactionism. In other words, instead of treating the *prima facie* duality of phenomenal and physical, which formed our starting point, as something to be eliminated at all costs, we should rather accept it as a reflection of a still more fundamental duality in nature. If we do this we shall no longer need to force the parapsychological evidence into a deterministic framework to which it is so ill-adapted but can acknowledge it as an empirical demonstration of the fact that the laws of mind do not necessarily or invariably coincide with the laws governing material objects.

Perhaps one reason why interactionism has had, on the whole, a very bad press among philosophers is that the phenomenal entities seemed such unlikely candidates for the role of the causal agent in mental acts. How, for example, it was asked, could anything as intangible as a 'volition', considered as a pure datum of introspection, actually bring about an overt response? To this there is, I think, no satisfactory answer so long as we continue, in the Empiricist tradition, to equate mind with the content of consciousness. But, one of the more significant aspects of parapsychology, in this connection, is the emphasis it places on the unconscious. Even depth-psychology and hypnosis could never quite succeed in persuading philosophers of a positivistic bent that there was any need to take the unconscious seriously, since, in the last resort, one could always identify unconscious mental events with neurological events. But in parapsychology we are constantly confronted with phenomena that cannot be explained as the effects either of neurological events or of conscious mental events. We are thus driven by a consideration of the empirical facts to postulate a transcendental cause behind both bodily behaviour and conscious experience. This leads to a conception of Mind, which though nowadays looked upon as excessively extravagant, has a long and respectable philosophical history. On this view voluntary behaviour, for example, would be explained as due neither to the experience of 'willing' nor to electrical impulses in the motor-cortex but to a transcendental mind or 'self' acting upon the automatisms of the body.[19] Likewise, perception would no longer be explained as a case of brain-events automatically generating sense-data but as the 'self' or 'witness'[20] using the mechanisms of brain and sense-organ to attain an awareness of the world.

COMMENTS BY LORD BRAIN

This chapter is concerned with a statement of the Identity Hypothesis which I am unable to accept. The author says that this consists of a belief that 'the world consists exclusively of physical entities and physical space–time events. What, all this while, we have been calling the phenomenal facts are, it transpires, merely particular physical facts, i.e. brain-states and brain-processes, that happen to become known to us in a very special way, namely by direct acquaintance. This, in a nutshell, is the whole hypothesis'. This, it seems to me, is simply a statement of materialism since it regards mental events as actually, or potentially, explicable in terms of physical events, that is to say it gives the primacy to physical events. Since, however, we have direct knowledge of mental events, and only indirect of the events which constitute their physical basis, this appears to me to be invalid. Moreover, as regards the physical events occurring in the nervous system we have at present only the most elementary knowledge of them at comparatively simple levels of organization, and none at all of the ultimate physical basis of thinking, willing and remembering. Both on logical and empirical grounds, therefore, it would seem better to give the primacy

[19] In support of this view cf. H. Zanstra, *The Construction of Reality* (Pergamon Press, 1962), or R. H. Thouless and B. Wiesner, 'The Psi Process in Normal and Paranormal Psychology' (*Proc. of the S.P.R.*, **48**. 1947. 177–96, or *J. of Parapsych.*, **12**. 1948. 192–212).

[20] I have borrowed this expression from J. R. Smythies, *The Analysis of Perception* (Routledge & Kegan Paul, 1956), pp. 115–9.

to mental events. If, therefore, I have reason to think that I can exercise choice it is no reason for rejecting that view to argue that physical events at an elementary level in the nervous system are determined, even if that be true, because we do not know what physical laws describe the behaviour of the many millions of nerve cells acting together which underlie the higher mental activities, and as far as I can see there is no ground for believing that they must follow the same laws as elementary events. Incidentally, what evidence there is suggests that in some respects the activity of the nervous system at some higher levels is probabilistic.

Discussing the two-language theory Beloff says 'the fatal weakness of a two-language theory, however, is that if the physical and the phenomenal are really just two different languages they ought to be mutually translatable'. I have already suggested that, even if it proves possible to translate the mental language into the physical one, it by no means follows that the physical language will be simply that with which we are already familiar in physics. At present the two languages are not mutually translatable, but it does not follow from that that such translation is inherently impossible. The reason may simply be that we do not yet know enough about either or both languages. For this reason I cannot accept Beloff's conclusion that if we at present 'need any concepts that cannot be analysed in terms of the concepts used in the interpretation of physical events' for the interpretation of human behaviour and experience, 'we are clearly committed to some form of dualism'. We certainly do need such concepts, but there is no *a priori* reason for concluding that it will never be possible to translate them into concepts describing physical events. Beloff appears on general grounds to favour dualism, that is to say that brain and mind are in some sense separate substances, but this view seems to have implications which he does not develop. In evolution it is very difficult to find any point in the scale of life at which mind cannot be said to exist. The behaviour of bees and birds, for example, exhibits features which, if they occurred in human beings, we should describe as mental, and I know of no reason for denying consciousness in some elementary form to comparatively simple organisms. If this is so, at what point in the scale of evolution does mind make its appearance, and what on the dualistic hypothesis is the status of the mind of the bee or a bird? Is it an individual mind, and does it survive the destruction of the creature's body, or is it part of some universal mind, and what is the bearing of our conclusions on this point upon the status of the human mind if it is substantially independent of the body?

COMMENTS BY C. J. DUCASSE

The paper presents fairly the two versions of the mind–body Identity Hypothesis on which it comments.

But it seems to me that the paper does not question as sharply as they call for some weak points in the hypothesis. For example, p. 36, line 1 ff: Precisely what do the Identity theorists mean when they call an event 'physical'? And then, are any events at all, that are 'physical' in such sense as is assigned to the word, known otherwise than *indirectly*; i.e. known otherwise than through the mode of knowing called 'perceiving' (which consists in *interpreting* sensations)? Precisely what is meant by 'direct' knowing of a *physical* event? Or is not this simply a question-begging, arbitrarily language-perverting locution? For, to *introspect* a physical event is, in English as distinguished from Identitese, an internally contradictory locution.

Again, just how does Central-State Materialism define 'belief', and how does it claim to be able to know whether a person P does or does not have a particular belief B, at a time when P's behaviour is not a manifestation of belief B but of some other?

As regards the long terminal paragraph on p. 53: To speak of a volition as 'intangible' is only to use 'intangible' as a smear word (since nobody would claim that volitions can be *touched*). The *only* thing the causality relation requires of a candidate for the status of cause or of effect is that the candidate be an *event*, no matter whether it be material, mental or transcendental.

Again, occurrence of a volition is one thing, and introspection of it is another, which seldom occurs, and which, when it does, is not what causes the effect for which a cause was sought.

Again, if a volition, in virtue of its 'phenomenal' nature, is alleged to be unfit to function as cause, then consistency demands that, in the converse direction, a pain, whose nature is likewise 'phenomenal', should be regarded as equally unfit to be an effect of a physical event, e.g. of a pin-prick.

The Empiricist tradition has *erred* in its equating of mind with the *content* of consciousness (and I would add, that to equate mind with the *content* of both consciousness and subconsciousness or unconsciousness would be equally an error). For such equating ignores the crucial distinction between the *nature* of a mind which consists of a set of dispositions, and the *history* of a mind which consists of such events as constituted exercise of ones or others of its dispositions at particular times. Postulating 'a transcendental mind or "self" acting upon the automatisms of the body' is gratuitous as a substitute for volitions in causation of 'overt response', i.e. bodily events; for, that no substitute for volitions is needed at all for this becomes evident as soon as one duly adverts to the basic fact that the *only* thing the causality relation requires as to the nature of its terms is that they be *events*, to wit, changes, or endurings unchanged.

The scientifically important thing about paranormal phenomena is that they are evidence that material things, and also minds, do have some dispositions additional to those which the orthodox physics and the orthodox psychology of today are yet aware of.

COMMENTS BY ANTONY FLEW

Since it is only at the end of his paper and very briefly that Dr. Beloff begins to outline as an alternative his own sort of Cartesianism, we shall not try to come to grips with it here. The bulk of his paper is devoted to the sympathetic presentation and examination of the Identity Hypothesis: which he considers—rightly, I think—to be a programme 'implicit in the very nature of the scientific enterprise itself' (p. 42). The Identity Hypothesis (I.H.) he states as the claim that: 'What . . . we have been calling the phenomenal facts are . . . merely particular physical facts, i.e. brain-states and brain-processes, that happen to become known to us in a very special way, namely by direct acquaintance' (p. 36). A tougher variant, which might appropriately be called 'the Australian Heresy', is Central-State Materialism (C.S.M.): 'The crux of this version is that it does away entirely with phenomenal entities of any kind' (p. 38).[21]

(1) In his Section 3 (*a*) Beloff deploys against I.H. an objection which has often been opposed to the older thesis of Epiphenomenalism. The objection is: 'that it makes it impossible to ask why (as opposed to when or under what conditions) we should ever have to come to *feel* anything or *be aware* of anything whatsoever . . . since consciousness confers no biological advantages, one may speculate that . . . evolution could just as well have culminated in a race of wholly insentient automata' (p. 47 and p. 48). Now it certainly is a consequence of both I.H. and C.S.M. that consciousness is not an extra and isolable causal factor for the evolution of which a separate explanation might possibly be required.

In the latter case this would presumably be because C.S.M. is committed to discarding phenomenal entities (i.e. sense data, etc.). Beloff

[21] Beloff might perhaps have given still further support to his forcefully argued and persuasive contention that 'the logical outcome of taking Ryle seriously can only be Central-State Materialism' (p. 41) by noticing that Professor Smart is not the only Australian Heresiarch to have been one of Ryle's research students.

does not himself apply the present objection to C.S.M. directly; for he prefers, very properly, to concentrate his attack on I.H. as the weaker, and hence less vulnerable, version of the opposing thesis. But it is hard to see why anyone who is prepared to discard phenomenal entities should have to think of it as a further objection to this bold rejection that it must commit him to denying that there is any room for an account of their evolution. If you deny the reality of some class of objects, and think that you can deal with the immediate objection that such things do in fact exist, then you surely have no call to fash yourself about any further objection that you are committed to denying that there is any room for an explanation of their evolution!

In the former case the reason would be that I.H. is concerned to maintain precisely that what are called the phenomenal facts are simply identical with particular physical facts. Hence there cannot possibly be room for two different evolutionary accounts; any more than—to adapt the favourite example of spokesmen of I.H.—there is room for different accounts of the origin of the Morning Star and the Evening Star.

(2) Beloff is surely entirely wrong to reject Feigl's claim 'that as against Epiphenomenalism, where mental events are indeed no more than "nomological danglers", the Identity Hypothesis restores to them their commonsense causal efficacy' (p. 47). It is not true that if I.H. is correct 'the analogy would be the case in which one was presented with a clockwork mechanism where one could obviously ignore any optical properties or effects that one might observe as quite irrelevant to the dynamics of the situation' (p. 47.). If the Morning Star produces some effect so does the Evening Star. If one is dealing with an identity there can be no question of one thing being relevant and the other not. There just is only one thing to be either irrelevant or relevant. That is what *identity* means.

COMMENTS BY H. H. PRICE

It seems to me that the difficulty about the relation between phenomenal and physical entities is only a part—though of course an important part—of the traditional mind–body problem. So even if the Identity Hypothesis could solve this difficulty and get round the objections which Dr. Beloff has so forcibly pointed out, it would not thereby have done all or anything like all that an acceptable theory of the mind–body relation has to do.

Let us consider Beloff's own formulation of the difference between the phenomenal and the physical (p. 35). He says it is a difference between what can be known in one way (by introspection, direct acquaintance, etc.) and what can be known in another way (indirectly, conceptually, etc.). Now even if the entities known in the first way could somehow be reduced to entities known in the second, we shall still have to ask whether knowledge itself—of either sort—can be satisfactorily analysed in physicalistic terms. We may try to analyse 'knowledge' in a dispositional manner (though this is much less plausible for the first sort of knowledge than for the second). Even so, it is not very plausible to suggest that *all* the occurrent manifestations of such a disposition are purely behavioural. We also need the notion of 'being aware of' or 'being conscious of'.

Nor must we think of consciousness as a kind of medium or stuff 'in' which various sorts of entities swim about like tadpoles in a pond. This is sometimes a useful metaphor, but it cannot be taken literally. The 'of' which follows the words 'awareness' or 'consciousness' is not literally equivalent to 'containing'. Indeed, the expression 'aware of . . .' denotes something so fundamental that it cannot be analysed in terms of anything else. Is this a paradox? It ought to be regarded as a platitude. But platitudes are just what we philosophers tend to forget. (It is a kind of occupational disease.) To remind us of such a platitude and provide us with a terminology for talking about it may be a first rate philosophical achievement.

This is just what Brentano did when he introduced the concept of 'intentionality'. According to Brentano, intentionality is the distinguishing mark of the mental. Every mental event is 'of' something or 'directed upon' something. It has to have an object or accusative. For instance, there cannot be inspection unless there is something inspected, nor wishing unless there is something wished for, nor believing unless there is something believed. On the other hand, no physical event ever has intentionality.

This doctrine of Brentano's is highly relevant to the mind–body problem, and if it is correct, the Identity Hypothesis must be false. My only complaint against Beloff's otherwise admirable paper is that he says nothing about intentionality.

Mr. Quinton, however, discusses it at considerable length (see Sections 13 to 16 of his paper). I agree with him in thinking that Brentano overstated his case, and failed to draw certain distinctions which need to be drawn, especially the distinction between mental dispositions and their occurrent actualizations. Again, Beloff himself is surely right in pointing out that unconscious mental events must be provided for, as well as conscious ones (p. 53). In the study of paranormal phenomena, at any rate, I am sure we cannot get anywhere without using something like the conceptual apparatus of the Depth Psychologists; and the sense in which mental events have intentionality when they are beneath the threshold of consciousness is no doubt puzzling and needs analysis.

Nevertheless, unless there are *some* events which do have intentionality in Brentano's sense, it is difficult to see how there could be anything mental at all.

The main object of these remarks is just to persuade Beloff to make some comments on Quinton's discussion of intentionality.

REPLY TO LORD BRAIN BY JOHN BELOFF

I do not think that the question of the relative merits of a monistic as against a dualistic metaphysic devolve upon what answer we give to the question as to where in nature mind and matter co-exist. Speculation on this latter question has ranged all the way from panpsychism, which held that every particle of matter had its psychic component, however primitive, to the notorious doctrine of Descartes, according to which no organism below man could be credited with a mind. The fact is, of course, that we still have neither the knowledge nor the criteria on which to base a rational answer to this problem. But even if we had, even if we could say authoritatively that, for example, all animals but no plants had mental attributes, I still do not see how this would commit us either to a dualist or a monist ontology. This latter question, must, it seems to me, be decided on other grounds.

REPLY TO ANTONY FLEW BY JOHN BELOFF

Professor Flew writes: 'If one is dealing with an identity there can be no question of one thing being relevant and the other not.' This is obviously true if the identity in question were a logical identity, but in the case of I.H. what we are dealing with is an empirical identity between two quite different aspects of one and the same entity. I am not so sure, therefore, whether his reply really does meet my objections. Let me put it this way. The shape and colour of an apple are just as much part of the apple as its mass, but they are certainly not relevant to an explanation of why the apple falls to the ground. In somewhat the same way (the analogy, I know, is not very close but there seems to be no real parallel) *if* it is the case that our behaviour could in principle be fully explained in terms of, say, the distribution of electrical charges in the brain cells, then the fact that such a distribution sometimes has an introspectible aspect, such as we might describe subjectively in terms of our desires or aversions, would add nothing to the explanation of that behaviour, any more than knowing the shape or colour of the apple adds anything to the explanation of its fall. And this, despite Feigl, does not strike me as compatible with the commonsense view.

On the evolutionary question, I am afraid it still does seem to me very puzzling as to why, of all physical events, certain brain processes only should have this secondary conscious aspect. Postulating an identity does not remove this difficulty. Thus, we may say that the object we see is identical with the object we touch, but we can still be called upon to explain why an object that is tangible is not always visible. The identity theorist, on the other hand, offers no intelligible explanation as to why *any* physical events should be introspectible. For him, it is presumably just a matter of brute fact, and, although every empirical theory must have its brute facts, they ought not, one feels, to obtrude themselves at quite such an advanced level in the cosmological scheme. I quite agree with Flew that C.S.M. (as distinct from I.H.) does not have to face this particular difficulty, but its solution, to deny the reality of consciousness as such, strikes me as almost on a par with that of the naturalist who, being unable to account for the origin of the giraffe, simply denied that such an animal existed!

SOME ASPECTS OF THE BRAIN–MIND RELATIONSHIP[1]
Lord Brain

THE relationship between the brain and the mind has interested thinkers for many centuries and it has many implications. We live in an age of specialism and I think one of our greatest needs is that specialists should do their best to explain what is happening in their own spheres of work which is of wider relevance. It is certainly much more rare than it used to be for philosophers to contribute to the understanding of modes of thought which belong to other disciplines. This may well be because these have become so specialized and technical that they can be understood only by the specialists concerned. These specialists, feeling the need for philosophical guidance, sometimes themselves turn philosopher. But I think we are all the poorer, and not least the specialists concerned, if philosophy retreats into its ivory tower, a tower whose inhabitants, like those of the Tower of Babel, seem preoccupied with problems of language. So my object here is to report some recent advances in our knowledge of the brain which seem to me to have a bearing upon its relation with the mind, and only rather indirectly shall I hint at what may be some of their philosophical implications.

Just over half a century ago, William McDougall published a book, called *Body and Mind*.[2] He began his preface by saying that his primary aim was to provide for students of psychology and philosophy, within a moderate compass, a critical survey of modern opinion and discussion upon the psycho-physical prob-

---

[1] The Ludwig Mond Lecture delivered at Manchester on March 16, 1964.
[2] W. McDougall, *Body and Mind* (London, 1911).

63

lem—the problem of the relation between body and mind. The main body of the volume, he said, was occupied with the presentation and examination of the reasonings which had led the great majority of philosophers and men of science to reject animism (that is, a belief in mind or soul in some respects independent of the body), and of the modern attempts to render an intelligible account of the nature of man which, in spite of the rejection of animism, shall escape materialism. This survey led him to the conclusion that these reasonings were inconclusive and these attempts unsuccessful, and that we are therefore compelled to choose between animism and materialism; and, he said, 'since the logical necessity of preferring the animistic horn of this dilemma cannot be in doubt, my survey constitutes a defence and justification of animism'. I read the book a few years after it was published and looked at it again the other day. It is still a good historical account of the controversies about the body–mind relationship, but it strikes me now that the debate between animism and materialism with which McDougall himself was so much concerned is today as much a matter of history as the rest of the book. I do not mean of course that it is not still being vigorously debated, as are many other ancient controversies. But it seems to me that we ought not to be looking at the body–mind relationship today in the same way as William McDougall, who was perfectly justified in tackling it in terms which had been current and respectable for many centuries.

Why is this? For three reasons. When McDougall was writing, although psychology had been established as a science for many decades, and the foundations of neurophysiology had been laid by Sherrington about the turn of the century, virtually nothing was known about the mental functions of the brain. Indeed in 1911, when McDougall published *Body and Mind*, he, though a qualified doctor and a distinguished psychologist, could have known little more about the psychophysiological aspect of the brain–mind relationship than an educated layman. Both knew that if you hit a man hard enough on the head you rendered him unconscious, but neither knew why. Both knew that if the brain decayed, the mind decayed too. The doctor knew this at first hand, because he could see the decayed brain, while the layman had to take his word for it, but neither could explain the fact in any more detailed terms than the general observation, that the mind was in some unexplained way dependent upon the brain. Perhaps the doctor could go a little further than the layman, in that his experience, or the experience of others recorded in the literature, suggested that in a very broad sense, some parts of the brain had more to do with the mind than others, particularly perhaps the frontal lobes situated behind the forehead. But observations in support of this were at that time so fragmentary that they amounted to hardly more than the ideas embodied in Gall's phrenology, and Gall, in spite of being almost entirely unscientific, nevertheless should be regarded as the founder of the concept of cerebral localization, that is, the idea that certain functions are localized in certain areas of the brain.

The first reason, then, why the problem looks so different now is that the last fifty years have witnessed a remarkable expansion of our knowledge of brain function, particularly in the field of psychophysiology. This has come about in a variety of ways, and, as often happens in science, knowledge has grown by a kind of geometrical progression, new observations in one field stimulating those in another. We owe a great deal to new electrophysiological techniques, which have made it possible to stimulate single nerve fibres and record responses from single nerve-cells, and so explore in animals the organization of the nervous system in relation to a wide range of environmental stimuli, of which I shall be giving some illustrations later. Similar technical developments have made it possible to produce in animals minute areas of damage to the brain, and observe the effects of these on their behaviour. The human nervous system, being organized basically on the same lines as those of other mammals, these experimental observations on animals have greatly illuminated the effects of disease in man, and have been correlated with the human pathological observations. Then, a large part of the activity of the nervous system is chemical, and comparatively recently we have begun to learn about that, while pharmacological developments have led to the production of a wide range of new drugs, which have profound effects on human behaviour and states of mind. So here is a new field in which animal experiment and the human observation go hand in hand. Nor has the clinical neurologist been backward. A century ago great clinicians like Hughlings Jackson were observing the mental disturbances produced by disease of the brain, but in the absence of the neurophysiological and pathological advances I have been describing, they could do little more than give a clinical account of the resulting symptoms. Today, however, the clinical neurologist, aided by the technical advances of neurosurgery, is able to make his clinical observations against the background of a systematized knowledge which his predecessors of even fifty years ago entirely lacked, and it is fitting in this regard, that I should commemorate my friend, Geoffrey Jefferson, neurosurgeon and philosopher, who made such notable original contributions in this field.

The second sphere of advance which has greatly altered the look of the whole problem is that of the physicist. The matter which in the past seemed to provide such a solid basis for materialism, is no longer what it was, and it seems to have become much more difficult to disentangle it from mind, in particular, the mind of the physicist himself, than used to be the case, and that has important implications when we come to consider the old antinomy between mind and matter. And thirdly, the development during the last fifty years of what I may broadly call linguistic philosophy suggests that some of the old philosophical problems may spring not from the nature of things but from our use of language to describe them. And this also may have important implications for the problem we are considering.

Let me now present some account of the nervous system. This is composed of nerve fibres which, when excited, convey nerve impulses, that is electrical changes, from one end to the other. These nerve-impulses are of a very simple kind compared with the vast complexity of the mental life which they sustain. Here then is our first problem, or rather series of problems, namely, how do these nerve impulses convey information and how does their central organization in the brain make it possible to handle the information and react appropriately? Let us begin at the periphery—the surface of the body. Here there is already a high degree of specialization in the organization of the receptors, which are stimulated by outside events, and in turn excite the nerve-fibres to transmit messages to the brain. A good deal of this specialization is still not fully understood, but I can illustrate the principles involved by means of recent work on the eyes of the frog and the cat.[3] It has been shown that the organization of the retina

[3] D. H. Hubel, *J. Physiol.*, 1959, **147**, 226; *J. opt. Soc. Amer.*, 1963, **53**, 58.
    D. H. Hubel and T. N. Wiesel, *J. Physiol.*, 1959, **148**, 574; *J. Physiol.*,

of the frog's eye is such that individual nerve cells can be classified in terms of the stimulus to which they respond. What stimulates the frog's retina is of course what we may term a visual object. But the individual cells respond to particular aspects of the object. Thus one class of cell responds to a sharp edge and another class to a convex edge. Yet a third responds to changing contrasts, a fourth to dimming, and a fifth measures the intensity of the light. Thus the frog's vision is organized even at the most peripheral level to respond to, and convey information about, changes in the frog's environment, to which it is important that it should react. Similarly, in the cat, there are nerve-cells in the retina, which are excited only by movement, and by movement in a particular direction. I cannot now discuss the complex organization of the retina which renders these highly specific responses possible, but it is not peculiar to the retina: it exists in all forms of sensation, and differs in different species of organism, each having been evolved under the influence of natural selection with a nervous organization capable of responding to those events in its environment which are biologically important to it.

I must at this point observe that, whatever the nature of the stimulus in the environment, whether it is a sight or a sound, a touch or a smell, all it can do to the living organism is to excite nerve impulses in nerve fibres, and, though such nerve impulses differ in certain respects, they are on the whole very much alike, so that there is probably nothing in the nerve impulse itself to indicate whether it is conveying information about touch or pain, sight or sound. So here we meet the idea of 'coding' in the nervous system. Specific nerve impulses are regarded as a coded form of information about the physical event which excites them. But this information does not necessarily or perhaps usually become conscious: in other words, it is not necessarily decoded. What it does in the case of the frog's vision, for example, is to evoke the appropriate reaction—a flick of the tongue if the coded information 'means' a fly, a dive into the pond if a large moving shadow 'means' danger, perhaps a heron, and the code acquires 'meaning'

1960, **154**, 572; *J. Physiol.*, 1961, **155**, 385; *J. Physiol.*, 1962, **160**, 106; *J. Physiol.*, 1963, **165**, 559.

H. R. Maturana, J. Y. Lettvin, W. S. McCulloch and W. H. Pitts, *J. Gen. Physiol.*, 1960, **43**, July Supp. p. 129.

through the organization of the nerve impulses, which is partly innate and partly the result of learning (a product of experience).

When we come to higher levels of the nervous system and higher levels of activity we cannot at present offer much more than hypothesis, but it is generally assumed that there are physiological processes probably involving very large numbers of nerve-cells which underlie the recognition of patterns and the abstraction of common elements in situations otherwise diverse— what in the realm of speech I have called schemata. The complexity of these operations must be very great, as indeed is that of the nervous system itself. The brain has been estimated to contain ten thousand million cells, and one cell may be capable of being influenced by a thousand others.

Let us now consider briefly the storage of sensory impressions and other mental experiences by memory. There is still much which we do not know about this, but some facts seem to be well established. In the first place, there is a remarkable difference between short-term and long-term memories. It is a common experience nowadays, when unfortunately head injuries are all too common, for a person, who has sustained a head injury severe enough to cause loss of consciousness, to find that he cannot remember the events which immediately preceded the injury nor the occurrence of the injury itself. Yet his recollection of everything that happened up to, let us say, half an hour beforehand, is perfectly clear and accurate. Experiences such as these show that memories are most vulnerable to brain damage immediately after the events which they record, but then they become much more stable. The same point can be demonstrated in another way. It occasionally happens that, as a result of disease which damages a certain area of the brain, a patient is left with a permanent loss of the capacity for short-term memory, though he has no other evidence of mental impairment, and his memory for all that happened before he became ill is unimpaired. Such a person is totally unable to remember what happened to him only a few minutes ago. If he is seen in hospital, he will have forgotten how he got there. Nevertheless, apart from this disability he may be able to lead a normal life, and I have heard of one such, who was even able to conduct a business by having all the information he needed to remember written down, and so made immediately available for him. In his case, notebooks and card indices were a substitute for the damaged part of his brain. From observations such as these we must conclude that the organization of our experience takes time, and we now know broadly what regions of the brain are concerned in this organizing activity. We do not, however, know how memories are stored. Some theories would explain this in terms of organization of the nerve fibre pathways, others would invoke molecular changes in macromolecules, and there is something to be said for a combination of these views.

There is another point which needs to be mentioned in connection with memory. Linguistically we speak of memory as though it were a unitary activity: we say that I remember my childhood, what I had for breakfast today, your name and how to ride a bicycle, but memory is not a unitary activity as far as the nervous system is concerned. As I have already said, a patient may remember his childhood but not what he had for breakfast, and disease of the brain may impair memory in many different ways. A patient may not remember the names of objects he sees, or the words he wants to use. He may even have forgotten the nature of an object he sees, though he can recognize it if it is placed in his hand. He may forget how to do things, such as lighting a cigarette, sitting down in a chair, or putting on his clothes. And all these varieties of loss of memory may occur in isolation. Evidently in the brain memory is not a unitary function nor is there any single part of the nervous system in which all memories are stored.

Now I would like to turn to consider emotion. Here again, although we have still much to learn about the organization of the nervous pathways which are active when we experience emotion, we do know in broad outline what happens in the brain. This knowledge has been derived from a very wide range of observations made on both animals and man. Emotion is closely linked with the instinctive drives, and animal experiments have shown what parts of the brain are particularly concerned with these. We do not know, of course, what emotion animals experience, but we can observe their behaviour, and we are accustomed in everyday life to infer that they experience rage or fear or some other emotion. The effects of brain damage or stimulation upon animal behaviour have received a great deal of study. In man and animals there appears to be a close rela ionship between emotion and the temporal lobe of the brain which lies just above and in front of the ear. An epileptic attack may be regarded as an uncontrolled discharge of nervous impulses, and what the patient experiences during the attack will often depend upon the particular site in the brain at which the abnormal discharge begins. When it starts in one temporal lobe, this experience may be a feeling of fear, occurring by itself and unrelated to any object. Other feelings such as sadness and loneliness have been described, and Professor Penfield, who has done a great deal of work in this field, has observed that when fear is a symptom produced by an epileptic discharge in the temporal lobe, the same experience may be reproducible by electrical stimulation of the appropriate area of the brain in the course of an operation when the patient is not under a general anaesthetic. On the other hand, Penfield says that so far as his experience goes, neither a localized epileptic discharge nor electrical stimulation is capable of awakening the emotions of anger, joy, pleasure or sexual excitement.[4] Removal of the temporal lobes causes profound changes in animal behaviour.

So far we have been considering emotion in terms of its anatomical organization in the nervous system, but there is also a biochemical aspect of emotion to be considered. We may not call hunger and thirst emotions, but there seems no reason apart from linguistic convention why we should not. The feelings associated with hunger and thirst are certainly simpler than those associated with some other emotions, and superficially the reactions they evoke in us may appear to be simpler too—just eating and drinking; but in order that we may eat and drink we must earn a living, and though there may well be other motives for the work we choose to do, earning our daily bread is surely as elaborate a manifestation of an instinctive drive as there well could be. My present point, however, is that we experience hunger and thirst largely as the result of biochemical changes in the blood, to which specialized small regions of the brain are sensitive. And it has been shown experimentally in cats that normal sexual activity depends upon the sensitivity of another small localized area of the brain to biochemical substances secreted by the sex glands and carried to the brain by the blood. These fundamental drives—to eat, drink and reproduce—essential for the survival of the

[4] W. Penfield and H. Jasper, *Epilepsy and the Functional Anatomy of the Human Brain* (London, 1954), p. 451.

individual and the race, depend not only upon the activities of nervous pathways to outside stimuli but also upon their sensitivity to information reaching them in a biochemical form through the blood stream.

There are still one or two points to be made about the neurological basis of the mind. The operation of prefrontal leucotomy was introduced some thirty years ago for the treatment of certain mental disorders. Its importance for our present purpose is that, independently of its effect in relieving symptoms, especially mental tension, the more extensive forms of the operation used at first were likely to produce changes in the personality, from which it was possible to infer some of the normal functions of the frontal lobes of the brain in relation to psychological life. It was noted that after extensive operations on both frontal lobes, the patient tends to become distractable, shallow, and a victim of changing concrete stimuli, and the same kind of disordered behaviour is manifested by animals after experimental lesions. If I may quote what I have said elsewhere on this subject:

> In considering the functions of the frontal lobe, then, we encounter two interweaving strands, time-sense and emotion, and here we reach the roots of the personality, in which we can either say that emotion is binding together the past, present and future, or that the time-sense is essential to the integration of emotion with the rest of the mental life. Perhaps these are two different ways of saying the same thing.

All these observations have one very important implication for our ideas of the brain–mind relationship. By studying the effects of local brain damage on such mental functions as memory, emotion, speech, thought and perception, we are learning more and more about how these functions are organized in the brain, but it turns out that brain damage breaks them down in ways which do not correspond to our ideas of the organization of mental activity, but which are explicable only in terms of brain activity, and there is in most instances no evidence that the mind has any independent power to compensate for the loss of these highly specific brain-dependent functions.

Now let us consider the other term in the brain–mind relationship—mind. What do we mean by mind? The shorter Oxford English Dictionary defines it as 'the seat of conscious thoughts, volitions, and feelings; also the incorporeal subject of the psychical faculties'. It would be difficult to beg more questions in so few words. 'Seat' implies some sort of location or at any rate, basis, and the word 'conscious' links mind with consciousness. But this 'seat' we are told, is also 'incorporeal' so it is not a bodily seat. Webster's New International Dictionary says much the same. Mind is 'the subject of consciousness, or the soul considered as such a subject; that which feels, perceives, wills, thinks; also, consciousness itself; especially an individual consciousness; the sum total of the conscious states of any individual;—often in distinction from body.' Perhaps we should not reproach dictionaries, which after all exist to reflect current usage, for defining mind in Cartesian terms, which have now been fashionable for three centuries. Both these definitions, however, take for granted that mind is in some way to be identified with consciousness, and that is the first question I want to consider, for much depends on how we answer it.

The idea of unconscious mind is of respectable antiquity, going back at least as far as Leibnitz. What McDougall has to say about it is interesting. He has a section devoted to 'Unconscious Cerebration', a significant combination of words, in which he considers those philosophies which regard the existence of unconscious mental processes as supporting materialism. McDougall's consideration of these ideas is not altogether happy, and finally involves him in the use of the term 'unconscious consciousness'. Freud at that time was only beginning to impinge on British psychology, but is given a brief summary towards the end of the book.

If there is no mind without consciousness, we are not entitled to apply the term 'mental' to any activities of an organism of which it is not at the moment conscious, and the term 'unconscious mind', as Hughlings Jackson[5] suggested, is self-contradictory. There is, however, another possibility. If we can discover other criteria of mental activity than consciousness, we can say that there exist mental activities, of which we are sometimes conscious and sometimes not—the process of consciousness then being one mental activity among others. Much psychological thinking during the whole of the present century has been based upon this second view. I want to consider this question, not in the

[5] J. H. Jackson, *Selected Writings* (London, 1931) 2, 85.

abstract, but in the light of current work on psycho-physiology and animal behaviour.

There is of course a linguistic problem here, which I must leave to the philosophers to disentangle, and which I can put only in my own words. When Hughlings Jackson, like the dictionary, identifies mind with consciousness, he is, I think, guilty of a confusion which arises from an incomplete analysis of consciousness. If we regard consciousness as implying a mental act, function or state, it is one which involves a relationship, and most people I suppose are nowadays sufficiently realist to admit that one term of the relationship may be non-mental. We must, therefore, distinguish the conscious experience from its content. It must also be true that not all the ingredients of a conscious experience are conscious.

Now consider an experience which it will be agreed is one of the most characteristic activities of mind, namely, thinking. The thinker assembles his data, reasons from them, and draws his conclusions. This is all a conscious process. It may be argued that thinking, and being conscious of thinking, are the same thing but there is evidence that this is not so. Thinking depends upon the activity of many millions of nerve-cells and at present we understand only the merest outline of its physiological basis. But from a physiological point of view it seems unlikely that the product of the activity of these cells necessarily always becomes conscious. In other words, as far as the organization of the nervous system is concerned, we have to distinguish between the process of consciousness and its content. Doctors recognize this in their everyday work, for their experience shows that the function of consciousness may be affected in itself. There are not only patients who are fully conscious or completely unconscious, but intermediate degrees of impairment of consciousness, in which the patient is partially conscious but not efficiently so, and in such states of partial consciousness no single element in the content of consciousness is affected alone, but all conscious functions, perception, memory, emotion and thought, tend to be impaired in a general way. By contrast, there are many patients who are not suffering from an impairment of the process of consciousness but who have lost part of its normal content. Thus, if the brain is so damaged that the patient cannot feel with one hand, or has lost the vision of half of what he looks at, the content of his consciousness is to that extent impaired, but not his consciousness as a process.

Thus in the organization of the nervous system there is a distinction between the process of consciousness and its content. The psychological function which best describes the activity of the former part is the maintenance and direction of attention. This can be illustrated by a familiar experience. You are sitting with a book in a room in which there is a clock. Before you start to read, you hear the clock ticking. You then become immersed in the book, and, when you put it down, not only do you hear the clock ticking again, but you realize that you have not heard it while you have been reading. Thus your consciousness of the tick of the clock depends upon the direction of your attention.

Now let us return to thinking. Thinking is a more active process than hearing the tick of the clock, but it may still be true that thinking is one process and being conscious of it is another. If this is so, we should expect to find evidence that a process identical with that which we call thinking, when we are conscious of it, may go on when we are unconscious of it. This of course has long been recognized. The most dramatic examples are cases of problems solved during sleep, and the sudden intuitions which sometimes come to scientists and present solutions of difficulties without their being able to say how they have arrived at them. And surely a little reflection will make us all aware of the importance of unconscious thinking in everyday life. The crossword puzzle is a good example. When you have found only two letters out of a ten letter word and those somewhere in the middle of it, the right word may suddenly present itself to you when all your conscious efforts to work it out have failed. Again, when you have forgotten someone's name, it is usually a waste of time to try consciously to remember it, but it may later emerge spontaneously. Moreover, even when you do not know the right name, you will reject wrong ones offered, so that you are somehow unconsciously testing these against a pattern which nevertheless you cannot consciously evoke. Indeed it is surely obvious that our everyday thinking and remembering have come to depend upon activities which, though they may once in our lives have been conscious, are no longer so, just as we are no longer conscious of how we maintain our balance while riding a bicycle.

We have no means of discovering to what extent animals are conscious nor what their conscious experiences are like. But at least as far as vertebrates are concerned, there is at no stage of evolution any basic change in the organization of the nervous system which would suggest that at that point consciousness made its appearance. In other words, however complex consciousness may have become in man, there is no biological reason to think it absent at lower levels of the evolutionary scale.

Now let us look at some of the things which creatures with very much simpler nervous systems than man can accomplish. We know that the honey-bee, with an extremely simple nervous system, is able not only to find its way back from a source of honey to the hive but also to communicate its direction and distance to other bees by a system of signs. We know also that migrating birds are able to orientate themselves by means of the sun. Now let me quote some comments on this by Professor W. H. Thorpe[6]: Observation, he says, suggests

> that the sun-orientation mechanism of birds is, in its correlation of inborn faculties of experience, extraordinarily similar to that of the honey-bee. In both, there is presumably innate appreciation of direction and speed of movement of the sun, together with an accurate internal clock. In both there is the innate ability to relate a 'desired' direction to the space–time standards innately provided, to extrapolate from the observed situation and to relate to it the knowledge of general topography and special landmarks gained from individual experience. In both there is an 'appreciation' of the relation between '*direction*' of a light source and the '*direction*' of a movement (foraging flight, migration flight, homing flight). But the honey-bee does better than the bird in two respects. Firstly it can and must 'transpose' between sun direction and gravity direction, and secondly it must be able to transmit information by transposition between foraging flight and the straight run of the dance. [That is, the dance, the movements of which convey information about the source of the honey to other bees.] So far as we know, birds cannot and do not need to transfer information in any such way, and so lack these additional faculties which the honey-bee possesses.

Here then we find the birds and the bees doing exactly the same things which the navigator does with his sextant, chronometer and elaborate calculations. It seems improbable that the birds and the bees are conscious of thinking in the way in which the navigator is, and of course their sextants and chronometers are built

---

[6] W. H. Thorpe, *Learning and Instinct in Animals* (London, 1956), p. 329.

in, but they may well have some conscious experience which corresponds to an impulsion to take the right direction, and is the result of unconscious calculation from the relevant information received, processed and provided by the nervous system. The question is, should we apply the term mental to the navigator's activities and deny it to the birds and the bees except in so far as the latter may be conscious, however dimly, of their surroundings and of an impulse to react to them in a certain way?

Fifty years ago, then, McDougall in considering the relations between the mind and the brain had to deal with them almost entirely in the abstract. How the mind was influenced by brain changes was largely unknown, and the brain itself as a physical object was supposed to be subject to the simple mechanical laws then current in physics. Today we know a good deal about the organization of psychological functions in the brain, and we know that localized damage to the brain, if it affects the mind, is likely to do this selectively, and in a way that can be understood only in terms of brain organization. As we have seen, memory, for which we have only a single term, and which we should be inclined to regard as a unitary mental function, turns out to be a series of different activities with a very complex organization in the brain.

Then the nervous activity which underlies all brain function turns out to be inherently simple, but organized in an increasingly complex fashion, to much of which the term 'coding' is appropriate. Information and coding, however, prove to have a wide range of applicability in life itself and may constitute a most important unifying concept. Thus the molecular biologists speak of a genetic code, and a good deal is now understood about the nature of the code by means of which DNA organizes amino-acids to form proteins. The organization of increasingly complex patterns, therefore, seems to be basic to life itself, and the genetic code, which determines the fundamental structure of the nervous system, is also involved in the process by which the nerve fibres concerned with input into the nervous system reach their appropriate receptor organs, and so are organized for their life-long task of coding particular forms of information.

At the same time, the basic ideas of physics have moved on from the idea that all physical activities are to be explained in terms of the interactions of enduring units, and we are taught to think much more in terms of relations and probabilities. This is especially true of the quantum theory; for example, Bridgman[7] says: 'An electron is an aspect of a total situation, the major part of which is the rest of the apparatus. We should not talk about "electrons" as such but rather say: under such and such conditions the apparatus *electrons*.' These ideas are important for our understanding of the highest brain functions. It is already clear that neurophysiology today is increasingly using terms like coding and information, which have psychological implications, to describe the activity of the nervous system, even at its simplest levels. Language is one of the highest activities of mind, and a distinctively human one. Nevertheless, the complex symbolism of language is ultimately a form of coding, and we may expect that its physiological basis will prove to be explicable in terms of simpler nervous activities.

Now I come to my final question—does McDougall's animism look any different today? His point of view was essentially that which Dr. Johnson put into the mouth of Imlac in Rasselas.

> Matter can differ from matter only in form, density, bulk, motion and direction of motion; to which of these, however varied or combined, can consciousness be annexed? To be round or square, to be solid or fluid, to be great or little, to be moved slowly or swiftly, one way or another, are modes of material existence, all equally alien from the nature of cogitation.

But this reductionism fails to recognize that the organization of simple units may produce unforeseen and indeed, unforeseeable characteristics. Hence there are descriptions which are applicable to organized wholes but not to their parts. Thus we may speak of a substance as coloured but it is meaningless to speak of its atoms as either coloured or colourless. Similarly, as Hanson[8] points out, 'if you speak of me as a man, but someone else speaks of me as a collection of cells, then though the denotatum of your talk be physically identical, the two of you diverge conceptually. You are not speaking the same language.'

I would hold, therefore, that the fact that I can speak of another person both in brain language and in mind language does not, in spite of what Popper says, imply that brain and mind are

[7] B. W. Bridgman, *The Way Things Are* (Cambridge, Mass., 1959).
[8] N. R. Hanson, *Patterns of Discovery* (Cambridge, 1958).

separate entities. As we have seen, however, it seems inappropriate to restrict mind language to conscious activities. If so, two things seem to follow. First we must accept the concept of the unconscious mind. Although this plays an important part in some schools of psychopathology, we are not thereby committed to any particular interpretation of it, nor indeed to the restriction of the unconscious mind to the explanation of abnormal mental states. It is simply the lost origin of emotional reactions which have become habitual. Some psychologists, however, would go further than that, for example, Jung, who regards the unconscious mind as the source of symbols and modes of thought which individuals or groups of individuals may have in common. In this sense, the unconscious mind may play a vitalizing role in art and religion. Scientists also have frequently acknowledged their debt to the unconscious, when they have used it to explain the emergence of intuitions which do not appear to be the immediate product of conscious rational thought, but which may nevertheless be important for the progress of science. If we accept the idea of unconscious mental activities, there is wide scope for their scientific study. But where, if anywhere, are we to draw the line? We have already seen that even relatively simple organisms are capable of behaviour of great complexity which finds a parallel in our own conscious acts. And we have seen also that we must use the concepts of information and coding to explain genetic activity and embryonic development. The process at work guiding the growth of nerve fibres and linking them with their appropriate receptor organs seems similar to that which will be concerned in their ultimate function of transmitting information in the fully developed organism. McDougall's materialist opponent might maintain that all these facts are to be explained in terms of physics and chemistry, which, no doubt, is true. But when we have reduced everything to the ultimate units of matter, whatever they may currently be, have we really done any more than is involved in explaining a cathedral by saying that it is built of bricks? This is a modern version of the old puzzle of the relation between the whole and the parts, but both in physics and biology, it now begins to look as if, while the whole can be 'explained' in terms of the parts, the parts can be 'explained' only in terms of the whole. At the moment we lack the necessary concepts to take this much further.

To end with a speculation, I suspect that our difficulties arise in part at least from our analysis of events into a four-dimensional space–time. We can *describe* events in this way, indeed we are compelled to do so by our own biological organization, but I fancy that there are living events which we shall fail to understand until we can describe them also in terms which may involve additional co-ordinates. Then we may transcend both the old materialism and the old animism.

COMMENTS BY C. J. DUCASSE

My basic criticism of Lord Brain's paper is that he neglects to say how we know at all that there is a material world (of which brains and sense organs are parts). So long as the terms 'material', 'mental', 'matter', 'mind', 'life', which are key terms in the whole discussion, are not, *ab initio*, defined sharply and in a non-arbitrary manner, no responsible inferences concerning the mind–body relation are possible at all. Brain (p. 66) speaks of nerve impulses as 'sustaining' mental life; on p. 69 he speaks of memories being 'stored' in the nervous system. But such use of terms is metaphorical and vague. Again, it is indispensable to distinguish between 'memory', which is a capacity; and particular 'memories', which are episodes. The particular memory I had just now of the visual appearance of the cat which visited my garden yesterday consisted of *a mental image*; and to speak of a mental image being 'stored' in the nervous system is as incongruous as it would be, for instance, to speak of packing a mental image in a cardboard box and mailing it to Canada! A certain state of the nervous system might be causally necessary to, or causally sufficient to, occurrence of that mental image. But causation does not constitute or entail identity, but on the contrary *precludes* it.

COMMENTS BY J. R. SMYTHIES

The evolutionary problem that faces the dualist hypothesis (raised by Lord Brain in his comment on Dr. Beloff)—i.e. '*when* did mind appear in the universe?'—could be dealt with perhaps as follows. If we postulate that any individual consists of a body in physical space and a collection of sense-data, etc., in mental space then clearly this formulation could fit crabs and gorillas as well as men. Only man can introspect the content of his consciousness and report what he finds in language because only man has a sufficiently developed language and because only man has the intellectual capacity to do so. But this does not mean that other organisms may not occupy in part their own mental spaces or parts of mental space, i.e. have some form of existential consciousness. The problem then becomes 'at what point in time did causal interactions commence between events in physical space and the events in the various "mental" spaces (Price) or the various sections of "mental" space (Broad)?' On this theory such interaction is going on now and clearly no such interaction went on before there was any life on earth. Therefore at what point did it start? The answer is that we don't know. We can picture an evolving physical world, and, in addition, an evolving world of images and 'hallucinatory' sense-data in which events of some kind were going on. As brains developed in the physical world the mechanism for some form of causal interaction between the two systems developed. The sense-data and images in this mental world could then gradually come to be organized into collections, each causally related to only one brain, forming the contents of one consciousness. However, since it is clear that the earth is only one of innumerable planets when life could, and probably does, exist, and since on the theory of continuous creation the Universe may have always existed, it is perfectly possible that complex interactions have always gone on between local parts of the mental world (or the various mental worlds) and brains on various planets in the physical world. (The mental world could best be pictured in this case in Broad's sense as an *n*-dimensional manifold enveloping the physical world.) These interactions presumably develop at some point in time when both the physical apparatus of the brain and the mental apparatus of consciousness have evolved sufficiently for such causal interaction to take place, and this interaction might itself evolve very slowly. A lowly physical organism might be associated with a very small eddy of images in the mental world that leave little trace behind, whereas each human existential consciousness seems to be a most complex system. Thus it is possible that the concept of evolution (in the sense of change from the simple to the complex) may apply not only to the physical world (as a local phenomenon) but also to the mental world *and* to the causal interactions between them.

MINDS, MATTER AND BODIES
C. J. Ducasse

THE word 'mind' occurs in various ordinary statements and phrases. Some of them would be: 'I have a mind to go', 'He changed his mind', 'Mind you do not slip on the ice', 'I don't mind rainy weather'. What 'mind' means in these sentences is no part of the present essay's concern, which is instead with the meaning of 'mind' used as a substantive in phrases such as: 'a healthy mind in a healthy body', 'the relation between mind and matter', 'Why the mind has a body' (title of a book by C. A. Strong), 'having a keen mind (or a retentive, or a poetic, or a scientific, etc., mind)'.

1. *Two questions, and the answers proposed.* Two questions immediately arise about 'mind' as employed in these phrases. One is as to just what kind of substantive entity the term 'a mind' is conceived to designate there. The other is whether any substantive entities of that conceived kind exist.

To the first question, the answer here proposed is that a mind is essentially *a more or less well-integrated set of capacities*, of certain types to be explicitly mentioned farther on. And to the second question, the answer—likewise to be amplified in the sequel—is that a mind *exists* in so far and only in so far as one or more of its capacities are *being exercised*. In the absence of such exercise, the set of capacities which together constitute the 'nature', i.e. the 'what' or 'description' of a particular mind, only 'subsists', i.e. is conceivable; but does not exist. A mind therefore exists only in so far as it has a *history*—its history being the series of such exercises as its capacities have had, are having, and will possibly have.

Two parallel questions evidently arise concerning the nature and the existing of 'material things'; and parallel answers to them are proposed—the difference between 'minds' and 'material things' being a difference in *the types of capacities* in terms of which the generic nature of each is defined.

2. *Some key terms defined.* In the attempt I shall make to explicate and support the answers proposed in brief above to the two questions raised about 'a mind' and about 'material things', certain terms will play key roles. It is therefore important that the sense each of them will be taken to have be first made quite clear. The chief of those terms are 'a substant', 'a capacity', 'exercise of a capacity', 'an event', and 'causality'.

The term *'a substant'* will designate anything, whether mental or material, whose nature consists wholly of a more or less well-integrated set of *capacities.* Some of the material things commonly called 'substances'—e.g. glass, lead, water—would be substants as just defined; but so would a tree, a table, a human body, which on the contrary would not in ordinary usage be called 'substances'. Moreover, the term 'substance' has been used in various technical senses in philosophy. All this has made it ambiguous and therefore unsuitable for designating what, comprehensively, the term 'a substant' was defined above as designating.

The term *'capacities'* will be taken as essentially synonymous with 'capabilities', 'powers', 'abilities', 'faculties', 'dispositions'. And, that a substant S has a capacity or disposition A will be taken to mean that S is such that, under circumstances of kind K, occurrence of an event of kind C in a relation Q to S regularly causes occurrence of an event of kind E in a relation R to substant Z, which may or may not be the substant S itself. If Z is S itself, then the capacity is an *internal* one; but if Z is not S itself, then the capacity is an *external* one. Possession by S of the capacity A to play the *active* role defined—that of *agent*—implies of course possession by Z of the capacity B to play the corresponding *passive* role—that of *patient*.

Exercise of a capacity of a substant S consists in occurrence of a case of the causation which the definition of the capacity concerned specifies.

An *event* is either *a change* or *an unchange*; i.e. an enduring of a state for some time unchanged.[1]

Occurrence of an event is thus inherently 'at' some time and

[1] The term 'an unchange' was proposed by Dr. Ch. Mercier, *Causation and Belief* (Longmans, London, 1916), p. 38.

'at' some place; and since at a strictly punctual, i.e. strictly dimensionless time or place neither changing nor lasting, i.e. no event, can occur, it follows that occurence or existence of an event is *occupation* of a *span* of time and of a *region* of space by the change or the unchange which is the event. In this statement, however, 'space' is not, as is usual, qualified tacitly as physical; but is used in a sense which on the contrary admits also of psychical space, as the ordinary use of 'time' does admit of psychical time as well as of physical.

The warrant for thus treating space in the same manner as time—indeed, what logically requires that it be so treated—is the reciprocity of the relation which obtains between space and time: *time* is the possibility of *both* occurrence and non-occurrence of one very same event at one very same place; and *space* is the possibility of *both* occurrence and non-occurrence of one very same event at one very same time. This reciprocity obtains no matter whether the event concerned be a mental or a material event.

We come next to the notion of *Causality*, which as we have seen inheres in that of Capacity and hence also in that of Substant. The vast importance, practical as well as theoretical, of the Causality relation is made evident by the numerousness of the verbs of causation employed by all of us every day—transitive verbs such as 'to break', 'to bend', 'to push', 'to ignite', 'to create', 'to kill', 'to remind', 'to persuade', 'to motivate', etc. Philosophers have therefore at various times inquired into the nature of that relation.

The analysis of it as empirical regularity of sequence, which Hume proposed, is the most famous but is patently invalid since on the one hand some empirically regular sequences are admittedly not causal; and on the other, one single experiment can—as noticed even by Hume—show the sequence occurring in it to be a causal one.

Yet, as the late Professor Arthur Pap pointedly remarked, most critics of the regularity theory of causation 'are silent about an alternative *analysis* of the concept of causation'.[2] The continuing employment of it by philosophers—often at crucial points in their

---

[2] 'A Note on Causation and the Meaning of "Event"' (*Jl. of Philosophy*, Vol. LIV, No. 6, March 14, 1957, p. 155). Cf. the present writer's comments thereon in the June 20 issue of the same volume of the same journal.

arguments—notwithstanding that, without a valid analysis, their idea of causality is then perforce only nebulous, might therefore well be termed the great modern scandal in philosophy!

Because of limitations of space, it is not possible to introduce here the detailed analysis of Causality which the present writer has formulated and defended elsewhere; but at least its chief contentions must be stated in brief since, if sound, they provide the light needed to clarify some of the chief questions at issue in this essay—for instance those of the relation between minds and matter, and of the relation between a mind and its body.

The most important of those contentions are the following:

(*a*) Only an *event* can be a cause or an effect.

(*b*) Causation is the observable relation which obtains between the three terms of any strict experiment: If, in a given state of affairs *S*, *only two* changes (whether simple or complex) occur during a given period, one of them *E* occurring immediately after and adjacent to the other *C*, then, *eo ipso*, *C* proximately *caused E*, and *E* was the proximate *effect* of *C*.

This irreducibly *triadic* relationship between *C* and *E* in *S* is what the experimental Principle of Single Difference specifies; and one may well ask what any particular experiment makes manifest to observation, if not that a given concrete change *C* in a given concrete state of affairs *S did cause* a particular other concrete change *E* in it. The principle is not a 'method' for ascertaining a relation other than the one it describes, which *is* causal connection itself.

Hume, it is true, declared that no connection is ever perceived between a cause and its effect; but he then confesses that he does not even know what, under the name of 'connection', he denies is perceived. He holds that relations of sequence are perceived, but fails to see that sequence, when it has the special features mentioned above, which constitute it an *experiment*, is *causal connection itself*. This is where Hume's professed empiricism failed to be thoroughgoing.

(*c*) Causation, as defined in (*b*), constitutes *necessitation* of the change *E* in *S* by the immediately antecedent change *C* in *S*— necessitation, however, *not logical* but *etiological*: the head of Charles I was causally *deducted*, not logically *deduced*, by the blow of the axe; and the spectators *perceived* the blow's *making* the head come off. That, as Hume assumed, 'necessity' always means *logical* necessity is simply not true. Even the higher animals *perceive* causation in certain cases.

(*d*) Causation, as defined in (*b*), entails that causal regularities are not causal because regular, but because each of the sequences that recurred was, *in its own individual right*, a causal sequence. Hence, a sequence could be unique in the history of the universe, and yet be a causal sequence; and every event could have had a cause and have an effect, and yet the case might be that no causal sequence ever recurs; i.e. that, as a bare matter of fact, there do not happen to be any causal regularities of sequence.[3]

(*e*) As defined in (*b*), however, Causality entails logically both *uniformity* and *universality* of causation: it entails both that the same cause, if it ever recurs under the same circumstances, has always the same effect; and that every event that occurs was caused and has an effect.

(*f*) The Causality relation is wholly neutral as to whether the cause-event and the effect-event are both physical, or both psychical, or either one of them physical and the other psychical. The Causality relation requires only that both the cause and the effect be *events*.

(*g*) The question as to *how* one given event caused a given other never has any meaning other than: *through what intermediary causal steps*. Hence the question as to *how*, if asked concerning a case of *proximate* (instead of *remote*) causation, is absurd as being implicitly self-contradictory.

(*h*) *Purposive* causation and *mechanical* causation are causation in the very same sense of the term, defined in (*b*). The difference is in *the special nature of the cause-event* in purposive causation. The event which causes purposive activity is *not the future event* the activity will cause, but is *the present desire for future occurrence of it*.[4]

---

[3] Cf. H. W. B. Joseph, *Introduction to Logic*, p. 404: 'We mean by the causal relation something that might hold between terms that were unique, and does hold between terms that are individual even though there are other individuals of the same nature.' Cf. also H. S. Jennings 'radically experimental determinism' set forth in an address, 'Some implications of Emergent Evolution'. *Science*, January 14, 1927.

[4] The supports which the writer has offered more fully for these various contentions concerning Causality may be found in Chapts. 7 to 10 of *Nature, Mind and Death* (Open Court Pub. Co., La Salle, Ill., 1951), and in the following papers: 'On the Nature and the Observability of the Causal Relation' (*Jl. of Philosophy*, Vol. 23, 1926, pp. 57–68); 'Of the Spurious Mystery in

3. *Kinds of items in fact denominated respectively 'material' and 'mental'.* The sense having now been made clear in which each of certain key terms is intended to be used in this essay, I turn next to the basic question as to *what the ultimately authoritative fact is,* which determines what types of capacities there are, which a mind on the one hand, and on the other a material thing, *can, cannot and must have.*

In the statement I shall now give of that basic fact, I shall continue to take as equivalent for the purposes of this essay the two terms 'material' and 'physical', and likewise as equivalent the two terms 'mental' and 'psychical'. And I shall use the term 'items' as designating indifferently substants, events, states, activities, operations, relations, etc.

The ultimately authoritative fact referred to is (i) that certain kinds of items *are in fact denominated* 'material' or 'physical', *not* 'mental' or 'psychical'; and (ii) that certain other kinds of items *are in fact denominated* 'mental' or 'psychical', *not* 'material' or 'physical'. For example:

(i) Some of the kinds of items denominated 'material' or 'physical' would, beyond question, be granite, air, water, iron, trees, human and animal bodies; liquidity, solidity, combustion; igniting, melting, drying; rain, earthquakes, tornadoes, etc.

(ii) On the other hand, some of the kinds of items denominated 'mental' or 'psychical' would, indisputably, be feelings, emotions, moods, attitudes, ideas, sensations, thoughts, mental images; craving, desiring, willing, imagining, perceiving, conceiving, hoping, wondering, remembering, expecting, believing, etc.; or, comprehensively, forms of consciousness, or mental states and activities.

4. *The types of capacities a mind, or a material thing, can, cannot and must have.* On the basis of the patent twofold fact which has just been stated and illustrated, and of the fact that, in the notion of 'capacity' as defined earlier there essentially enter a cause-event

Causal Connection' (*Philosophical Review*, Vol. 39, 1930, pp. 398–403); 'Of the Nature and Efficacy of Causes' (*Philosophical Review*, Vol. 41, 1932, pp. 395–99); 'On the Analysis of Causality' (*Jl. of Philosophy*, Vol. 54, 1957, pp. 422–6); 'Concerning the Uniformity of Causality' (*Philosophy and Phenomenological Research*, Vol. 22, Sept. 1961, pp. 97–101).

and an effect-event, we are now in position to distinguish *four generic types* of capacities; namely, a capacity is:

(i) *physico-physical* if both the cause-event and the effect-event are physical;

(ii) *physico-psychical* if the cause-event is physical and the effect-event psychical;

(iii) *psycho-physical* if the cause-event is psychical and the effect-event physical; and

(iv) *psycho-psychical* if both the cause-event and the effect-event are psychical.[5]

It follows that a *physical* substant *can* have capacities of the *first three* of these four types, *cannot* have capacities of the *fourth*, and *must* have capacities of the *first*; and that a *psychical* substant, i.e. a *mind*, *can* have capacities of the *last three* types, *cannot* have capacities of the *first*, and *must* have capacities of the *fourth* type.

This statement satisfies the engagement, made at the place in Section 1 where 'a mind' and 'a material thing' were initially defined each as a set of capacities 'of certain types', to specify—as just has been done—*which types* of capacities these were, respectively in the case of 'minds', and of 'material things'.

5. *How the items of material kinds, and of mental kinds, are respectively identified.* The question immediately arises, however, as to what is the characteristic shared by the items of the first list of examples, which identifies all of them as 'physical'; and a parallel question has to be answered, as to what characteristic identifies as 'psychical' all the items of the second list.

The answers I now submit are:

(i) that, *fundamentally*, any kind of item is called 'physical' or 'material', the concrete instances of which are *perceivable*; and, *derivatively*, 'physical' or 'material' also the unperceivably minute constituents and unperceivable processes in them which it may be necessary to postulate in order to explain, predict and possibly control perceivable facts in whose case this cannot be done on the basis only of their perceivable relations to other perceivable facts. And

(ii) that, *fundamentally*, any kind of item is called 'psychical'

---

[5] Cf. W. E. Johnson's *Logic* (Camb. Univ. Press, 1924), Vol. III, Introduction, Sec. 9, pp., xxvi–xxviii.

or 'mental', the concrete instances of which are *introspectable*; and, *derivatively*, also 'psychical' or 'mental' any unintrospectable 'subconscious' or 'unconscious' beliefs, assumptions, attitudes, forgotten experiences, latent capacities, etc., which it may similarly be necessary to postulate in order to explain, predict and possibly control introspectable facts in whose case this cannot be done on the basis only of their introspectable relations to other introspectable facts, or to physical facts.

The task next confronting us, then, is that of defining the two key verbs, 'perceiving' and 'introspecting', and of making clear what essentially *the experienced* is, on the one hand in perceptual experiencing, and on the other in introspective experiencing.

6. *The epistemic primacy of sensations, and the problem of 'Perception'.* As first step in the attempt to perform that task, attention may be called to a passage in G. E. Moore's essay on 'The Status of Sense-Data' in which he supposes himself to be looking at two coins lying on the ground, one a half crown farther from him than the other, a florin, which thus looks larger than the half crown. Moore then mentions five propositions which he knows to be true concerning the two coins; e.g. that the half crown is really larger than the florin; that the face of each, which looks elliptical, is really circular; that each has another face; etc. Then he writes: 'my knowledge of all the five propositions . . . is based, in the last resort, on experiences of mine consisting in the direct apprehension of sensibles and in the perception of relations between directly apprehended sensibles. It is *based* on these, in at least this sense, that I should hever have known any of these propositions if I had never directly apprehended any sensibles nor perceived any relations between them.'[6]

If, in the passage just quoted, the plain English word 'sensations' is substituted for the esoteric and possibly misleading term 'directly apprehended sensibles', then the essence of the insight Moore formulates in that passage is seen to be that, *if we had no sensations, we would know nothing at all of a physical world.* And this, I submit, is perfectly evident and entails that whatever we know of the physical world, we have come to know it *by interpreting,* somehow, our sensations. *These* are therefore *epistemically basic.* Hence, that the physical world, as causative of them, is *ontolo-*

---

[6] *Philosophical Studies* (Kegan Paul, London, 1922), pp. 185–6, 188.

gically basic is itself known to us, if at all, only through our interpreting, somehow, our sensations.

The problem of the nature of 'perception' in the sense of perception of physical substants, events, processes, relations, etc., is therefore the problem of *the specific nature of that interpretive activity*, and of *the epistemic status of the interpreted occurrences or entities*, diversely termed 'sensations', 'sensibles', 'sensa', or 'sense-data'. Moore speaks of them as 'presented objects' (pp. 230–1) and insists that such a judgment as 'This is an inkstand' is a judgment *about* a given such 'presented object' in the sense that 'if there be a thing which is this inkstand at all, it is certainly *only* known to me as *the* thing which stands in a certain relation to this sense-datum. It is not given to me in the sense in which this sense-datum is given' (p. 234).

7. *Sense-data*. To speak as Moore thus does of *sensations* as 'presented objects' sounds queer; for sensations would ordinarily be categorized as *subjective* states or occurrences. The term 'sense-datum', on the other hand, with which Moore equates 'sensation', definitely is an 'object' term, whether the objects it designates be thought of more specifically as psychical, or as physical, or as 'neutral'.

Moore makes clear what he takes a sense-datum to be when he writes: 'It seems to me evident that I cannot see the *sensible* quality blue, without *directly seeing* something which *has* the quality—a blue patch, or a blue speck, or a blue line, or a blue spot, etc., in the sense in which an after-image, seen with closed eyes, may be any of these things.'[7] And Professor Broad even says that 'sensa have some of the characteristics of physical objects . . . they are extended, and have shapes, sizes, colours, temperatures, etc.'; but they also have some of the characteristics of mental states; for instance, 'they do seem to be private to each observer', and to be mental 'at any rate in the sense of being mind-dependent'.[8]

Such a conception of sensa or sense-data as objects entails that, like physical objects, they may seem to have characteristics they do not really have, and seem not to have some they really do have. But, as Professor Ayer has pointed out, 'one of the purposes which the introduction of the sense-datum terminology is intended to

[7] *The Philosophy of G. E. Moore* (Lib. of Living Philosophers, Vol. 4, Northwestern Univ. Evanston, Ill.), 1942, p. 659.
[8] *Scientific Thought* (Kegan Paul, London, 1923), p. 259.

serve is that it should enable us to deal with the problems which arise from the fact that *material things* can appear to have qualities that they do not really have, and can appear to exist when they do not.'[9] And, if the distinction between appearance and reality is made not only in the case of material things, but *also* in the case of 'sense-data' themselves, then the very same problems automatically reappear concerning sense-data, which sense-data were invoked to resolve concerning material things, but which sense-data have then been robbed of the power to resolve.

There is therefore no point in employing at all the term 'sense-datum' unless one definitely means by it something that both cannot appear to have characters it does not have, and cannot have characters it does not appear to have. 'Sense-data', and its synonyms 'sensa' and 'sensibles' are therefore treacherous words unless, in the case of what they designate, *reality consists in appearance, and appearance constitutes reality*. That is, unless, in *their* case, *esse est percipi*.

8. *Sensations, Introspection and Perception of physical events*. Moore believes 'that there must be some good reason' why 'the *esse* of sensible qualities is *percipi*'; but states that he does not know what that reason is.[10] It becomes discernible, however, after two things have been done.

The first is to discard altogether the term 'sense-data' since it perniciously begs the status of *objects* of consciousness—as distinguished from that of *states* of consciousness—for what it designates; and does so notwithstanding that, as pointed out in Section 7, if the sense-data terminology were to be capable of the function it was designed to perform, then *esse est percipi* would have to be true of sense-data. Moore's term, 'sensibles', is likewise objectionable: it begs for what it designates the possibility not only of being sensed, but also of existing without being sensed.

What makes Moore cling to the 'sense-data' terminology is that when, in the account (quoted in the preceding Section) which he gives of what he means by a sense-datum—for instance, a *patch*, or a *speck*, or a *line*, or a *spot*, that 'has' the quality blue he sees—he fails to notice that the quality blue he sees 'has' for

[9] *Foundations of Empirical Knowledge* (MacMillan, N.Y., 1940), pp. 68–9. Italics mine.

[10] *The Philosophy of G. E. Moore*, p. 660.

instance *linearity*, or it may be *spotness*, etc., in exactly the same sense of 'has' in which the line or the spot he sees 'has' *blueness*.

The crucial fact overlooked by Moore is thus that what one *sees* comprises not only qualities, but also *extensities, shapes, quantities, relations*. These are *seen* just as literally as are qualities *seen*; and the 'good reason' which Moore rightly believes must exist, why the *esse* of seen qualities is *percipi*, is likewise the good reason why the *esse* of seen extensities, of seen shapes, of seen quantities, and of seen relations, is *percipi*.

The other thing that must be done before the nature of that 'good reason' becomes evident is to discard also the erroneous tacit assumption Moore makes, that the status of 'presented objects' is intrinsic to sensations. For the truth is that sensations—and likewise the other kinds of states of consciousness—become *objects* of consciousness *only when they are being introspected* or, as some prefer to say in the case of sensations, *inspected*; that is, only when they are *being attended to*. Attention to one's *states* of consciousness is what confers on them, for the time being, the adventitious status of *objects* of consciousness.

It is evident, for example, that to *be sad* is one thing, and that to *introspect one's sadness*, i.e. to *attend to it*, is another thing, which not only is not requisite to one's being sad, but rather tends to dilute one's sadness with curiosity; for what normally generates sadness is attention to some saddening fact such, for instance, as the death of a loved person.

Attention to a present state of one's consciousness has, it is true, sometimes been held to be psychologically impossible. But it is not really so at all. What makes it perfectly possible is the fact, on the one hand, that, as pointed out earlier, every event and therefore every mental event takes some *span* of time; and on the other, that mental events of two or more different kinds—e.g. hearing *and* wondering *and* introspecting one's wondering—can perfectly well occur at the same time or at overlapping times. One's sadness thus can be present still, after one's attention to it has begun. The so-called 'specious present', which comprises some span of time, is the only kind of present time that is *real*, for it is the only kind at which events ever do or can occur. A strictly punctual, mathematically dimensionless present is much rather what is specious—indeed, *spurious*—both psychologically and physically.

Attention to the seen quality blue does not, as in the case of sadness, tend to dissipate its object; but attention to the blue seen is not in the least requisite to one's *seeing* the blue. Indeed, at most times, we do not attend to our sensations, but only *employ* them, automatically, as *signs*, learned by us in the past, that certain other sensations impend; the anticipating of which—according as we desire them or are averse to them—causes us to engage in such purposive activity as we believe will permit or promote their occurring, or as will on the contrary prevent it.

The *proximate* cause of a sensation, however, is never any of the other psychical states or activities of the person having the sensation. Yet a sensation, like any other occurrence, does have a *proximate* cause of some kind. We denominate it 'physical'. That is, 'being physical' means *fundamentally* (as distinguished in Section 5 from *derivatively*) *being an occurrence of such kind as is proximately causing a sensation.*

That a given sensation is a *sign* that a certain other sensation impends, however, implies that, since one sensation never proximately causes another, there is a causal connection between the 'physical' proximate cause of the given sensation and the 'physical' proximate cause of the sensation of which the given sensation is a sign. This introduces the notion of a 'physical' capacity; and this in turn the notion of a 'physical' substant, whose exercise of its physico–psychical capacities is what proximately causes sensations.

The interpreting of one's complexes of sensations *as proximate effects of non-psychical occurrences is what 'perceiving physical facts'* consists in, whether these be physical events, physical processes or physical substants. To perceive visually for instance an apple is to sense visually together certain colour-qualities and certain shapes, sizes and relations; and to interpret this complex of visual sensations as complex proximate effect of exercise by a non-psychical substant of certain of its physico–psychical capacities.

In the perceiving of physical facts, as just described, the relation of the psychical to the physical is *epistemic*. But there are many occasions on which the relation of the psychical to the physical is not epistemic but is instead *telic*: desire to experience eventually a certain sensation complex (or as the case may be, not to experience it) is often efficacious but never *proximately* efficacious to that end; for, as stated earlier, one's sensations are never proximately caused by any other of one's mental states or activities. Yet the desire, like any other event, has effects; and if it is efficacious, it can then only be by its proximately causing some non-psychical event which, as before, we denominate 'physical', and which in turn causes one or more likewise 'physical' others, one of which proximately causes occurrence of the sensation one had desired to experience eventually (or as the case may be, prevents occurrence of the sensation to the eventual experiencing of which one was averse).

9. *Sensation, Sensing and the Criteria of the Mental.* The meaning of 'physical' has now been analysed in terms of (*a*) the kind of psychical occurrences called 'sensations'; (*b*) the fact that these, like occurrences of any other kind, have some proximate cause; and (*c*) the fact that the proximate cause of a sensation is never normally a psychical occurrence. (I say 'normally' as distinguished from perhaps sometimes 'paranormally'; in which case, however, the ostensible sensation would be not really a sensation but a hallucination.)

The question now remains as to what ultimately identifies sensations themselves as being psychical, not physical nor perhaps 'neutral'. The answer will constitute the 'good reason' Moore believed must exist why *percipi* (or more strictly, *senti*) is the *esse* of qualitative sensa; and of course is likewise the *esse* of sensa of the other kinds to which attention was called in Section 8; to wit, sensed extensities, sensed shapes, sensed quantities, and sensed relations.

The answer to that epistemologically crucial question is, I now submit, that whereas an occurring sensation's *being attended to* confers automatically on it the adventitious status of *object*—to wit, of object of inspective attention—the *occurring itself* of a particular sensation is not the occurring of an *object* of sensing, but of some *determinate mode*—or as we may prefer to say, determinate form, modality, modulation, or specificity—of *sensing*; sensing being itself one of the species of what has been variously called 'immediate experiencing', or (by S. Alexander) 'enjoying' or (by Moore) 'direct apprehension' or (which seems to me best) 'intuing', 'intuence' or 'intuent experiencing'.

Moreover, if sensing a blue is thus a (determinate) mode or species of the genus, sensing, then obviously the blue cannot exist without being sensed; nor can sensing exist, i.e. occur, without having some determinate modality.

A blue which is being simply sensed is thus not an *object* of sensing, but is a sensing—and more specifically a seeing—*bluely*; and of course a seeing not only bluely but also *briefly* (or as the case may be, more or less *lastingly*); also *herely* (or perhaps *therely*); also *abundantly* (or perhaps *scantily*); also *linearly* (or perhaps *spotly*); etc. And all this would equally be true if, as in Moore's supposition, the blue were being not *sensed* but instead *after-imaged.*

Evidently, moreover, that seeing blue is seeing bluely would not warrant saying that one's sensing, or one's after-imaging, 'is blue' in the sense in which a given flower is blue; for in the latter case, what the expression 'is blue' predicates of the flower is *not a quality* but *a capacity*—the capacity, namely, to cause intuence of a *quality* of the kind called 'blue' in a person whose eyes are focused on the flower while in daylight. And to assert that a sensation or an after-image has *that capacity* would patently be absurd.

At this point, something must be said first about a certain statement of Professor Broad's concerning sensations, sensa, and sensing; and then about the meaning of two of the terms that were used in the submitted account of what a sensation is intrinsically.

In *Scientific Thought* (p. 259) Broad writes: 'sensations are analysable into act and sensum, and the sensum must therefore be distinguished both from the sensation and from the act of sensing . . . yet these two factors are not capable of existing separately from each other.'

I submit, however, that—unlike looking, listening, sniffing, which are acts but are physical—*sensing* is not an *act*: it is not a *doing*, but an *undergoing*. It belongs to the *passive* pole of the mental, not to the *active* pole.

This fact is epistemologically crucial, and the overlooking of it by eminent writers on the subject of Sensation has been fertile of gratuitous puzzles and hypotheses.

I turn now to the first of the two terms alluded to earlier, whose sense as employed in the account of what a sensation is needs to be made quite clear. It is the adjective 'determinate', as qualifying 'modes of sensing'. It is used there in the sense W. E. Johnson gives it in Chapter XI, 'The Determinable', of Vol. I of his *Logic*; the relation between *determinate* and *determinable* being that of an *infima species* of a genus to the intermediate, i.e. the determinable, species of that genus.

Johnson's discussion, however, unjustifiably employs the names of various colours—'red',— 'yellow', 'blue'—as illustrations of names of determinates; whereas 'blue', for instance, is evidently not the name of a determinate colour, but of a determinable which has sub-determinables; e.g. Prussian blue, cerulean blue, etc. A truly determinate colour, on the other hand—e.g. a determinate cerulean blue—is determinate not only thus as to *hue*, but also as to *brightness* and as to *saturation*. Only such a *completely* determinate blue would be an *infima species* of blue.

Moreover, the only species of blue that admit of being sensed, i.e. *seen* (instead of only conceived) are its various *infimae species*. This is a cardinal point; for what *individuates* a determinate blue is not its being determinate, but its being at some determinate place at some determinate time.

The other of the two terms whose meaning needs to be made unambiguous is 'experiencing'. One speaks of experiencing, e.g. *a tornado*; and also of experiencing the *fear*, which the experiencing of the tornado causes one to experience. The crucial difference here is that, in the case of experiencing the tornado, 'experiencing' means *perceiving* as analysed in Section 8; the tornado therefore being an *adventitious* (external, objective) accusative of 'experiencing' in the sense of *perceiving*; whereas in the case of fear, fear is a *connate* (internal, subjective) accusative of 'experiencing' in the sense of *intuing*. And whereas the *esse* of a tornado does *not* consist in its being experienced, the *esse* of fear does, on the contrary, consist in its being experienced.

Just this, then, is the ultimate criterion of the 'mental' or 'psychical' character of something *experienced*: If something experienced is a *connate* accusative of the experiencing, as is the case with fear, or pain, or blue, or bitter taste, etc., then, *eo ipso*, it is 'psychical', its *esse* is its *experiri*, and the experiencing is *intuent* experiencing. On the other hand, if something experienced is an *adventitious* accusative of the experiencing, as is the case with a tornado, or a desert, or a tree, or a kangaroo, etc., then, *eo ipso*, it is 'physical', its *esse* is *not* its *experiri* but is its occupying some place at some time, and the experiencing is *perceptual* experiencing, i.e. perceiving.

The psychical or mental, however, comprises not only intuings—all of which are cases of *undergoing*—but also cases of many kinds of *intentional, purposive doing*, i.e. of *acting*; for instance,

95

inferring, recalling, reflecting, imagining, supposing, postulating, etc. The question then arises, as it did in the case of intuings, as to just what identifies as 'psychical' or 'mental' such various kinds of purposive or intentional doing.

I submit that the criterion of the 'mental' or 'psychical' character of something one is intentionally doing, i.e. of an *act*, is that, if the act is of an *introspectable* kind, i.e. is a form of *thinking*—as is the case with inferring, or recalling, or supposing, etc.—then, *eo ipso*, the act is 'mental', whereas if the act is of a *perceivable* kind, i.e. is a form of *behaviour*—as is the case with walking, throwing, pushing, etc.—then, *eo ipso*, it is a 'physical' act.

10. *The Mind–Body Relation.* I come now finally to the problem of the relation between a mind and its living body. It is best approached through a question which, from the materialistic point of view of the natural sciences, appears silly; but which, in the light of the contents of various of the preceding Sections, not only is seen to be quite legitimate, but turns out to be fertile of insight into the nature of the mind–body relation.

That question is: Which living human body, out of the hundreds and hundreds one perceives, is *one's own*?

One of its marks is that one never directly sees its eyes, nor any parts of its head other than its nose, orbital arches, and parts of its cheeks and lips. Also, one never directly sees most parts of its back.

These marks, however, appear to be accidental rather than decisive, since, if certain others were absent from the body those mentioned characterize, but were present in a body other than it, that *other* body would be the body one would call one's own.

Those decisive other marks are that the body one calls one's own is:

(1) the only one in which certain of one's mental states directly cause or inhibit certain body changes; for example, the only body in which one's being ashamed causes blushing automatically; or one's deciding to move its finger causes it automatically to move;

(2) the only body, stimulation of whose sense organs causes one to experience the corresponding kinds of sensations. For instance, if one is seeing several human hands wearing gloves, and each is pricked with a pin, the particular one the pricking

96

of which causes one to feel pain is the hand one calls one's own;

(3) the only body, certain kinds of damage to which causes loss of certain of the capacities of one's mind;

(4) the only body in which new capacities—e.g. capacity to play the piano—can be generated by one's persistent will to have it acquire them.

It turns out, therefore, that when in the question 'How is a mind related to "its" body?' one explicates the meaning of 'its', the question then reads: 'How is a mind related to the only living body with which it directly interacts?' That is, the question, when its meaning is analysed, is seen to contain its own answer!

Moreover, that this answer, to wit, Interaction, does *not* leave unanswered the question as to *how* a bodily event causes a sensation, or *how* a mental event causes a bodily one, follows from the fact to which attention was called in the account of Causation in Section 2, that the question as to the *how* of causation has no meaning other than 'through what intermediary causal steps'; so that to ask it concerning cases of *proximate* causation is to be guilty of a 'category mistake'.

COMMENTS BY LORD BRAIN

In this chapter the author defines 'mind' as a set of capacities for certain introspectable characteristics forming part of cause-and-effect events. Mind may be a convenient way of describing these capacities, but surely the substant (to use the author's term) to which they belong is a person, and we should say that mind is a generic name for certain capacities of persons. A person then has the mental capacities of feeling, thinking and acting, and the physical capacity of falling down a precipice, and these are not the capacities of two substants, but two types of capacity of one. The different modes of causation described hold good as between a person and physical events outside his body, but the postulation of two substants surely begs the basic question. Cause is defined as implying sequence in time. In physico–psychical causation, therefore, the physical event precedes the mental event, and in psycho–physical causation the reverse is true. It is agreed that a bodily event causes a sensation, but, if brain and mind are different substants interacting, the bodily event must precede the mental

97

event, but this is nowhere demonstrated nor, as far as I know, has it ever been demonstrated. On a monistic view the two are simultaneous, but a chain of bodily events could still be described as causing the simultaneous bodily-mental event which constitutes the sensation. The way in which the problem is stated does not distinguish between a monistic and a dualistic view, and therefore provides no proof of interaction.

COMMENTS BY ANTONY FLEW

With Professor Ducasse also there have been previous engagements.[11] On this occasion I will make only three points, briefly. The *first* is to question the distinction which Ducasse tries to draw in his first paragraph. For there does not appear to be a difference, or, if there are differences, they do not correspond with his description of his examples. In characterizing the second set, those which are supposed to involve the notion with which he is concerned here, he speaks of 'mind' used as a substantive. But certainly in one, and possibly in two, of the four examples of the first set 'mind' is also used as a substantive: certainly in 'He changed his mind'; and rather less so in 'I have a mind to go'. The idea in the background seems to be: not the old error, so rightly and so effectively blown upon by Berkeley, that every (grammatical) substantive must refer to a (logical) substance; but a different insistence, which may nevertheless be seen as a sophisticated variation upon the same theme, that a substantive is only really and truly such in so far as it does fulfil this function. This would explain: both why Ducasse cheerfully includes in his first set examples in which 'mind' is employed as a grammatical substantive; and why in his next paragraph he proceeds to raise the question of 'just what kind of substantive entity the term "mind" is conceived to designate' in the second set. Yet this still will not do. For there is no good reason why any of the phrases cited—except for the self-consciously artificial book title *Why the Mind has a Body*—should be construed in this way. To say that someone 'has a keen mind' is not to attribute to him the possession of a substantive entity, but only to assert that he is endowed with the appropriate capacities; and similarly, with all the other specimens.

It might at first blush appear that this is all that Ducasse himself wishes to maintain, for in his third paragraph he states that he proposes to argue 'that a mind is essentially a more or less well-integrated set of capacities'. But this apparently innocuous thesis has to be regarded in

[11] See, for instance, *Journal of the Society for Psychical Research*, Vol. XLI (1962) and Vol. XLII (1963), Nos. 714 and 716.

a very different light as soon as we see him proceeding to explain: 'The term, "a substant", will designate anything, whether mental or material, whose nature consists wholly of a more-or-less well-integrated set of *capacities*. Some of the material things commonly called "substances" —e.g. glass, lead, water—would be substants as just defined; but so would a tree, a table, a human body, which on the contrary would not in ordinary usage be called "substances"' (p. 82: italics and punctuation as in original). My *second* point is that Ducasse has no warrant thus to lump minds and material things together into the same ontological category. For material things such as he has listed are not bundles of capacities; they are what possess these capacities. Minds, on the other hand, may indeed be considered to be, in his sense, bundles of capacities; but by that same token they cannot themselves be what has those capacities.

My *third* point is that if the first two are accepted, then the question and the answer considered in Ducasse's Section 10 are, after all, neither of them legitimate. He asks: 'Which living human body, out of the hundreds and hundreds one perceives, is *one's own*?' (p. 96). His answer is: 'when in the question "How is the mind related to 'its' body?" one explicates the meaning of "its", the question then reads: "How is the mind related to the only living body with which it directly interacts?" That is, the question, when its meaning is analysed, is seen to contain its own answer!' (p. 97). Now no doubt one could suggest circumstances in which there could be a question as to which of various bits of various human bodies were one's own: in a Websterian tragedy, perhaps; or in a Rugger scrum. Equally, one can perfectly well ask what precise sorts of consciousness are related to what specific kinds of physiological state; and also, perhaps, one can ask how these relationships should be thought of. But to ask—with Ducasse—how my entire body is to be recognized as mine, or how I (as one thing) am related to my body (as another) is to mistake it that we are confronted with two separate and separately identifiable sorts of things: on the one hand minds, or people; and on the other, bodies. We are not.

COMMENTS BY H. H. PRICE

1. *The meaning of the word 'physical'.* There are two discussions of this point in Professor Ducasse's paper, one in Section 5 and the other in Section 8. In both he distinguishes between fundamental and derivative senses of the term. In Section 5 he says that in the fundamental sense any kind of item is called 'physical' or 'material' the concrete instances of which are perceivable, and in Section 8 that 'being physical' means

fundamentally 'being an occurrence of such a kind as is proximately causing a sensation'. The example he gives is the visual perception of an apple.

The two definitions may seem to be equivalent, because perceiving, on Ducasse's view, consists in the causal interpretation of sensations. When we perceive the apple we interpret a complex of visual sensations 'as complex proximate effect of exercise by a non-psychical substant of its physico–psychical capacities'. But what are we to make of the word 'proximate'? Surely the *proximate* cause of the visual sensations is not an event in the apple, but an event in the percipient's brain. In that case, should we have to say that the apple itself is physical only in the derivative sense, not in the fundamental sense?

There is a similar difficulty about attributing physico–psychical capacities to the apple (for the definition of these, see p. 87). Does an apple have physico–psychical capacities at all? On the face of it, the only physical entities which have them are the brains or central nervous systems of certain sorts of organisms. The most we could say of apples is that they have physico-*physiological* capacities, and even this is rather difficult when we consider the distance-receptor senses. In sight, for instance, it seems that what has physico–physiological capacities is not the apple itself, but the light-rays reflected by it.

2. *'Physical' and 'Spatial'*. 'Being spatial' is not included in Ducasse's analysis of the fundamental meaning of the word 'physical'. I think this omission will surprise many of his readers. Few of us perhaps would agree with Descartes when he (apparently) *identifies* 'being physical' with 'being spatial'. But we do usually suppose that being spatial is an essential part of the meaning of the word 'physical' or 'material'. Everything which is physical (at least in the fundamental sense of 'physical') must surely be spatial, though it does not follow that everything spatial is physical.

This point is relevant to Ducasse's theory of perception as well. We do in fact interpret our visual and tactual sensations as caused— proximately or not—by spatially extended and spatially located entities. How or on what grounds do we do it? Ducasse does not think of visual and tactual sensation as acquaintance with sense-data which are themselves extended. He prefers an 'adverbial' or 'internal accusative' terminology (p. 94). He would say, I think, that when we experience a visual field we are sensing voluminously or in a voluminous and patterned manner. But why do we suppose that this voluminous sensing is caused by an entity which is itself voluminous, or by several voluminous entities which themselves form a spatial pattern, e.g. by an apple on a plate with a knife beside it? It seems to me that a special principle will have to be introduced at this point, the principle that there is at least as much internal multiplicity in the cause as there is in the effect, or something of the sort. Such a principle could perhaps be derived deductively from Ducasse's analysis of the notion of causality itself in Section 2.

3. *Mind and Memory.* Ducasse has not said much about memory in his paper. The only reference to it, I think, is in the passage about forgotten experiences in Section 5. Let us consider Leibniz's phrase *mens momentanea seu carens recordatione.* To me it seems self-contradictory. Of course, Ducasse himself does not think that minds are or can be momentary entities. He insists that every mind has a history. But is it enough that it should *have* one? To count as a mind, must it not in some way 'retain' at least part of the history which it has had up to now? There is at least a temptation to say that 'retention of its past'—or some degree of such retention—is one of the essential characteristics of a mind.

No doubt this is rather a difficult point. Some might prefer to say that memory in a wide sense of the term is an essential characteristic of *living* entities (not merely of minds or mind-possessing entities). Moreover, the very queer form of paranormal cognition called 'psychometry' suggests that even non-living material objects can sometimes preserve a memory—or something like it—of their own past history. Perhaps memory is not a *distinguishing* characteristic of minds after all. Nevertheless, I suggest that it is an essential one.

4. *Which body is my own?* (Section 10, p. 96). Many contemporary philosophers (Mr. P. F. Strawson for instance) will no doubt say that this is an absurd question, equivalent to 'which person is myself?' It is therefore worth while to point out that there are paranormal experiences in which the subject really does ask 'which body is my own?' and is genuinely puzzled by the question. They are what psychical researchers call 'out-of-the-body experiences'.[12] Here the subject seems to himself to be seeing his physical organism from without, just as if it were the body of another person. For instance, he seems to see it lying inert on the ground or in bed or on the operating-table in a hospital, as if he were up above and looking down on it. The recumbent and inert body certainly is the one which he *ordinarily* calls his own and is in the place where his own body might be expected to be. But for the time being it fails to fulfil the four conditions laid down by Ducasse. It also fails for the time being to fulfil another condition. The body which I call my own is the centre of my perceptual world, in that the point of view from which I perceive things is located on its surface.

---

[12] See also H. H. P.'s comments on Mr. Quinton's paper p. 234. The reader will find an excellent account of out-of-the-body experiences (with detailed discussion of a number of cases) in Professor C. D. Broad's *Lectures on Psychical Research* (Routledge & Kegan Paul, 1962), Ch. 6.

But in an out-of-the-body experience the subject's point of view is located elsewhere.

Moreover, in some though not all 'out-of-the-body' narratives the subject reports that he seemed to himself to be 'in' *another* body, which did for the time being more or less fulfil Ducasse's four conditions, and did also serve for the time being as the 'centre' of the subject's perceptual world. This may lead him to ask 'which of these two bodies is my own?'. In one such narrative, however, the subject speaks as if he were a disciple of Mr. Strawson, and was so much puzzled that he could only say he had split into 'two me's'.

Unfortunately, out-of-the-body experiences are not very common. But I think they have some relevance to the conceptual difficulties we encounter when we discuss the mind–body problem, and it seems highly desirable that every philosopher should have one or two out-of-the-body experiences in the course of his career.

COMMENTS BY J. R. SMYTHIES

The difficulties that Ducasse raises over the use of the term 'sense-datum' in Section 7 arise in part because he does not keep separate the employment of this term by different philosophers who have based their usage on different definitions—i.e. the *ostensive definition* of Moore and myself and the *epistemological definition* of Price, Ayer, etc., as given classically in terms of the perception of a round, red tomato by Price in the opening paragraphs of *Perception*. If we stick to the ostensive definition we are not primarily concerned with the difference between appearance and reality, nor with problems about what we can be certain of in perception; but our analysis is based merely on the *phenomenology* of our sensory fields as these present themselves ('appear', 'occur', etc.) to direct introspection. If we start off with an unambiguous ostensive definition of sense-data—as I have attempted to do—we can use this then to define 'mind' to account for one important meaning of this complex word in the sense of *conscious* mind. We can say that X's mind is X's collection of sense-data, images, thoughts, emotions and his Ego. 'Mind', of course is used in *other* senses to include his capacities, intelligence and certain features of his personality—psychological aspects of 'mind'; whereas my definition covers its much-neglected existential (even *anatomical*) aspects. I take 'Ego' to be that, in Newton's words, 'which in us perceives and thinks.'; or that which in Ducasse's analysis actually *does* the introspection he talks about. Sense-data can hardly introspect themselves—so either 'introspect' becomes an impersonal verb—but Ducasse never uses it as such—or it requires some subject. Ducasse uses the personal pronouns, e.g. 'I'. But 'I' usually stands for my total being—for all of me—and therefore confusion is liable to arise if 'I' is also used to describe that *part* of 'total me' that is capable of *inspecting* other parts of 'me', i.e. my sensations. Or we can consider Hume's complaint that when he searched around in his mind he could never find there anything but sensations and thoughts. Hume's Ego would be, I suggest, that which *did* this searching. The main *evidence* for its existence for each of us is the manner in which we experience the events of our own consciousness.

REPLY TO LORD BRAIN BY C. J. DUCASSE

Lord Brain states that, on a monistic view of the relation between the body and the mind of a 'person', 'a chain of bodily events could still be described as causing the simultaneous bodily-mental event which constitutes the sensation'.

On a monistic view, however, the causative chain would *ex hypothesi* be *also* a chain of mental events; and one wonders which ones Brain would say these are; also, just what analysis of the notion of causation, which he employs, he would offer.

In commenting on the question whether, in causation of a sensation by a bodily event, the bodily event does, or does not, precede the mental event, Brain speaks of *two* events—one bodily and the other mental. I submit that, no matter whether they are simultaneous or sequential, they are anyway quite distinguishable: the mental one is observable only by the 'person' in whom it occurs, and only in the manner called Introspection; but the bodily one—nerve currents between the particular sense-organ and the particular region of the brain cortex concerned—is not perceptually observable by him at all.

To put a hyphen between 'bodily' and 'mental' in characterizing a sensation does not make one out of the two quite unlike events mentioned. A statement made long ago by Friedrich Paulsen is relevant here still today: 'I understand by a thought a thought and not a movement of brain molecules; and similarly, I designate with the words anger and fear, anger and fear themselves and not a contraction or dilation of blood vessels. Suppose the latter processes also occur, and suppose they always occur when the former occur, still they *are* not thoughts and feelings.'[13] The basic hard fact to a statement of which Section 3 of my essay is devoted is essentially the same which Paulsen points out in his statement just quoted.

[13] *Introduction to Philosophy*, trans. F. Thilly (Henry Holt & Co., N.Y., 1895), pp. 82–3.

The monistic view Lord Brain favours seems to be identical with the 'double aspect' version of psycho–physical parallelism. I have considered it elsewhere, reaching the conclusion that, when critically examined, it is seen to be only a vacuous metaphor.[14]

One last comment on the monism to which Brain adheres is that it rules out *a priori* as impossible because self-contradictory that the mind or any part of it should survive the body's death. But the many eminent scientists and philosophers who in the publications of the Societies for Psychical Research and elsewhere have considered and weighed the empirical facts alleged to be evidence of the mind's survival have not found the supposition of such survival internally contradictory. What is so is the monistic supposition that two quite distinguishable and independently conceivable things are nevertheless only one.

REPLY TO ANTONY FLEW BY C. J. DUCASSE

Professor Flew's account of what I say in the first paragraph of my essay is inaccurate. What I say there I am *not* concerned with is the meaning of 'mind' in the sentences I first list—in some of which indeed, as Flew notes, 'mind' is used as a substantive. But when I go on to state what my essay *is* concerned with, I do not just, as he writes, 'speak of' '"mind" used as a substantive', but I specify that the essay's concern is 'with the meaning of "mind" used as a substantive *in phrases such as: . . .*'

What I contend is that, in the 'phrases such as: . . .' which I list, 'mind' designates a *substant* of a certain kind, to wit, a mental or psychical substant; that glass, lead, water, trees, human bodies, etc. are substants of another kind, to wit, material or physical substants; and that a substant is anything, whether mental or material, whose *nature* consists wholly of a more or less well-integrated set of *capacities*, no matter which of them, or whether any at all of them, are being exercised at a given time.

Flew's second criticism is that material things such as I have listed 'are not bundles of capacities; they are what possesses these capacities'. But he omits to say then just what, for example, is the lead which 'possesses' fusibility, pliability, inelasticity, visibility, specific gravity

---

[14] *A Critical Examination of the Belief in a Life after Death*, pp. 72–3 (pub. Charles C. Thomas, Springfield, Ill, 1961), in Part III of which the various theories of the mind–body relation are scrutinized; and where, in Sections 2, 3 and 4 of Ch. XII, the case for Interactionism as the only theory ultimately tenable is presented.

11.34, etc., but which, he alleges, is something other than the whole they together constitute. Would he contend, similarly, that for instance a week is something that 'possesses' its days but is itself other than the seven of them together?

Flew's criticism of the answer I propose to the question as to which of the many human bodies I perceive is my own ultimately consists only of the dogmatic assertion that 'to ask . . . how my entire body is to be recognized as mine, or how I (as one thing) am related to my body (as another) is to mistake it that we are confronted with two separate and separately identifiable sorts of things: on the one hand minds, or [!] people; and on the other bodies. We are not.'

My reply would be, (a) that I have not spoken of being 'confronted' with . . . minds . . . and . . . bodies; (b) that I contend that a human body is a physical substant and a human mind is a psychical substant; (c) that, while a human body is living, it has and exercises not only physico–physical capacities, but also physico–psychical and psycho–physical capacities; (d) that, when it dies it loses the latter two kinds of capacities, and also loses some but retains and exercises some of its physico–physical capacities; (e) that, while it is living and in normal condition, the mind concerned in that body's exercise of its physico-psychical and psycho–physical capacities has and exercises the logically converse capacities of being affected by and of affecting that body; and (f) that, when that body dies, that mind automatically ceases to exercise these two kinds of capacities, and either also all of its psycho–psychical capacities—i.e. ceases altogether to be—or else continues to be, exercising various of its psycho–psychical capacities.

These six statements together set forth my answer to the question as to whether a human body and the human mind with which it interacts during that body's life are 'separated' and 'separately identifiable'.

REPLY TO H. H. PRICE BY C. J. DUCASSE

Professor Price is of course right in saying that, in visual perception of an apple, the proximate cause of one's visual sensations is an event in one's brain; and further, in saying that the apple is physical in the derivative, not the fundamental sense of 'physical', since, in the latter sense, 'being physical' means being an occurrence that is proximate cause of a sensation.

Accordingly, the part of my Section 8 commencing on page 92, line 22 should be rewritten to read as follows:

this in turn the notion of a 'physical' substant; some physical substants having physico-physical capacities only; certain others (to wit, certain brain tissues) having also physico-psychical capacities, exercise of which is what proximately causes sensations; and certain other physical substants (to wit, certain other brain tissues) having not only physico-physical, but also psycho-physical capacities; i.e. capacities to be proximately affected by certain psychical occurrences.

The interpreting of one's complexes of sensations *as remote effects of non-psychical occurrences* is what perceiving physical facts consists in. To perceive visually for instance an apple is to sense visually together certain colour-qualities, shapes, sizes and relations; and to interpret them as remotely caused under the existing circumstances (presence of an eye, optic nerve, etc.) by exercise of a relevant capacity (capacity to reflect light) of a substant physical in the derivative sense of 'physical'; that substant being what an apple is in so far as perceivable only visually.

In the perceiving of physical facts the relation of the psychical to the physical is thus *epistemic*: perceiving is a knowledge-yielding process. But the knowledge it yields is a case of knowledge in the sense of *knowledge that*. . . . which may be called 'scient' knowledge as distinguished from 'intuent' (or 'experient') knowledge; that is, from knowledge in the sense intended in such expressions as having known pain, or dizziness, or nausea; or indeed having known, or knowing, any particular one of the many determinate olfactory, gustatory, tactual, or kinaesthetic sensory qualities that have no proper names and therefore can be referred to only by mention of the particular perceivable substant exercising its capacity to cause remotely a particular one of those determinate sensations—for instance, the odour 'of this rose', or the taste 'of this wine', etc. In all such cases the relation of the psychical to the physical is still epistemic: occurrence of the sensations is knowledge-yielding; but in the intuent as distinguished from the scient sense of 'knowing'.

There are many occasions, however, on which the relation of the psychical to the physical is not epistemic but is instead *dynamic*, either automatically or telically.

Examples where it is *remotely dynamic automatically* would be the psychosomatic causation of blushing, or paling, or trembling; or of stomach ulcers; or of other good or bad physiological effects of various emotions; or of the harboring of conflicting—or on the contrary harmonious—beliefs or impulses.

On the other hand, the psychical is *remotely dynamic telically* in cases where desire to experience eventually some particular sensation-complex, (or as the case may be, not to experience it) is efficacious to its end. In such cases the desire proximately causes some event physical in the derivative sense (to wit, an event in a brain tissue) which remotely causes eventually an event physical in the fundamental sense; namely, an event in another part of the brain, which proximately causes the desired sensation-complex.

As regards Price's criticism, that 'being spatial' is not included in my analysis of the fundamental meaning of the word 'physical', what I would say is that although it is not included explicitly, it is so tacitly, in virtue of the fact that 'physical' (both in the fundamental and in the derivative sense) is defined in terms of causation; and that space, and indeed time also, are intrinsic to causation in the analysis of it I offer. (See page 83 of my essay.) I would add only that it is imperative to distinguish between psychological and physical space and time; and that physical space and time are perceived dimensions of the physical facts that are perceived, as 'perceived' is defined in my rewriting of the part of Section 8.

As regards Mind and Memory, I would say that memory—capacity to remember—is one of the capacities of minds. And so is capacity to forget. But the capacity of a mind to remember some items of its history is exercised almost constantly by it while awake; whereas many of the other capacities it also has are exercised only occasionally; and some of them never.

As regards the question 'Which body is my own?' I would say that the unconscious body which, in an out-of-body experience I would see on the bed from a point external to it, is at that time mine only in a sense similar to that in which a coat I am not wearing or an automobile I am not operating at a given time can nevertheless be mine. The fact seems to me to remain that if, out of various bodies I observed while out of body, a particular one were such that whenever a rose is put under its nose I experience its odour, whenever a pin is struck into its skin I experience pain, whenever I decide that its forefinger wiggle it does wiggle, etc., then I would be fully warranted in judging that particular body to be truly mine.

REPLY TO J. R. SMYTHIES BY C. J. DUCASSE

Price's definition of 'sense-data', to which Smythies refers as 'epistemological', is, and I think is intended by Price to be, as purely phenomenological—or, to use Smythies' term, as purely ostensive—as Moore's definition in terms of a blue patch, speck, or line after-image seen with closed eyes. For a blue patch after-image seen with closed eyes is, *ex vi termini*, an image occurring *after* and *because of* one's having seen something with the eyes open; and is therefore implicitly just as 'epistemological' (if epistemological at all) as is the visual sensation-complex seen when one looks at a tomato—or indeed as are Moore's 'directly apprehended sensibles' seen when, as supposed in his 1923–4 paper on 'The Status of Sense-Data', what he looks at is a coin lying on the ground. Price, like Moore and Smythies, is not defining 'sense-data' in terms of what may be causing them or be signified by them (which would be making the definition epistemological) but simply instructs us how to find sense-data.

But instructions as to *how to find* something A have any relevance only for a person who *is searching for* A: A then having *ex hypothesi* the status of *object of*, i.e. of aim or goal of, his search. This object status, however, is not intrinsic to sensations, which are inherently *states of* consciousness and only rarely and adventitiously *objects of* consciousness in addition. That status is *conferred on* a sensation automatically when the sensation is made object of, i.e. topic of, introspection. For it is one thing for a sensation simply to occur, and another thing for it not only to occur but in addition to be introspected, i.e. attended to, inspected. In the great majority of cases we do not introspect either our sensations or the visual images we see with eyes closed, whether these be after-images, or be the changing cloudlike images we ordinarily see when our eyes are shut. In most cases, they simply *occur* and, in themselves, are neither right nor wrong, neither correct nor incorrect; for they are not images *of* anything.

As regards the relation of the Ego to the Mind, the fact is simply that the Mind is one and the same thing with the Ego. For clearness as to the identity of the Ego and the Mind, however, what is indispensable is the distinction between the following two questions: (*a*) What is meant by 'a mind'? and (*b*) Do any cases of what is meant by 'a mind' exist? (Cf. What is meant by 'a centaur'? and 'Do any centaurs exist?')

As regards question (*a*), the answer is that a mind is a more or less well integrated set of capacities ('dispositions') of certain kinds (specified in my essay); and as regards question (*b*) the answer is that a particular mind, defined as consisting of a particular set S of such capacities, *exists* at a time T in so far as any of them are being exercised at time T.

This entails that the collection of sensations, images, thoughts and emotions, of which Smythies speaks, constitutes the *history*, i.e. the *existence in time*, of a mind whose particular *nature*, i.e. *definition* or *essence*, consists of the particular set S of capacities—many of which, however, never get exercised; e.g. in the case of most of us the capacity to do homicide.

A mind M as conceived in the manner stated above *is* the Ego that *does*, for instance, the introspecting, i.e. the attending to, a particular one, P, of its own *states*; for 'attending to' P is exercise of the capacity C of M to bring the state of consciousness P from the margin of consciousness to the focus of consciousness when some event that causes exercise of M's capacity C occurs in the circumstances then present. No Ego, in the sense of something distinct from a mind as defined above is either needed for, or capable of, explaining any state or activity of consciousness that occurs.

The objections to employing at all the term 'sense-data' are: (*a*) that the term is not needed since the plain English word, 'sensations', already exists and does designate what Moore, Price and apparently Smythies too, mean by 'sense-data'; and (*b*) that, as Ayer has pointed out, 'sense-datum' has in fact sometimes been used in a manner that makes 'sense-datum' mean not a *state* of consciousness, but an *object of* consciousness, which then, like material things, can appear to have characteristics it does not really have, and can appear to exist when it really does not.

A RATIONAL ANIMAL
Antony Flew

1. I propose in this chapter to examine two theses. Though they are two it is convenient to consider both in one paper. For they can be seen best as two opposed, but equally wrong, accounts of the relations, or lack of relations, between two different kinds of explanation which may be offered for various human ongoings. When so described these theses—and hence, of course, their contradictories too—sound like paradigms of philosophy in the strictest sense: and so indeed they are. Yet each—and its contradictory likewise—in fact constitutes also an example of the sort of wide-ranging, exciting, and ideologically relevant contention which professional philosophers nowadays are often supposed to eschew. For if the first was right it would become—to put it no stronger—very difficult to go on maintaining that man is a part of nature; and, surely, this must in some interpretation be a presupposition of anything which deserves the name of a scientific world-outlook.[1] If the second was right it would enable us to dispose at one blow, and in a new way, of the problem of reconciling physiological determinism with the constantly realized possibility of free, rational and responsible human conduct; and this again would be an achievement of obvious ideological importance. Though we shall be here concerned chiefly with the two theses in themselves, we shall also give some attention to their important corollaries.

[1] For a development and defence of a scientific programme which includes this contention that man is a part of nature see Paul Oppenheim and Hilary Putnam, 'Unity of Science as a Working Hypothesis' in *Minnesota Studies in the Philosophy of Science*, Vol. II, edited by H. Feigl, M. Scriven and G. Maxwell (University of Minnesota Press, Minneapolis, 1958).

To explain what these two theses are one must first sketch a distinction between two sorts of question, two kinds of answers, two classes of concepts, two categories of explanation. This distinction is so fundamental, and each of the alternatives embraces so many necessary subdivisions, that it is perhaps wise to speak here of categories rather than, more modestly, of classes, sorts, or kinds. On the one side there are the questions, answers, concepts, and explanations which refer to mechanisms and other things incapable of purpose, intention, and rationality. (*Mechanism* here is being used in that very broad sense in which all electrical processes, as well as more old-fashioned arrangements of wheels, pumps and pendula, would certainly count as mechanical: and *incapable of rationality* has to be construed in such a way that actually to be either rational or irrational presupposes a capability of rationality.) The home of this first category of concepts and explanations is the sphere of technology and of the physical and biological sciences, although no one disputes that there is at least some scope for them in considering some aspects of the human organism. Obviously a mechanical explanation would be appropriate to a question about the occurrence of a 'reflex action'; notwithstanding that some would insist that this is precisely and only because 'reflex actions' are not—as indeed strictly speaking they are not—really actions at all.

On the other side we have those questions, answers, concepts and explanations which refer to reasons, purposes, wishes, intentions and so on. These belong to the human studies, such as history, and to everyday discourse about conduct. But in this case it is at least not obvious that they have any proper place outside their metropolitan territory. For such rational and purposive notions can, surely, have application only to persons or to other entities or putative entities thought of as either partially or preeminently personal. To ask what *is* (not what *ought* to be) the purpose of our life on earth, or to demand some justification for some at present humanly unalterable natural phenomenon, is to presuppose that there is some Super-person who regards us as his instruments, and who is responsible for things being as they are. In recent years many philosophers have been paying a great deal of attention to these distinctively personal notions; and some of their work can contribute to the understanding and resolution of certain issues arising in and around the various psychological disciplines.[2]

Now the two theses which we propose to discuss form a pair. Both accept as fundamental the distinction just outlined: but the one maintains that the two categories are so different as to be logically incompatible; while the other urges that they are so far separated that members of the first have no logical relations at all with members of the second—not even incompatibility. As an example of a statement of the first of these take Peter Winch's manifesto, in *The Idea of a Social Science*: 'I want to show that the notion of a human society involves a scheme of concepts which is logically incompatible with the kinds of explanation offered in the natural sciences'.[3] Or, again, consider A. C. MacIntyre's claim that 'human behaviour can only be understood in terms of such distinctive concepts as purpose, intention, consciousness, rationality, morality, and language. And these concepts rule out the possibility of causal explanation, in the sense in which mechanical explanations are causal explanations'.[4] The second thesis is stated explicitly, in A. I. Melden's *Free Action*, in the assertion that 'absolutely nothing about any matter of human conduct follows logically from any account of the physiological conditions of bodily movement'.[5] It is convenient to have labels for these two propositions. Since arbitrarily affixed letters and numerals are hard to remember, let us nickname the first the Conflict and the second the Co-existence Thesis.

2. (*a*) The Conflict Thesis is found most often, and most interestingly, as the usually unrecognized presupposition of the more immediately exciting contention that a comprehensive scientific naturalism has to be self-refuting; in the sense that a fully exhaustive account in terms of physiology (and perhaps ultimately of physics and chemistry) of all the ongoings in and of the

---

[2] See, for instance, A. C. MacIntyre's *The Unconscious* and R. S. Peters' *The Concept of Motivation* (both published by Routledge & Kegan Paul, London, 1958), and also the philosophical works recommended in the preface of the former book.

[3] (Routledge & Kegan Paul, London, 1958), p. 72.

[4] '"Commitment and Objectivity": a comment' in *The Sociological Review Monograph No. 3: Moral Issues in the Training of Teachers and Social Workers*, p. 91.

[5] (Routledge & Kegan Paul, London, 1961), p. 201. But, as my colleague Professor MacKay has suggested to me, compare and contrast p. 215.

human organism must preclude the possibility of our knowing such an account to be true. Though rarely noticed in the journals this proposition appears to have been and to be both widely and respectably held.[6] For example: in *Beyond Realism and Idealism*, W. M. Urban claims: 'in . . . deriving mind and knowledge from nature, as science conceives it, he [the "naturalist"] must assume that his own account of nature is true. But, on his premises, the truth of this account, like that of any other bit of knowledge, is merely the function of the adjustment of the organism to its environment, and thus has no more significance than any other adjustment. Its sole value is in its survival value. This entire conception of knowledge refutes itself . . .'.[7] Again, in a similar context in his very widely circulated study *Miracles*, C. S. Lewis urges: 'A theory which explained everything else in the whole universe but which made it impossible to believe that our thinking was valid, would be utterly out of court. For that theory would have been reached by thinking, and if thinking is not valid that theory would, of course, be itself demolished. It would have destroyed its own credentials.'[8]

That this contention does take for granted the truth of the Conflict Thesis comes out most clearly from a third formulation, by a scientist who has since disowned the whole argument, J. B. S. Haldane: 'If my mental processes are determined wholly by the motions of atoms in my brain, I have no reason to suppose that my beliefs are true . . . and hence I have no reason for sup-

---

[6] But see: G. E. M. Anscombe, 'A Reply to Mr. C. S. Lewis' Argument that "Naturalism" is Self-refuting' in *Socratic Digest IV* (Oxonian Press and, later, Blackwell, Oxford, 1949—); Margaret Knight, 'Consciousness and the Brain' in *Science News 25* (Penguin Books, Harmondsworth, 1952); and Antony Flew, Ernest Gellner, and Antony Flew again on 'The Third Maxim', 'Determinism and Validity', and 'Determinism and Validity Again', in the *Rationalist Annuals* for 1954, 1957 and 1958, respectively (C. A. Watts, London).

[7] (George Allen and Unwin, London, 1949), p. 236.

[8] (Collins Fontana, London, 1960), pp. 18–19. This and later references are given to the first paperback edition, not to the original hardcover version (Geoffrey Bles, London, 1948). In the paperback the third chapter, which is devoted to the present argument, has been largely rewritten in an attempt to meet the criticisms which Miss Anscombe deployed in the article mentioned in Note 6, above. Neither the author nor his publisher provide any indication either that these substantial changes have been made, or why.

posing my brain to be composed of atoms.'[9] Haldane is obviously presupposing that there cannot be room simultaneously for accounts: both of the physiological mechanics of the origins of a belief; and of the evidence which was sufficient to warrant the believer to hold it to be true. Of course Haldane's minimum presupposition here is considerably narrower than the full Conflict Thesis: for that covers the entire category of rational and purposive concepts; whereas Haldane is immediately concerned only with the sub-category of those required for the logical assessment of human discourse.

(*b*) To establish that the Conflict Thesis actually is false let us begin by considering an example. Suppose a man called Jones emits from his mouth noises within the range of variety which would be rendered in the notation of the English language as: 'The massacre in the Katyn forest was the work of the Russians'; or 'In Euclidean geometry the square on the hypoteneuse is equal to the sum of the squares on the other two sides'. The most usual response, and the one which would almost always be at least logically appropriate, would be to construe these ongoings as significant utterances; and to respond with questions or other remarks about the truth of the corresponding propositions, or about the reasons—which may not be the same as Jones's reasons—for holding them to be true. This is one sort of response: and the relevant notions are those of the truth of propositions, the validity of arguments, evidence for conclusions, logical grounds and logical implications, and so on. For ready reference we may label the kind of assessment which is involved in this sort of response Subject Assessment.

A second sort of response is to treat the Jones performance as an action: which, usually, it will have been. Here the appropriate remarks refer to Jones's purposes, motives and intentions; and questions may also be raised about whether what he did was moral or immoral or morally neutral, legal or illegal, good or bad manners, and so on. Thus we may, for instance, ask: 'Why did he make a remark which he must have known would touch all the Communist delegates, and their fellow-travellers, on the raw?'; or 'Do you have to keep rubbing in the fact that you did geometry

---

[9] *Possible Worlds* (Chatto & Windus, London, 1927), p. 209. Haldane disowned this argument in an article published in *The Literary Guide* (predecessor of *The Humanist*) for April 1954.

at O level, or to be so pedantic about its being Euclidean?' A mnemonic label for the kind of assessment which is involved in this sort of response might be Action Assessment.

One rather special case of Action Assessment, which in the present context perhaps deserves separate mention, is that seen in the work of the psychoanalyst. For the psychoanalyst is professionally committed to treating every utterance, and indeed every piece of non-verbal movement too, as an expression of his patients' (probably unconscious) intentions, motives, and purposes.[10] 'To achieve success the analyst must above all be an analyst. That is to say he must know positively that all human emotional reactions, all human judgments, and even reason itself, are but the tools of the unconscious, that such seemingly acute convictions which an intelligent person like this possesses are but the inevitable effect of causes which lie buried in the unconscious levels of his psyche.'[11] The passage occurs in a long study of one case by Dr. Charles Berg, a leading Freudian. It is, one might add, surely significant that even compulsive symptoms, at least when it is thought that they are susceptible of some analytic interpretation, should be called obsessive acts or obsessive actions.

A third possible response is to think of Jones as an organism, and of his utterances as so much acoustic disturbance: which indeed he is, and they are. Then the appropriate questions will be about the mechanisms responsible for the production of these particular disturbances on this particular occasion; though it would be unrealistic to expect to get any but the sketchiest and most inadequate answers for a very long time to come. This third response can be labelled the Physiological Approach. Whereas both Subject and Action Assessments require notions from the second of the two categories distinguished earlier, the Physiological Approach demands only those of the first. What the Conflict Thesis maintains is that where Subject or Action Assessment is possible the questions of the Physiological Approach cannot arise: and, of course, the other way about also.

---

[10] For a development and defence of this interpretation of psychoanalysis see Antony Flew, 'Motives and the Unconscious' in *Minnesota Studies in the Philosophy of Science*, Vol. I, edited by H. Feigl and M. Scriven (University of Minnesota Press, Minneapolis, 1956).

[11] Charles Berg, *Deep Analysis* (George Allen and Unwin, London, 1946), p. 190.

Now against this we want to urge that there is no fundamental inconsistency between any of these three approaches, and
that it is perfectly possible and proper to raise questions of all three
sorts on and about one and the same occasion. A man may wish
to hold and to express a certain belief; that belief may be true, and
he may himself have sufficient reasons for believing that it is; and
yet there may be physiological sufficient conditions for the occurrence of those acoustic disturbances which are, correctly, interpreted both as expressions of his beliefs and as manifestations of
his wishes and purposes. That we can thus be simultaneously,
both rational beings, and moral agents, and living animal organisms, is one of the great basic facts about the multiple and complex nature of man.

(c) What then is the case for the Conflict Thesis? The curious
fact is that we have not been able to find any sustained and developed argument, which we could try to meet systematically.
One might have hoped that Winch was going to provide this,
after his announcement: 'I want to show that the notion of a
human society involves a scheme of concepts which is logically
incompatible with the kinds of explanation offered in the natural
sciences.' Unfortunately the arguments which he then proceeds to
offer do not in fact support the Conflict Thesis; and, more seriously from our point of view, when it comes down to detail
Winch does not even try to show that they do. What he really
does try to show is that purposive and rational concepts are fundamentally different from the mechanical notions of the natural
sciences; that the former are both characteristic of and essential
to social and human studies; and that Mill was wrong in thinking
'that there can be no fundamental logical difference between the
principles according to which we explain social changes'.[12] But
to show, as Winch tries to do, that there could be no sufficient
account of any social phenomenon in exclusively natural scientific
terms, and without any reference to the plans and purposes of the
people concerned; or even to show that no rational and purposive
notion can be either derived from or reduced to the purely
mechanical; is not at all the same thing as demonstrating that
explanations involving concepts of these two different categories
must be logically incompatible. To show that A is incomplete
without B, or that B is neither logically derivable from nor

[12] Winch, *loc. cit.*, p. 71.

reducible to *A*, is not to show that *A* and *B* must be incompatible. This should have been obvious. However, in view of the present popularity of contentions about the differences between the two categories, Winch has perhaps performed an unpremeditated service in providing an occasion for underlining this particular piece of obviousness.

Unlike Winch, MacIntyre does not even claim to be deploying a case for the Conflict Thesis. First he gives his statement of what he calls 'the fact that human behaviour can only be understood in terms of such distinctive concepts as purpose, intention, consciousness, rationality, and language. And these concepts rule out the possibility of causal explanation, in the sense in which, for instance, mechanical explanations are causal explanations.' He then adds: 'In the space available to me I can only assert this. I cannot argue for it.' So he proceeds simply to bring out what he sees as the point of the contention, and some of its consequences:

> If I am right the concept of causing people to change their beliefs or to make moral choices, by brainwashing or drugs, for example, is not a possible concept. It is not, for part of our concept of having a belief or making a choice is that beliefs and choices cannot be produced or altered by non-rational means of such a kind. If one were to hypnotize someone so that he as a result of our hypnotic suggestion took one alternative rather than another, then the agent could simply not be said to have chosen. If one were to discover a drug as a result of which a man permanently became unable to say other than what he believed to be true, one would not be in a position to call the man truthful. For the essence of being truthful is that one could be a liar and isn't. Thus where human concepts such as those of morality or rationality have application, causal explanations of a physical kind have not.[13]

This is a most useful contribution; though in the opposite sense to that intended by the author. Let us consider choice first. Now, though choice is a far trickier concept than MacIntyre seems here to realize, it is no doubt true enough that a man could not properly be said to have acted by his own choice if his behaviour was the result of such physiological manipulations by some other person. Certainly it would be monstrous to hold the victim rather than the manipulator responsible; except in so far as he had consented to

[13] MacIntyre, (footnote 4), p. 91.

be manipulated, and had thus become to some degree an accessory before the fact. But from this it does not follow that, if some pattern of behaviour has certain physiological sufficient conditions, and if therefore it could be produced by someone else by producing those conditions (as in principle if not in practice it presumably could); then that pattern of behaviour cannot ever correctly be described as something done by the agent's free choice. Nor does it follow that the action cannot then ever be something for which that agent may fairly be held responsible.

The crucial and constantly neglected difference between the two cases is that in the former the behaviour actually is the result of manipulation by another person, whereas in the latter it either might or might not be. It is one thing to offer the excuse that someone was in fact the unconsenting victim of manipulation. It is quite another to say only that there were physiological sufficient conditions of his behaviour, which might in principle have been manipulated. The presence of sufficient conditions, whether physiological or other, is presumably a necessary, but it is certainly not a sufficient, condition of manipulation. Manipulation requires also an active manipulator.

MacIntyre is supposed to be elucidating the concept of choice, and bringing out that there cannot be physiological sufficient conditions of a genuine choice. Yet the most that has actually been shown is that you cannot properly be said to have acted in a certain way if your behaviour was in fact the result of the manipulation of such sufficient conditions by someone else. Now it might perhaps be urged in MacIntyre's defence that he has made a point of saying that he is not going to argue for the Conflict Thesis, but only to display some of its consequences. This would, I think, be too charitable. For he certainly has chosen to try to illuminate this very wide claim by appealing to the rather special case in which the behaviour actually is the result of manipulations.[14] This concentration, and his peculiar interpretation of the

---

[14] Compare the similar, and similarly unfortunate, concentration on such manipulation cases in his 'Determinism' in *Mind*, 1957: criticized in Discussion Notes by both Antony Flew and M. C. Bradley in *Mind*, 1960. The particular discussion of which this forms a part began in Flew and MacIntyre (eds.) *New Essays in Philosophical Theology* (S.C.M. Press, London, 1955), Chapter VIII and continued later in Chapters V and VII of my *Hume's Philosophy of Belief* (Routledge & Kegan Paul, London, 1961).

significance of this special case, strongly suggests that he is inclined to think that the whole wide claim of the Conflict Thesis—at least in its application to the particular concept *choice*—would be adequately based on the narrow and very modest observation that, if a man's behaviour results from manipulations performed without his knowledge or consent, then he could not truly be said to have acted by his own free choice.

We turn now to belief. MacIntyre contends: 'If I am right the concept of causing people to change their beliefs . . . by brainwashing or drugs . . . is not a possible concept . . . part of our concept of having a belief . . . is that beliefs . . . cannot be produced or altered by non-rational means of such a kind.' One is tempted to remark, adapting an old Central European saying, that a thesis which has a friend like this has no need of an enemy. MacIntyre is absolutely right that the Conflict Thesis does carry these implications. For since it states that such 'rational' ideas as that of belief are logically incompatible with those of mechanical explanation it surely follows that if it were true a belief could never be produced in such a 'non-rational' way. But this consequence does not in fact hold. The thesis from which it is derived must therefore itself be false also.

If it did hold it would presumably rule out as logically impossible all indoctrination by such non-rational techniques. The account of Pavlovian conditionings in Aldous Huxley's *Brave New World* would be not a nightmare fantasy but contradictory nonsense. We could know a priori that William Sargant's preliminary studies of 'the mechanics of indoctrination, brainwashing, and thought-control' must be radically misconceived and aborted.[15] These would indeed be rich and strange fruits of philosophy. How odd that it never seems to have occurred to any of the apologists labouring for those recently accused of 'brainwashing' their prisoners to urge that these charges could not be true; because self-contradictory.

Again if this consequence did hold, one of the criteria for the use of the term *belief* would have to be essentially backward-looking. Yet this is surely not the case. The actual criteria are concerned with the present and future dispositions of the putative

[15] The phrase quoted is taken from the front cover of the paperback edition of Sargant's *Battle for the Mind* (Pan Books, London, 1957); the book is subtitled 'The Physiology of Conversion and Brainwashing'!

believer; and not at all with how he may have been led, or misled, into his beliefs. You can perfectly well say that Murphy believes that it is better that the peoples of less happier lands should continue to be poor and hungry, rather than that they should pursue policies of restrictive population planning, without thereby implicitly denying either that this is something which Murphy wishes to believe, or that his belief results from early indoctrination. Still less are you committing yourself by this straightforward reporting of Murphy's lamentable views to the even more rash denial that there are any non-rational sufficient conditions for his conviction. Indeed if the statement that someone believes something really carried the negative implication which MacIntyre is claiming that it does carry, it would be difficult to see how anyone could ever be in a position to know that anyone believed anything.

The reason which MacIntyre fields in support of this particular contention is: 'If one were to discover a drug as a result of which a man permanently became unable to say other than what he believed to be true, one would not be in a position to call the man truthful.' This will not do. What MacIntyre is supposed to be supporting is the contention that under certain very general conditions a man could not properly be said to believe. These general conditions are that there are physiological sufficient conditions of his behaviour. What MacIntyre offers as a reason is that under certain very specific conditions a man could not be said to be truthful. These very specific conditions are that he has been given a drug which has made him permanently unable to say other than what he believes to be true. This consideration, whether or not it is correct in itself, provides no support whatsoever for MacIntyre's conclusion. For if MacIntyre's drug affects only the subject's ability to say what he does not believe then it does not as such affect his beliefs. This makes the case irrelevant. Yet if the drug were to be allowed to affect what the subject believes then this very supposition would itself contradict the thesis which it is supposed to be supporting.

(*d*) It would seem that in the previous subsection 2(*c*) we have, by showing that it implies something which is surely false, delivered 'the killing blow' to the Conflict Thesis. It is worth considering briefly some of the implications for the further and more immediately interesting contention explained in subsection 2(*a*), above. Now to do justice one must recognize that there is a sort of deflationary metaphysics—often presented as if it were a consequence of the findings, methods, or presuppositions of some form of scientific inquiry—against which a contention of this kind can be both sound and decisive. But this objection does not necessarily presuppose the Conflict Thesis.

Consider again the passage, quoted in 2(b), above, in which Dr. Berg maintains that a psychoanalyst 'must know positively that all human emotional reactions, all human judgment, and even reason itself, are but the tools of the unconscious, that such seemingly acute convictions which an intelligent person like this possesses are but the inevitable effect of causes which lie buried in the unconscious levels of his psyche'. The most, perhaps excessively, charitable interpretation of this passage is to construe it as intended only as a statement of the limitations of interest required of an analyst in his working hours: every utterance as well as every non-verbal movement is to be treated solely as a symptomatic act; and the only questions to be asked, whether silently or aloud, are those belonging to the realm of Action Assessment—as extended by the introduction of the notions of unconscious motivation, planning and so on. If so, fair enough; no doubt.

But the temptation, to which others if not Dr. Berg certainly have succumbed, is to take it that the discoveries, methods, and presuppositions of psychoanalysis warrant or demand the deflationary metaphysical claim that there is no room anywhere for Subject Assessment; that there is no proper place—even among those fortunate enough to enjoy rude mental health—for the notions of logic, evidence and validity; that no one ever has, and knows he has, good and sufficient reasons for believing any proposition to be true. To do this is to provide one more example of the illegitimate conversion of the necessary limitations of a professional interest into an aggressively contractionist metaphysic.[16] Against this move it is a decisive objection to urge that any system of ideas which really did carry this implication would thereby undermine its own claims to consideration. Psychoanalysis cannot possibly have shown that all argument is just so much unwarranted rationalization, because the supposed demonstration would be self-discrediting in just the way in which it has

[16] For further examples and for some development of this idea see Section 5 of my 'Crime or Disease' in *The British Journal of Sociology*, 1954.

been supposed that any naturalism must be which insists that man is a part of nature.

Similar, and similarly misguided, claims might be made on the basis and on behalf of physiology; or even of physics and chemistry. Someone might say—they often have said—that people are merely very, very, complex organisms the workings of which are, in principle, comprehensible in physiological and ultimately, in physical and chemical terms. The word *merely* is the one which has to be watched here. It is a word which often gets slipped in unnoticed, though it may be crucially important. (Try the experiment. Say to a group of students: 'Man is an animal'; and notice how many will, in all good faith, be willing to misreport you as having said that man is merely an animal.)

Confronted with this claim that people are merely very complex organisms, and so on, the first thing to get clear is what this particular *merely* is intended to exclude. (As a tip for the avoiding of confusion and cross-purposes the advice to ask this sort of question in this case is as good, but even less commonly given or heeded, than the recommendation to insist on discovering what individuals or states characterized as free are supposed to be free from.) If, for instance, the point of the assertion was to reject the idea that people are incorporeal substances, which as such might significantly be said to survive disembodied, then nothing has been said which gives purchase to the sort of objection which we are presently considering. But if the intention really was to deny that Subject Assessment and the notions peculiar to it have any proper application to any of these very complex organisms; then it will once more be relevant, fair and decisive to object that this denial itself was and had to be expressed through the utterance of a proposition which, were that denial well founded, could not properly be said to be either known or not known, either true or false, either probable or improbable. Is the physiologist not himself a man?

This sort of objection to ill-starred contentions of this kind does not presuppose the truth of the Conflict Thesis. With the similar objection that any comprehensive scientific naturalism must be similarly unsupportable the situation is different. For to make that charge stick you have to try to show that such a view must be committed to the denial which we have seen to be disastrous. But this ruinous commitment will be inescapable only if the claim which is essential to such a naturalist—that people are complex organisms the workings of which are, in principle, comprehensible in physiological-mechanical terms—must necessarily preclude the proper application of Subject Assessment to any of their ongoings: in short, only if the Conflict Thesis is true. However, as we have already argued, that thesis is false. So there is no ground here for rejecting the claim: that people are organisms, consisting of parts all the ongoings of all of which can, in principle, be subsumed under the notions appropriate to a Physiological Approach; but that these organisms also have other aspects, including most importantly those which both justify and require Subject Assessment and Action Assessment.

If such a claim is correct then the sort of analogies which might illustrate and illuminate the relations, and lack of relations, between physiological questions and questions of the other two sorts are those of the relations, and lack of relations, between the physical and the musical consideration of a particular musical performance or between an engineering and a logical interest in a particular Turing machine. In the former case, investigations of the sort described by Sir James Jeans in *Science and Music* do not in any way prejudice a concern with the distinctively musical characteristics of musical performances.[17] It would be quite wrong to insist that physics has shown, or might show, that music is merely so many phons and decibels of acoustic disturbance: at least if that *merely* is to be interpreted as denying the legitimacy of any consideration of the same ongoings which introduced such terms as *harmony, con brio, counterpoint,* and so on. It would be equally wrong to urge that the possibility and necessity of a Musical Assessment of these ongoings showed that even in their purely physical aspects they could not be comprehended within the terms of a natural science. (And it would be downright fantastic to suggest that a logical irreducibility of musical to physical concepts meant that musical characteristics must belong to some incorporeal, though nevertheless substantial, musical soul!)

In the other case, a Turing machine might be specified as one which fulfils a certain 'logical' programme. But the engineers might be able to meet this specification in radically different ways: there could, for instance, be both electronic Turing machines as well as others which were, in the narrower sense, purely mechani-

[17] (Cambridge University Press, Cambridge, 1937).

cal. This analogy has been developed fully, although not in exactly the same context, by Hilary Putnam.[18]

3. The Coexistence Thesis states that 'absolutely nothing about any matter of human conduct follows logically from any account of the physiological conditions of bodily movement'. This has perhaps seemed plausible because it has been confused with other and weaker contentions. Thus, in the passage from which the quotation is taken, Melden has been urging 'that there is a radical disparity between these two modes of explanation'. (See Section 1, above). Unfortunately some 'psychologists are obsessed with the desire to establish their inquiry on a parallel footing with the natural sciences'. But 'as bodily movements items of overt behaviour are physiological occurrences for which physiological occurrences would appear to be sufficient causal conditions'. Where this is what psychology has studied its 'alleged explanations of human action have succeeded only in changing the subject, in substituting explanations of bodily movements for explanations of action'.[19]

It is one thing, and surely right, to urge that an action, qua action, would not have been appropriately or sufficiently explained were even the fullest account to have been given of the physiological sufficient conditions of all the movements involved of and in the agent organism. It is quite another and, as we shall try to show, wrong to maintain that from such an account no inferences at all could be drawn to consequences about conduct.

The possible confusion here is like one to be found in, or in a misinterpretation of, R. S. Peters. P. C. Dodwell, in an article on 'Causes of Behaviour and Explanation in Psychology', writes of Peters' *The Concept of Motivation*: 'Peters is not denying that physical processes are necessary conditions of an organism's behaving in one way or another, only that such conditions could ever be sufficient, taken on their own.'[20] Now there certainly are passages which might seem to demand this construction: 'we could never give a sufficient explanation of an action in causal terms. . . . A precise functional relationship could never be established. Of course . . . we could lay down certain very general

---

[18] 'Minds and Machines' in *Dimensions of Mind*, edited by Sidney Hook (New York University Press, New York, 1960: and a paperback edition by Collier Books, New York, 1961).

[19] Melden, *loc. cit.*, pp. 200–1.   [20] *Mind*, 1960, p. 2.

necessary conditions. . . . But this would not be a sufficient explanation of his action; only a statement of some of its necessary conditions.'[21] But other passages suggest that Peters would be quite prepared to accept that there may be not merely necessary but sufficient physical or physiological conditions of all the movements involved in the performance of actions on particular occasions: 'In cases where an explanation in terms of conscious reasons is sufficient—e.g. taking a bishop in order to checkmate the king—there are obviously also causes of the action like movements in the muscles and central nervous system. The point is that if it is an action it is not *sufficiently* explained in terms of such causes.'[22]

Probably what Peters really wanted to maintain was: that wherever the ongoings in and around an human organism are susceptible of Action Assessment they have not been sufficiently explained until they have been explained as actions; and that actions qua actions cannot be sufficiently explained simply in physical and mechanical terms; but not that these same ongoings cannot have physiological sufficient conditions. Yet even on the most friendly reading it is hard to acquit him completely of all relevant confusion. For, in the passage from which the first of our quotations comes, he starts by agreeing with D. W. Hamlyn: 'that we can never specify an action exhaustively in terms of movements of the body or within the body'; proceeding to give as his reason that a person performing on different occasions what would nevertheless be characterized as the same action would 'vary his movements in a great variety of ways'.[23] From this we could, no doubt, infer: that there will be no one set of conditions which are together both necessary and sufficient for the occurrence of an action *on all the occasions on which it might occur*; that we can at most hope to find some conditions which are *always* necessary; and perhaps also that 'a precise functional relationship could never be established' between any of the terms appropriate to the description and explanation of actions qua

[21] Peters, *loc. cit.*, pp. 13–14: italics as in original.

[22] Peters, *ibid.*, p. 59: italics as in original.

[23] Peters, *ibid.*, pp. 12–13. The Hamlyn paper to which Peters is referring, and which I am glad to find this occasion to mention, is 'Behaviour', first published in *Philosophy*, 1953, and since reprinted in *The Philosophy of Mind*, edited by V. C. Chappell (Prentice-Hall, Englewood Cliffs, N.J., 1962).

actions and those found or to be found in a purely physiological account. Yet, even granting all this, we cannot validly deduce that there are not, on any particular occasion on which any action is performed, causally necessary and sufficient conditions for the occurrence of all the movements which happen to be involved. The fact, if it be a fact, that action types have no necessary and sufficient physiological conditions does not by itself involve that there can be no such conditions for action tokens.

Nor, suppose we grant the impossibility of establishing a precise functional relationship, can we infer from this that absolutely nothing about any matter of human conduct follows logically from any account of the physiological conditions of bodily movement. In a recent published discussion of determinism P. F. Strawson urged that if such contingent functional relationships could be established, then there could be 'physical laws of human action as well as physical laws of physical movement'. But since, on philosophical grounds, he believes that this is out of the question he concluded that the physical sciences 'could never yield deterministic explanations of human action'. J. F. Thomson disagreed: for 'if we assume, as it were, unlimited success in physical explanation of physical movements, then it's by no means clear to me that people in general would find your point about absence of correlations an adequate defence against determinism'. To this objection Strawson responded crushingly: 'I cannot help it if people are confused'.[24]

This is altogether too short a way both with determinism and with dissent. To establish that there can be no neat correlations between accounts of sorts of physical movements and descriptions of kinds of actions would by no means be to show that no inferences at all can be made from one to the other. For, as Warnock argued in a later paper in the same volume, even if it were impossible from any descriptions of mere movements to deduce that an action had been performed, it might nevertheless be quite possible from some such descriptions to draw definite conclusions about actions which had certainly *not* been performed. And this possibility is in fact realized. It is not hard, for example, to think up descriptions of physical movements from which we could infer that the individual so described had not sat down in a

[24] *Freedom and the Will*, edited by D. F. Pears (MacMillan, London, 1963), pp. 66–7.

chair, committed adultery or bowled an over overarm. This is by itself sufficient to show that the Coexistence Thesis is false.

We cannot, therefore, hope to overcome the difficulties of reconciling physiological determinism with the fact of free, rational and responsible conduct by taking the short cut which Strawson thought he saw. The category to which mere bodily movement belongs is not so far removed from that of action for possible discoveries about the former to be necessarily irrelevant to questions about the latter. Fortunately there appears to be another and viable route, though longer and more laborious. In which case we shall not be required, if we wish to defend the reality of responsible human action, to reject what seems to be a presupposition of physiological science; and to embrace, however ruefully, what Warnock calls 'the excitements of superstition'.[25]

COMMENTS BY C. J. DUCASSE

I agree with much of what Professor Flew says but there are one or two places where I think he is mistaken. Take for instance, on p. 118, his statement in the last paragraph, beginning '. . . it is no doubt true enough . . .' and ending '. . . an accessory before the fact.'

What Flew overlooks is that each of us is continually becoming to some extent a different person as a result of, among other causes, the nature of the persons he comes in contact with, what they happen to say to him and do to him, etc., as well as in consequence of the aging of his body, of infirmities due to accident or to disease, etc. Each of us, without formal hypnotism, gets automatically suggested into various beliefs and disbeliefs by advertisements, newspaper headlines, the tone of voice in which we hear various names uttered, etc. What Flew refers to as 'manipulations'—whether with esoteric mind-changing drugs, or with such run-of-the-mill ones as coffee, alcohol, aspirin, perfumes, are only other such transforming influences as those mentioned above, except that—like advertisements and the talk of salesmen—they are

[25] G. J. Warnock, 'Actions and Events' in Pears, *loc. cit.*, p. 79. This other route, as Warnock says 'has had its sponsors here and there since at least the time of Hobbes' (*ibid.*, p. 70). One of many modern discussions is mentioned in Note 14, above. Hobbes blazed this trail with a pamphlet first published, against his will, in 1646 under the engagingly immodest title *Of Liberty and Necessity: A Treatise, wherein all controversy concerning Predestination, Election, Freewill, Grace, Merits, Reprobation, etc., is fully decided and cleared* (*The English Works of Thomas Hobbes*, edited by Sir William Molesworth, Vol. IV: John Bohn, London, 1839–40).

deliberately intended to make the recipient a different person in certain respects the manipulator desires.

Now, let us call A what a person was, say, a week ago; and call B the more of less different person he has become today in consequence of such influences of one or others of those kinds as in the meantime have affected him. Suppose that B steals, but that A was honest. It would be as inappropriate to praise B for what A was, as it would have been to punish A for B's future stealing. But it is not inappropriate to punish B for B's stealing; for, no matter how B got to be a thief, a thief is what B now *is*; and the moral justification of punishment of B is that (or if) it will transform today's thieving B into tomorrow's honest C.

A person is morally responsible for what he does, if and only if awareness by him of what the consequences of various courses of action open to him would be influences him to reject one course because he is averse to what the consequences of it would be, and to adopt another course because he desires the consequences it will have. If a person's future conduct is not influenced by such punishments or rewards, then he is morally irresponsible (e.g. infants, idiots, etc.), and punishment or reward are equally inappropriate because futile. Similarly, it is appropriate to whip a dog in the act of biting the postman; but it would be stupid to whip him today for having bitten somebody ten days ago; for he would not then associate the whipping with his biting, and the whipping would teach him nothing.

I relished particularly Flew's account of what I would call the occupational disease of psychoanalysts!

COMMENTS BY D. M. MACKAY

Professor Flew, in his stimulating discussion of MacIntyre's notion of 'manipulation', appears to concede that 'if a man's behaviour results from manipulations performed without his knowledge or consent, then he cannot truly be said to have acted by his own free choice'. Although this is almost my only point of disagreement with his paper, it raises a more general issue which I feel to be worth discussing.

My difficulty is that many of our choices, as viewed from outside, 'result from' not just one but a whole chain-mesh of circumstances, which must often include the actions of other people 'performed without our knowledge or consent'. Presumably none of these is 'manipulating' me unless he knows and intends the effect he has on my choice. But even if he is, and does, I do not see how this knowledge and intention of his affect the *freedom* of my choosing.

Consider a philanthropist, for example, moved to send money to Mr.

A by a circumstance which A has unwittingly brought about. No question here of 'manipulation' by A. But now suppose that A discovers how it all happened, and decides this time to 'try it on', with a similar result. We would, I think, judge him now a manipulator; yet the philanthropist's decision, reached (*ex hypothesi*) in the same way as before and in similar circumstances, would surely be no less 'of his own free choice'.

Obviously the 'manipulation' contemplated by MacIntyre and Flew is more drastic. The problem is to define more closely just what *kind* of manipulation it is that removes freedom and responsibility from the victim. In the case of Mr. A, we would certainly say that knowledge of the effects of his action gave *him* some responsibility for the form of the philanthropist's decision; but only an unwarranted doctrine of 'conservation of responsibility' (analogous to 'conservation of matter' in physics) could lead to any conclusion that this necessarily reduced the responsibility of the philanthropist. It is a noteworthy feature of responsibility that it is not always diminished by being shared.

The criterion that I would offer follows from the line of argument in Refs. 8 and 11 of my chapter. Responsibility for an act is annulled, I suggest, if or in so far as there exists an advance specification of its form upon which agent and observer *would be right to agree* before the event. It does not matter, on this view, whether or not either agent or observer ever gets to hear of such a specification. The question is simply whether it exists, and is binding upon them whether they know it or not, in the sense that both would be correct if they believed it, and in error if they did not.

By this criterion, manipulations are separated into two classes. The first, which includes hypnotic suggestion, physiological interference with the brain's motor system, *force majeure* and the like, do in principle give rise to definitive predictions (whether known by anyone or not) which would be valid for both agent and observer—in the kind of 'take it or leave it' way that predictions of (e.g.) astronomical events are valid for all.

Manipulations of the second class, however, give rise only to conditionally valid predictions, whose validity would be reduced or destroyed if the agent himself were to believe them in advance. Such manipulations shade gradually from impersonal 'rigging' of circumstances, to direct appeals calculated to sway decision, eventually becoming distinguishable from true dialogue only by the 'one-way' character of the causal relationship—(i.e. dialogue shades into manipulation when the normative system of one party ceases to be open to the address of the other—see ref. 15 of my chapter).

My suggestion would be that only the first class of manipulation necessarily eliminates the agent's freedom of choice; the second gives the manipulator a share in responsibility for the outcome, but does not necessarily prevent the agent from acting of his own free choice. To attribute freedom to a choice, in other words, is to deny the existence of a determinative future-tense specification of its outcome which is binding upon the agent whether he knows it or not. As I have argued elsewhere (*loc. cit.*), this 'logical indeterminacy' of a normal choice would hold even if the brain were as mechanically determinate as clockwork (which it is not).

COMMENTS BY H. H. PRICE

1. *The formulation of the Coexistence Thesis* (p. 125). It maintains that the two categories 'are so far separated that members of the first have no logical relations at all with members of the second—not even incompatibility'. But if they really have no logical relations at all, even the relation of compatibility would be absent (as well as incompatibility). Compatibility *is* a logical relation after all, and quite an important one. Surely the Coexistence Thesis does hold that the two sorts of description or explanation always are compatible with each other? Is not that the whole point of it?

Suppose however that the 'assessments' which Flew discusses later were regarded as mere expressions of emotion, as in the old 'Boo-Hurrah' theory of evaluative utterances. To adapt an example he uses on p. 124, let us compare the physicist's account of a musical performance with a series of utterances like 'Oh!' 'Ah!' 'Wonderful!' made by a member of the audience. Then there really would be no logical relations at all—not even compatibility—between the auditor's utterances and the physicist's written sentences. Nothing can be compatible with something else unless each of them is either true or false; and though what the physicist says is true or false, what the auditor says is neither.

But it is quite clear that Flew does not hold this old-fashioned Positivist theory of evaluative utterances. The assessments he speaks of *are* true or false. In that case they *can* have the relation of compatibility with the descriptions or explanations offered by a physicist or a physiologist; and according to the Coexistence Thesis, they always do have it.

2. *Beliefs.* On this subject, Flew's criticism of MacIntyre's version of the Conflict Thesis seems to me conclusive. But curiously enough, he says little or nothing about the treatment of beliefs in the Coexistence Thesis. In the excellent discussion at the end of his paper, he argues that the Coexistence Thesis is false. But he only considers its treatment

131

of actions. I wish to suggest that the 'Coexistentialist' view of beliefs is open to more or less parallel criticisms.

We must agree that the concept of belief *per se* is not a 'backward-looking' one (p. 120). But surely the concepts of reasonableness and unreasonableness, as applied to beliefs, *are* backward-looking ones. I have reason now to believe that it will rain before nightfall because of what I saw when I looked at the barometer an hour ago, or because of what I heard at breakfast-time on the wireless.

Now according to the Coexistence Thesis nothing that a physiologist could discover could be relevant to the reasonableness of my beliefs. But surely this is not true. In the example just given, he might have evidence that I was blind or deaf; and then I could not have got the evidence I claim to have for my belief about the weather (cf. 'He could not have committed the crime, because he was paralysed'). Again, a physiologist might be able to show by examination of my brain that my memory is very defective; so even if some belief of mine was reasonable when first acquired, it is not reasonable now, because I am quite incapable of remembering the evidence I had for it.

It might even be that I am in a state of 'derealization' (cf. Smythies' paper p. 249) and a physiologist might be able to discover this by examining electro-encephalographic records of what is going on in my brain. In such a state, I am likely to express *dis*beliefs about my physical environment, or doubts at any rate. But disbelieving a proposition *p*, or doubting it, can be assessed for reasonableness, just as believing it can. And if the physiologist can produce evidence which proves, or makes it likely, that I am indeed in a state of derealization (and surely this is conceivable in principle, whether or not it is practicable at present) you will then be justified in making an unfavourable assessment of my disbeliefs or doubts. I need not be unreasonable about other matters. For instance, I might believe correctly and with good reasons that the square root of 2 is a little more than 1·4. But it is likely that any disbelief or doubt I express about the external world will be unreasonable.

Let us consider another example which is very important in practice, the legal concept of 'being unfit to plead'. A man is in that condition if he is incapable of making reasonable statements in his own defence and reasonable replies to questions which are asked of him. And surely a physiologist might have good, even if not conclusive, evidence that Mr. Smith *is* incapable of doing these things, because the functioning of his brain is impaired, either temporarily (e.g. he has acute pneumonia) or permanently (e.g. he is in a state of senile dementia). Another and more painful example, very familiar to academic persons, is unfitness to take an examination. An examination candidate is expected to display reasonableness, as well as a more or less accurate memory of what he has been taught. We may have convincing medical evidence that at present he is incapable of displaying either, because of the bodily state in which he is.

We may also notice that when either kind of unfitness is temporary, it can sometimes be cured by physical or chemical means, and the capacity for reasonable conduct and reasonable believing can thereby be restored; on the other hand, bodily disorders can sometimes be cured by psychological means, in which a rational discussion of the patient's symptoms may quite well play an important part. These two medical facts are enough by themselves to show that the Coexistence Thesis is false.

3. *Mind–body Interaction.* Flew has deliberately abstained from discussing the mind–body problem in the traditional terms. Nevertheless, the Coexistence Thesis has *some* resemblance to the old theory of psycho–physical parallelism. At any rate it is committed to denying psycho–physical interaction. For if there were such interaction, a 'physiological account' would have some relevance to our rational activities, and *vice versa*. If the Coexistence Thesis is false, does it then follow that there is some truth in the Interaction Theory after all? Flew himself insists that we 'can be simultaneously both rational beings and moral agents and living animal organisms' (p. 117). What is the relation between these different parts or aspects of human nature? The Coexistence Thesis says they just exist side by side. But if the Coexistence Thesis is false, the relation between them must surely be much more intimate than that.

REPLY TO H. H. PRICE, C. J. DUCASSE AND
D. M. MACKAY BY ANTONY FLEW

I am grateful for the various comments of Professors H. H. Price, C. J. Ducasse and D. M. MacKay; and relieved that the issues which they raise, though most important, do not seem to upset the main contentions of 'A Rational Animal'.

1. *Professor H. H. Price. First,* about my formulation of the Coexistence Thesis, I have simply to concede that he is correct. To meet Price's criticism this formulation needs to be amended so that it maintains that the two categories of discourse have no logical relations, *save only that of logical compatibility.*

Second, he offers further reasons in support of my contention that the Coexistence Thesis is false. These I gladly accept, but with one reservation. The reservation is that some of the connections to which Price is drawing attention may be contingent and not logically necessary: (I am referring to the connections between, on the one hand, certain physiological facts and, on the other hand, the reasonableness or un-reasonableness of holding certain beliefs). For instance, Price mentions that certain 'bodily disorders can sometimes be cured by psychological means, in which a rational discussion of the patient's symptoms may quite well play an important part'. Perhaps, for our present purposes, such cases should be described as ones in which what removes the bodily disorders are the physiological ongoings involved in the rational discussion. This description would bring out, what is surely true, that the fact that this particular rational discussion requires these particular physiological ongoings is contingent: even though it is pre-sumably necessary that any rational discussion must involve some physiological—or at the very least physical—changes.

Third, Price notices that I have 'deliberately abstained from discuss-ing the mind–body problem in the traditional terms'; and that I want to insist that we 'can be simultaneously both rational beings and moral agents and living animal organisms'. He then asks: 'What is the relation between these different parts or aspects of human nature? The Co-existence Thesis says they just exist side by side. But if the Coexistence Thesis is false, the relation between them must surely be much more intimate than that.'

Certainly the abstention was deliberate: for, surely, the very incon-clusiveness of so much of the traditional discussion suggests that new approaches are needed; even though, at some stage, any such fresh beginnings have to be brought into relation with more ancient lines of inquiry. Certainly, too, the relations between these different aspects of human nature are much more intimate and numerous than mere coexistence. But in the present volume I do not want to commit myself further than I have already done in 'A Rational Animal', and in my later comment 'Some Objections to Cartesian Views of Man'.

2. *Professor C. J. Ducasse and Professor D. M. MacKay.* Ducasse and MacKay are both concerned with my too easy and inadequate attempt to distinguish between the causation which involves actual manipula-tion and that which does not. Their positive suggestions deserve far fuller consideration than would, unfortunately, be appropriate here and now. Perhaps it will be sufficient to concede that I should at least have added a further qualification to the sentence from which MacKay quotes.

I was arguing: 'MacIntyre is supposed to be elucidating the concept of choice, and bringing out that there cannot be physiological sufficient conditions of a genuine choice. Yet the most that has actually been shown is that you cannot properly be said to have acted in a certain way if your behaviour was in fact the result of the manipulation of such sufficient conditions by someone else.' What, as MacKay appreciates, I had in mind was a more drastic sort of manipulation than the weaker variety which he first indicates, a sort which would operate, as it were, directly on the physiological conditions of behaviour. Certainly, as he shows, that weaker variety is not necessarily incompatible with freedom of choice. To specify precisely what would or would not be involved in the stronger variety is not easy. But for the limited purposes of my argument against MacIntyre it should be enough: either simply to insert the word *physiological*, so that the passage reads 'if a man's behaviour results from physiological manipulations performed without his knowledge or consent, then he cannot truly be said to have acted by his own free choice'; or, more drastically, to make it run 'if a man's behaviour results from physiological manipulations performed without his knowledge or consent, and such that they render him unable to behave in any other way, then he cannot truly be said to have acted by his own free choice'. The more thorough, and more surely adequate, amendment produces a claim which if it were being offered as part of an analysis of *free choice* could scarcely be rated as illuminating. But in fact it is put forward only as a part of a refutation of MacIntyre's case for the Conflict Thesis.

THE CONCEPT OF CONSCIOUSNESS IN NEURO-LOGICAL EPISTEMOLOGY
Hartwig Kuhlenbeck

1. *The Meaning of Neurological Epistemology.* Neurological epistemology represents a particular aspect of theoretical neurology,
namely that aspect which is concerned with the origin, structure
and validity of knowledge. Until now, epistemology was custo-
marily considered a branch of philosophy. However, because
conscious experience and thought, on the basis of well substanti-
ated empirical data, may be regarded as a function of the brain,
there is a need to deal with epistemology on a neurological
basis. Many attempts at a classification of science have been under-
taken, but all such schematizations are not entirely logically
satisfactory in numerous respects, and must necessarily remain
arbitrary. This limitation then evidently obtains with regard to
any definition and subdivision of neurology.

Yet, for the purpose of the present argument, a rough delinea-
tion of the various aspects of neurology might be relevant. One
can distinguish applied and pure neurology. The former involves
clinical neurology in human and veterinary medicine, including
some aspects of neuropathology. Pure neurology becomes then
the study of form, structure, function, and chemistry of the
nervous system for its own sake, that is, as an end in itself.
Neuropathology, closely related to clinical neurology, can also
be dealt with as a subdivision of pure neurology. Again, neuro-
anatomy, neurophysiology and experimental neurology involving
both, could be distinguished. To this might be added theoretical

neurology, dealing with verbal, semantic, as well as with mathematical and philosophical aspects. Mathematical considerations are here meant to include the pertinent concepts of information, communication and control theory. Hence, theoretical neurology could be regarded as comprising attempts at unified, integrated formulation of all, or at least most, significant problems included in the field of 'neurology'. Psychiatry and psychology can thus likewise be conceived as intrinsic parts of neurology, pure and applied. Neurology or, if we prefer, neurobiology, and many additional 'separate' sciences are evidently so intricately interlocked, that any drawing of boundaries, or any classification becomes a question of more or less justifiable subjective, that is, personal emphasis. In accordance with this standpoint, neurological epistemology will here be considered a branch of theoretical neurology.

A neurologist may be justified to regard his field as a subdivision of the natural sciences, and to envisage the brain as an object, consisting of matter in the sense of classical physics and of chemistry. The material substratum of the functioning brain is in a labile chemical and physical condition, characterized as the living state, which, however, may still be interpreted as a purely material state.

Yet, some phenomena, which cannot be properly dealt with in terms of conventional natural sciences, may, nevertheless, reasonably be interpreted as entirely dependent functions of the brain. Such phenomena are the various aspects of consciousness, particularly those which H. Poincaré[1] has appropriately designated as 'qualités pures'. Because of certain peculiar semantic and logical difficulties unavoidably encountered in any approach to the problem of brain-consciousness contingency, some authors concerned with germane neurological, psychological, epistemological and logical questions choose to evade the issue by an indirect or even direct denial of consciousness. Discarding the term consciousness, or ignoring the data of conscious experience qua consciousness becomes, depending on additional details of the ratiocination's logical structure, either an indirect denial or merely a convenient fiction in the interest of economy of thought.

Traditionally, consciousness has been regarded as somehow

[1] *The Foundations of Science*, trans. by G. B. Halstead (Science Press, N.Y., 1913).

related to, or even in some respects synonymous with, a mysterious something designated as mind, which is of particular concern to philosophers. Philosophy often presupposes a reasoner or observer, conceived as a self, or ego, and possessed of a body. Outside this body there extends an external world. Body and external world are experienced through, or as, perceptions. Despite disruption and discontinuity of perceptions, a continuous and connected orderliness is experienced, such as would obtain if body and external world existed and persisted irrespective of perception. *Prima facie*, it seems therefore quite reasonable to postulate such a physical world, exhibiting not only general formal characteristics of space and time, but also specific attributes such as spatial configuration.

It could then be assumed that the self, ego or observer experiences this world by means of perceptions, mediated by the sense organs, and depending on the activities of the brain. Under these premises, perceptions would indeed have referents, that is, would stand for, something which is not perception, but a set of events in the postulated physical world. It goes without saying that such referent must not be confused with the semantic referent to the term perception, namely with our use of the word perception to stand for any sort of conscious experience.

Early attempts to qualify the attributes of the physical world led to a distinction between secondary and primary qualities. One of the best known definitions of primary and secondary qualities was given by *John Locke* in his 'Essay concerning Human Understanding'.[2] The primary qualities of bodies are those considered utterly inseparable from any imaginable state of such bodies, and comprise 'solidity, extension, figure, motion or rest, and number' (*Locke*, l.c. Book II, Chapter VIII, Section 9). The secondary qualities are those believed to be 'nothing in the objects themselves, but powers to produce various sensations in us by their primary qualities, i.e. by the bulk, figure, texture, and motion of their insensible parts, as colours, sounds, tastes, etc.'.

The distinction between primary and secondary qualities of bodies goes back in principle to *Democritus*; Scholastics, e.g. *St. Albert* (*Albertus Magnus*), were somewhat acquainted with it. The problem was again taken up by *Galileo, Descartes, Gassendi, Hobbes, Spinoza*, and by *Locke's* friend *Boyle*.

[2] Oxford University Press, 1894.

Locke, however, pointed out a significant difficulty inherent in any theory of perception based upon the assumption of primary and secondary qualities, namely the impossibility of discovering a logically satisfactory (conceivable, or intelligible) connection between the two sorts of qualities.

In Book IV, Chapter III, Section 13 of his 'Essay', *Locke* states:

> That the size, figure, and motion of one body should cause a change in the size, figure, and motion of another body, is not beyond our conception; the separation of the parts of one body upon the intrusion of another; and the change from rest to motion upon impulses; these, and the like, seem to us to have some connexion one with another. And if we knew these primary qualities of bodies, we might have reason to hope we might be able to know a great deal more of these operations of them one upon another: but our minds not being able to discover any connexion betwixt these primary qualities of bodies and the sensations that are produced in us by them, we can never be able to establish certain and undoubted rules of the consequence or coexistence of any secondary qualities, though we could discover the size, figure, or motion of those invisible parts which immediately produce them. We are so far from knowing what figure, size, or motion of parts produce a yellow colour, a sweet taste, or a sharp sound, that we can by no means conceive how any size, figure, or motion of any particles can possibly produce in us the idea of any colour, taste, or sound whatsoever; there is no conceivable connexion betwixt the one and the other.

These difficulties subsequently led to the argument of *Berkeley* and *Hume*. *Berkeley*[3] reached the conclusion that the elements of what is commonly interpreted as an independent physical world, namely 'material objects', exist only through being perceived. He may be said to have established the firm foundation of a consistent phenomenologic and positivistic approach to the problem of knowledge.

Hume[4] forcefully and convincingly denied the intrinsic difference between secondary and primary qualities. The pertinent passage in his 'first Enquiry' states:

[3] In *A Treatise Concerning the Principles of Human Knowledge*, (Everyman's Library, London, 1946) and *Three Dialogues between* Hylas *and* Philonous *in Opposition to Sceptics and Atheists*, (Everyman's Library, London, 1946).

[4] *Enquiries Concerning Human Understanding*, (Oxford University Press, 1902).

'Tis universally allowed by modern enquirers, that all the sensible qualities of objects, such as hard, soft, hot, cold, white, black, etc., are merely secondary and exist not in the objects themselves, but are perceptions of the mind, without any external archetype or model which they represent. If this be allowed, with regard to secondary qualities, it must also follow with regard to the supposed primary qualities of extension and solidity; nor can the latter be any more entitled to that denomination than the former. The idea of extension is entirely acquired from the senses of sight and feeling; and if all the qualities, perceived by the senses, be in the mind not in the object, the same conclusion must reach the idea of extension, which is wholly dependent on the sensible ideas or the ideas of secondary qualities.

In another very relevant comment *Hume* (l.c.) remarks:

Thus the first philosophical objection to the evidence of sense or to the opinion of external existence consists in this, that such an opinion, if rested on natural instinct, is contrary to reason, and if referred to reason, is contrary to natural instinct, and at the same time carries no rational evidence with it, to convince an impartial enquirer. The second objection goes farther, and represents this opinion as contrary to reason: at least, if it be a principle of reason, that all sensible qualities are in the mind, not in the object. Bereave matter of all its intelligible qualities, both primary and secondary, you in a manner annihilate it, and leave only a certain unknown, inexplicable something, as the cause of our perceptions; a notion so imperfect, that no sceptic will think it worth while to contend against it.

In my recent monograph[5], I have particularly attempted to show the intrinsic continuity displayed by the succession of *Berkeley, Hume* and *Kant,* to whom we owe a succession of concepts relevant to neurologic epistemology. To oversimplify this sequence: *Berkeley* showed that there is no matter, *Hume* showed that there is no mind and *Kant* clarified the distinction between phenomena (perception) and independent reality. By means of the *Brain-Paradox*[6] I believe I have provided an approximation to a 'logical proof' that the brain-consciousness problem is

[5] *Mind and Matter. An Appraisal of their Significance for Neurologic Theory* (Karger, Basel, 1961).

[6] Ibid., and also my 'Further Remarks on Brain and Consciousness: The Brain Paradox and the Meanings of Consciousness' (*Confinia Neurol.*, **19**, 462–85, 1959).

intrinsically unsolvable but allows a number of different approximate, more or less rational solutions which may be adapted to the needs of theoretical neurology.

These 'permissible' solutions involve undecidable and non-verifiable propositions requiring 'metalogical' postulates. Nevertheless, some of these propositions and postulates might be meaningful in dealing with various aspects of theoretical neurology for which an approach based on mechanism, behaviourism or logical positivism seems unsatisfactory or unsound, at least to those concerned with the significant *qualités pures* of consciousness, including axiologic values. I believe therefore that the present-day drift in approaching the complex neurological problems posed by the experienced fact of consciousness, namely a trend characterized by a one-sided emphasis on the partially valid concepts of behaviourism, logical positivism and operationalism, should no longer be allowed to remain unchallenged.

2. *The Definition of Consciousness.* If one defines, that is, delimits the *extension*[7] of the concept 'consciousness', it becomes evident that it includes everything one experiences in the state of vivid or dim awareness. *Prima facie*, this formulation appears circular, since awareness is consciousness, and it could be objected that a predicate applied to 'everything' is meaningless, or that we have here, as it were, a 'class of all classes' with its inherent logical weaknesses. One may, however, ask: what is *not* included in the term consciousness? Clearly, the state of consciousness is one's consciousness, that is, an individual, private state or manifold. It could be said that 'one' experiences this state, but it could also be claimed that this state is an integrated 'unit' or 'whole', and, as such, 'experiencing' *in toto*, this 'self-experiencing' 'whole' being the 'one'.

Under these premises, two large classes are not extensionally included in the concept consciousness, or better, consciousness-manifold. These two classes subsume (*a*) all possible, inferred, or presumed consciousness-manifolds other than one's consciousness, that is, other than the 'experienced' consciousness-manifold

---

[7] The extension of a concept is the class of entities, properties, states, etc. to which the concept refers. The extension of 'tree' is the class of all Trees. The intension of a concept are the qualities it defines. The intension of the 'Tree' connotes something like 'a large vegetable with roots, branches and biological characteristics'.

under consideration, and (*b*) all possible, inferred, or presumed events, 'entities' or 'somethings' 'existing' as not being manifestations of, or events in, a consciousness manifold. We have thus now three concepts: experienced consciousness, namely 'one's own'; inferred or assumed similar 'other consciousness'; and inferred or assumed non-conscious 'existence', whatever this may be. If, on the basis of fairly convincing evidence, we conclude, or postulate, that consciousness is a transitory state of brain activity, the 'orderliness' of non-conscious existence assumes, quite evidently, a paramount importance.

In order to avoid, as far as possible, ambiguities resulting from the use of the here relevant terms 'real' and 'reality', the following 'definitions' [8] should be re-emphasized:

(*a*) A 'thing' or 'event' is real in the first sense if it 'persists' or 'exists' when it is neither perceived nor imagined (i.e. 'perceived' by nonsensory perception such as thinking, etc.; this is explained further below).

(*b*) A 'thing' or 'event' is real in the second sense if it is correlated with other 'things' (etc.) in a way which experience (including 'logical' reasoning or rules) has led us to expect.

(*c*) A 'thing', etc., is actual when it is experienced, that is, while it is conscious, namely perceived or imagined here and now, i.e. while it occurs as an event in a private perceptual space–time system. A 'thing', etc., is actual in the wider sense (or potentially actual), if, while remaining undefined, it is assumed to pertain to the set of 'things' that can be experienced, or can occur, 'in consciousness'.

Proceeding from extension to *intension*, one might next ask: what are the properties, qualities or attributes which the word 'consciousness' symbolizes, or, what does 'consciousness' stand for, or, again, what is the referent, or what are the referents, of 'consciousness'? Now, when a state of consciousness obtains, there are, as E. Mach [9] concisely stated, colours, sounds, warmths, pressures, spaces, times and similar sensations, interrelated in a complex fashion with each other, and correlated with moods, feelings and intents. Following *Hume*, one could also designate

[8] Cf. Kuhlenbeck, *op. cit.*, 1961, p. 402.
[9] *Die Analyse der Empfindungen und das Verhältnis des Physischen zum Psychischen* (9th ed., Fischer, Jena, 1922).

these components of consciousness as perceptions or percepts and state that nothing is ever present in consciousness but a manifold of perceptions. In slightly modified terminology, we may roughly distinguish optic, tactile (in the wider sense), acoustic, olfactory and gustatory percepts. In addition, there are vague feelings, emotions, internal memory images, abstractions and thought. There are thus perceptions with sensory qualities, or sensory percepts, and perceptions, such as thoughts, which may almost entirely lack sensory qualities, and can be designated as nonsensory percepts.

Nonsensory percepts (memory images and thoughts) may symbolize, or be substituted for, patterns of sensory percepts. Again, in 'thought', unsensory percepts may be correlated with each other independently of sensory percepts. Percepts *qua* percepts are the ultimate actualities and are not experienced as representing something else, or in other words, are not experienced either as effects, or as referents to something that is not a percept, although, as previously stated, one percept can symbolize another one, or can stand as referent for another percept. Thus, being aware of being aware, or conscious of being conscious, allows an unlimited regress: I am aware that I am aware, and aware that I am, etc., etc.

With regard to the statements that consciousness is an 'occult quality', or a 'venerable hypothesis', it can be replied that consciousness is merely a descriptive term referring to experiences which any sufficiently adult normal human being can privately verify; the cited statements are easily reduced *ad absurdum* by using any concrete *qualité pure* of consciousness. We may then say: the statement that there exists an experience called 'blue colour' is a venerable hypothesis; or, the colour blue is an occult quality. In so far as the actuality of the optic experience blue is concerned, one can hardly insist that it is 'hidden' or 'occult'. If one naïvely uses here concepts of neurophysiology, one might, of course, indeed wonder why that experience blue is not located in the brain, but externally to the body, and whether 'blue' or better, a blue surface or shape within a visual field is something blue in the brain that one observer could demonstrate to another by inspection.

Scientific or logical or 'philosophic' arguments, even if 'triggered' by diverse inputs, including speech, from the environment, are, to a significant degree, initially private, and formulated by thought. In communicating such thoughts to others, and by reacting, in turn, to the thoughts of others, this argument presupposes (as *Pearson*[10] has stressed) the perceptions of the normal reasoning and related faculties of man.

If one looks for an 'invariant' common to all manifestations of consciousness whatsoever, it becomes evident that such invariant attributes indeed obtain: all consciousness-events whatsoever have the qualifications 'here and now', that is, occur as essential components of a private perceptual space–time system.

Space is that aspect of consciousness in which events (phenomena) display simultaneous (compresent) reciprocal relations, characterized as location, and, in many instances (visual or tactile percepts), as spatial configuration implying limiting surfaces, outlines or shapes. Even thoughts and feelings may be said to have a vague location, occupying a region of head and body representing an open (i.e. not delimited) neighbourhood. Since no impenetrability obtains, two different sounds, and two or more different emotions, etc., can evidently occupy the same region of space. This experienced, that is, perceptual space is private, namely restricted to an individual consciousness-manifold. It is not possible to trace a spatial vector connecting a neighbourhood element (point) in one's consciousness-manfold with a similar neighbourhood element in somebody else's consciousness-manifold. No path, in a given time, leads from one system into the other, and events in the two systems are absolutely incommensurable. Both systems have no dimensions in common. This, of course, includes perceptual time, which is the name for that aspect of consciousness wherein phenomena appear as a succession of events, characterized by different and comparable durations. Since, however, it can be assumed that, to a significant degree, the relationships between the diverse phenomena in two or more different consciousness-manifolds are invariants, one may formulate various concepts of public data, as discussed in my previous publications.[11] In a simplified 'definition', public data represent sets of orderly relationships between events in different consciousness-manifolds.

[10] *The Grammar of Science* (Everyman's Library, London, 1937).
[11] *Brain and Consciousness. Some Prolegomena to an Approach of the Problem* (Karger, Basel, 1957) and *op. cit.*, 1961.

Considering the continuity, despite disruption in consciousness, of spatially configurated, experienced events, from which latter the so-called primary qualities are abstracted, one may state: it is as if such events 'existed' or 'occurred' independently of consciousness. This, again, can be economically modelled by the postulate of a conceptual public space–time system in which physical events take place. As regards neurological events, the discrimination of conscious and unconscious cerebration clearly vindicates the use of the 'unconscious' in the justifiable aspects of *Freudian* and similar theories.

Again, in sphairal[12] thought-processes, such as, e.g., in attempting to recall a particular word, or in obtaining 'insight' into a certain complex abstract relationship without actually 'thinking' in words ('vorstellungsfreies Denken', cf. above), there obtains no more awareness of details than in the periphery of a visual field. This sort of nonsensory perception, ranging from sphairal thought, emerging out of a 'burst' of unconscious cerebration, to rigorously formulated verbal thought, has been vividly described by *H. Poincaré*[13] (1913) and numerous other authors.

Consciousness can thus be intensionally defined, in a satisfactory manner, as the designation for any private perceptual space–time system. The nature of consciousness as this sort of system clearly implies that consciousness is not located in the (perceptual) brain, but contrarily, that body, including brain, as well as 'external world', are 'located in consciousness'. This was already stressed more than 36 years ago.[14]

If one adheres to the opinion that the concept of consciousness should be used in neurology and cognate medical and natural sciences, then the distinction between perceptual and conceptual space (and time) becomes of fundamental significance for a rational approach to the pertinent problems. From another viewpoint, mathematicians and physicists, such as *Poincaré*,[15] *Lindsay and Margenau*,[16] and others, have emphasized that distinction. In some of my previous publications[17] I have pointed out similar

[12] i.e. outside the centre of attention in consciousness.

[13] *Op. cit.* 1913.

[14] H. Kuhlenbeck, *Vorlesungen über das Zentralnervensystem der Wirbeltiere* (Fischer, Jena, 1927).   [15] *Op. cit.*, 1913.

[16] *The Foundations of Physics* (Dover, N.Y., 1957).

[17] 'The meaning of "Postulational Psycho-Physical Parallelism"' (*Brain* 81: 588–603, 1958) and *op. cit.*, 1961.

distinctions made by additional authors, and also discussed the closely related views on perceptual and conceptual space expressed by a neurologist, namely *Brain*,[18] and a neuropsychiatrist *Smythies*,[19] with both of whom I fully agree in all the here relevant aspects.

Further detailed elaborations on the various aspects and implications of the consciousness-concept, particularly in connection with the formulation of 'psycho-physical parallelism', can be found in my cited publications.[20] In the present context, a few supplemental remarks on only three relevant topics may be appropriate, namely (*a*) on subject, object and self, (*b*) on 'space' and 'dimensions', and (*c*) on the word or concept 'mind'.

(*a*) The assumption of a reasoner or observer, conceived as an ego or self, and experiencing consciousness, is closely related to the traditional distinction, accepted by some philosophers, of a perceiving subject and a perceived object. The concept of a private perceptual space–time system or consciousness-manifold eliminates this distinction, or, at least, most of its various possible implications. If the manifold or system, taken as a 'whole', is designated as the 'subject', and its diverse manifestations, components, or 'elements' as 'objects', then the two eliminated terms can be conveniently re-introduced without contradiction, and without any further 'metaphysical' implications. The concepts of a hypostatized 'reasoner', 'observer', 'self', 'ego', and 'I' are likewise eliminated, in accordance with the anâtman concept of Buddhism, and with the views of *Hume* as well as of *Mach*. The difficulties and inconsistencies inherent to such 'ego'-concepts were also pointed out by *Kretschmer*.[21] Nevertheless, some formulations of an 'ego' and 'I' are necessary from the commonsense practical viewpoint, and semantically as well as logically convenient. They can easily be re-introduced, without contradiction, in the guise of auxiliary constructions, including even the various constructs used by psychoanalysts (cf. Kuhlenbeck, 1961 *et passim*).

(*b*) If one adopts the term 'perceptual space', in agreement with

---

[18] In *Mind, Perception and Science* (Blackwell, Oxford, 1951) and *The Nature of Experience* (O.U.P., 1959).
[19] In *Analysis of Perception* (Routledge & Kegan Paul, 1956).
[20] *Op. cit.*, 1957, 1958, 1959, 1961.
[21] *Medizinische Psychologie* (Thieme, Leipzig, 1926).

views expressed by *Leibniz*, as referring to the compresent togetherness of percepts, it is evident that, by a many-one transformation from a variety of conscious experiences, the invariant 'compresent togetherness' has been substituted by, or has become transformed into, the verbal symbolization 'perceptual space' which, therefore, becomes a 'conceptual space', although referring to an invariant of perception. In this sense, the designation 'perceptual space' can be fully justified.

Since there are various perceptual 'modalities', such as visual, tactual, etc., there are, clearly, many modalities of compresent togetherness, and one may, of course, as *Berkeley* and others have done, speak about separate visual, tactile, and even additional (acoustic, olfactory, gustatory, nonsensory or thought) spaces, of which, however, only the two first ones can, in human consciousness, manifest distinct directions and configurations, including definite 'limits', namely seen and felt 'shapes'.

Yet, in the 'normal' human consciousness-manifold or private perceptual space–time system, these different spaces are integrated into a unified system with 'common dimensions'. The central region of this integrated space is represented by the open neighbourhood provided by the sensed body including the system's brain, and corresponds, in all essential aspects, to the body schema of *Head* and *Holmes*,[22] and of *Schilder*.[23]

That the private perceptual space represents a unified system is evidenced by the transformation of visual percepts into tactile and proprioceptive percepts by means of drawing, writing and sculpturing. These transforms can then, again, be recognized visually. Moreover, blind sculptors, such as the once well-known Tyrolese artist, *Joseph Kleinhaus*, mentioned by *Schopenhauer*[24] may design, on the basis of tactile percepts, portrait-busts with visually distinguishable features. Furthermore, it is possible, with closed eyes, to recognize numbers and letters cut out of cardboard and placed in the palm of the hand. Likewise, it is not very difficult to read, without looking at the respective motions, numbers and letters traced by somebody else upon the skin of one's arm, leg or back. Depending on arbitrary definitions, the transformations

[22] *Studies in Neurology* (Frowde, London, 1920).
[23] *Das Körperschema* (Springer, Berlin, 1923).
[24] *Sämmtliche Werke*, Bd. III (1847). Ed. Grisebach (Reclam, Leipzig, n.d.), p. 77.

from tactile to visual space can be designated either as open or as closed transformations. Evaluating the private perceptual space as a single system, we have here, of course, a closed transformation.

Under these premisses, all compresent percepts, or, in other words, all manifestations of consciousness within a given manifold (private perceptual space–time system) bear spatial relations to each other. These relations, which shall be designated as locations, may manifest configuration, that is, separation by other perceptual 'objects', or contiguity by adjoining or touching each other. In addition, there are numerous instances where several 'objects' of perception may occupy one and the same region of space, by superposition, penetration, pervasion or permeation. This applies particularly, but not exclusively, to non-configurated percepts.

Thus, we may obtain superposition of two different pictures, reflected (catoptric) and transmitted (dioptric), in looking through a glass plate under appropriate conditions. Several different sounds may 'fill' the same space, and various different odours, tastes, sensations, feelings, as well as thoughts can, as open neighbourhoods, and with a very weak, indistinct characteristic of 'localization', permeate the internal space, including the open boundary zone, of the body.

Perceptual space is therefore, like topologic space, a set of 'elements' with continuity relations describable as local or neighbourhood relations. Every neighbourhood of an 'element' contains that element. In perceptual space, however, some neighbourhoods are without definable boundaries. Private perceptual space, moreover, is a *plenum*, namely one of the two essential properties (here and now) of consciousness-manifestations. In this respect, a certain analogy with *Einstein's* physical space–time concept does indeed obtain. 'Empty' perceptual space, devoid of any actual percepts, has therefore no logical 'existence' under the postulated premisses.

The conceptual model of perceptual space in neurologic epistemology must here deal with, and directly refer to, actually experienced relationships. Because of this requirement, no use can be made, at least for a solid intensional and referential basis, of space concepts transcending the capabilities of sensory inspection or direct introspection by an observer. This concept of experienced space introduces a reasonable degree of rigour, while avoiding those higher degrees of rigour necessary in mathematics, but excessive in the aspect under consideration, where an intuitive apprehension of 'elements' with their neighbourhoods and the corresponding oriented boundary zones of configurated percepts retains a paramount significance. It is true that the mathematician may formulate, as 'nonsensory' percepts, abstract concepts of interrelation which, however much they arise in perceptual actuality, have nevertheless an independent 'reality' (in the second sense) within the domain of thought. This, however, concerns mathematics or logic, or both, but neither neurologic epistemology nor, at another conceptual level, biologic morphology as elaborated by the Jena-Heidelberg School (*Haeckel, Gegenbaur, Fürbringer, Jacobshagen*).

The mathematician *Weyl*[25] has justly pointed out that the rational analysis of continua proceeds in three steps: (1) morphology, which operates with vaguely circumscribed types of form; (2) topology, which, guided by conspicuous singularities or even in free construction, places into the manifold a vaguely localized but combinatorially exact determined framework; and (3) geometry proper, whose ideal structures could only be carried with exactness into a 'real' continuum after this had been spun over with a subdivision net of a fineness increasing *ad infinitum*.

As regards both the space concepts of neurologic epistemology (perceptual space) and of biologic morphology (anatomical space), the steps (1) and (2) as characterized by *Weyl* appear, on the whole, much more relevant than those under (3).

In agreement with *Whittaker*[26] it may be assumed that Western geometry, as originated by the Greeks, resulted from an investigation of the properties associated with the experience of space. *Euclid*'s famed *Elements of Geometry*, written about 300 B.C., present these properties as logical deductions from a set of axioms which are asserted without proof. Three undefined but intuitively given 'categories' are posited, namely points, lines, and planes. To this are added the basic relations of incidence, betweenness, and congruence.[27] Now, while it is evidently

[25] *Philosophy of Mathematics and Natural Science* (Princeton Univ. Press 1949).

[26] *From Euclid to Eddington. A Study of Conceptions of the External World* (Dover, N.Y., 1958).   [27] Cf. Weyl, *op. cit.*, 1949.

possible to conceptualize experienced spatial relations in accordance with the well-known parallel postulate of *Euclid*, that is, in terms of *Euclidean* space, there are also numerous experienced aspects of perceptual space that manifest *non-Euclidean* features. I believe thus that perceptual space should not be conceived as homaloid, and I prefer to designate it, not as an *Euclidean*, but as an '*Euclidoid* mollusk-like or ameboid field'[28] In his clever *Dialogues on Space, Time and Causality*,[29] my old friend and comrade in arms of the First World War, *George Jaffé*, a theoretical physicist of wide practical experience, has competently emphasized some of the *non-Euclidean* aspects of perceptual space. *Jaffé* favours, to a considerable extent, *Berkeley*'s distinction of different perceptual spaces, while I am inclined to stress their integration within a given consciousness-manifold. Thus, I consider the private perceptual *Euclidoid* space to be a function of the experienced fusion of visual, tactile, auditory, etc. (including 'nonsensory' thought) spaces into a common three-dimensional integrated system, to which a time dimension is added, the total manifold then being designated as a four-dimensional private perceptual space–time system.

The concept 'dimension' is here used in the most elementary, '*Euclidean*' or '*Euclidoid*' geometric sense, as abstracted from common sensory experience, namely referring to the properties designated as length, area and volume in said *Euclidoid* space, with, or without, corresponding metric and vectorial implications. To this, in agreement with concepts of *Minkowski* and others, duration and change, namely time, is added as a fourth, vectorial dimension. Clearly, if one wishes to emphasize the distinctiveness of visual, tactile, acoustic, etc., spaces, one could introduce a substantially larger number of dimensions into the concept of perceptual space.

The solid space of the Greeks had three dimensions, but when geometry began to be studied analytically and algebraically, the restriction to three dimensions remained no longer necessary. Although *Descartes* established the foundations of analytical geometry, involving *n*-dimensional space, where *n* is any positive integer, *Michael Stifel* (1487–1567), Professor of Mathematics at the University of Jena, was one of the first to introduce the

---

[28] H. Kuhlenbeck, *op. cit.*, 1957, 1961.
[29] *Drei Dialoge über Raum, Zeit und Kausalität* (Springer, Berlin, 1954).

concept of an indefinite multidimensionality.[30] This 'complete free-dom'[31] became particularly significant after 1840, when *Cayley* and others made use of multidimensional manifolds, and *Hilbert*, about 1906, took for granted a countable infinity of dimensions.

These conceptualizations, again, are related to the further extension of the real number domain to complex numbers, and then, by *W. R. Hamilton*, to quaternions. *Grassmann* (1809–1877) developed still more generalized numbers among which quaternions figured as a minor detail. *Grassman's* hypercomplex numbers, by which *n*-dimensional space vectors can be expressed, include a multitude of possible 'laws' or 'rules' which likewise subsume the theories of determinants, matrices and tensors. These latter can be regarded as a further generalization of vectors.

Plücker (1801—68) originated an important concept of dimensionality, wherein this latter is not an absolute constant, but depends upon the 'elements', accepted as 'irreducible', in terms of which the space is described. Thus, a plane can be said to be a space of two dimensions because two numbers, or co-ordinates, are necessary and sufficient to locate any particular point in the plane. If, instead of either points or lines as 'irreducible elements' for plane geometry, circles are chosen, the plane becomes three-dimensional, since it takes precisely three numbers to identify a particular circle in the plane. Again, it requires precisely five numbers to identify a particular conic section, and the plane becomes five-dimensional in conics[32].

It becomes thus evident that the conceptualized four dimensions of private perceptual space–time in neurologic epistemology are not 'the' number of dimensions, but merely 'a' convenient and justifiable number of dimensions with well-established intensional, actual referents, used in dealing with the concept of consciousness.

(*c*) The exceedingly hazy, and highly ambiguous word or concept 'mind' was mentioned above in the introductory remarks on neurological epistemology as a mysterious something of particular concern to philosophers. If one attempts a critical analysis of this term, one is faced with semantic difficulties similar

[30] Cf. H. Kuhlenbeck, *op. cit.*, 1961, p. 407.
[31] E. T. Bell, *Mathematics, Queen and Servant of Science* (McGraw Hill, N.Y., 1951).   [32] *Ibid.*

to those obtaining with regard to 'thinking', 'knowledge', and, for that matter, 'game', and 'intelligence'.

Philosophers have used the word 'mind' with several denotations. Thus, mind frequently refers to a self or subject which perceives, remembers, imagines, feels, conceives, reasons and wills, and which may be functionally related to an individual body. *Berkeley*[33] for instance, speaks of a 'spirit or thinking substance', which perceives ideas and represents the 'soul', namely 'that indivisible, unextended thing, which thinks, acts, and perceives'. The assertion: '*Hume* showed that there is no mind' refers particularly to this sort of mind-concept.

Again, mind, 'generically considered', is supposed to be a metaphysical 'substance' which pervades all individual minds and which is contrasted with matter or material substance. I regard this concept as devoid of any usable and significant intensional or extensional 'meaning'.

A German philosopher, *Klages*, stated that 'der Geist ist der Widersacher der Seele'. Any translation of this strange remark, e.g. 'the mind is the antagonist of the soul', or 'l'esprit est l'adversaire de l'âme', completely fails to express the sphairal emotional 'overtones' contained in the German wording. However, the propositional content of this statement may amount to this: 'the conclusions of reason can be in conflict with affectivity', or 'reason may be antagonistic to emotion.'[34] The conflict between rational and emotional thinking becomes frequently very evident in the writings of philosophers. A conspicuous and interesting instance of such conflict is manifested, e.g. in the thoughts of *Miguel de Unamuno* (1864–1936). One might cite, in this connection, the well-known aphorism of *Blaise Pascal* (1623–62): 'Le cœur a ses raisons, que la raison ne connaît point.' (*Pensées*, Sect. IV, 277).

Invariants frequently implied in the word mind are 'orderliness' and 'logical structure'. These characteristics, however, are so universal, that they also apply to 'matter' and 'material events' in the ordinary sense. Here we have indeed predicates that can be practically applied to everything.

With respect to neurological events, mind has been defined as referring to cerebral activities preparing, initiating and controlling

---

[33] *Op. cit.*, 1713.
[34] H. Kuhlenbeck, *op. cit.*, 1961, Section 76.

the complicated forms of behaviour which 'we cannot explain in terms of reflexes or automatisms'.[35] One might here reply that any manifestation of behaviour, that is, any observable aspect of response or action whatsoever, can presumably, on the basis of recent progress in communication and information theory, be exhaustively 'explained' or described in 'causal' or 'statistical' terms and imitated, or reproduced, by automata. I would agree with the statement by *Pierce*,[36] that it is probably impossible to specify a meaningful and explicitly defined (behavioural) 'goal' which a man can attain, and a computer cannot, even including the 'imitation game' proposed by *A. M. Turing*. It is true that 'undecidable propositions', and the so-called 'decision problem' still pose here some difficulties, which, however, can be interpreted as not of a fundamental nature. There is no valid reason to deny the (not yet conclusively proved) possibility, or the probability, that a hardware artefact, seen from the viewpoint of an observer, could do anything a human brain can do.[37]

The formalistic, purely logical 'decision problem' has two aspects: (*a*) the so-called proof-theoretic decision, finding an effective test (decision procedure) by means of which it can always be determined whether a given formula is a theorem (implying possibility of proof); (*b*) the so-called set-theoretic decision problem, to find an effective test by means of which it can always be determined whether a given formula containing no free individual variable is satisfiable. In accordance with *Gödel's* completeness theorem, these two forms of the decision problem are equivalent, such that a solution of either would imply solution of the other. *Church* has elaborated a proof demonstrating that the generalized decision problem of the so-called first order pure functional calculus is unsolvable, although solutions exist for significant special cases.[38]

Sherrington[39] defined mind as referring to 'thoughts, memories,

[35] A. E. Fessard, 'Mechanisms of Nervous Integration and Conscious Experience' in *Brain Mechanisms and Consciousness*, ed. by J. F. Delafresnaye (Blackwell, Oxford, 1954), pp. 200–48.

[36] *Symbols, Signals and Noise. The Nature and Process of Communication* (Harper, N.Y., 1961).

[37] Cf. H. Kuhlenbeck, *op. cit.*, 1961, Section 80.

[38] 'Logic; Object Language; Syntax' in *Dictionary of Philosophy*, ed. by D. D. Runce (Philos. Lib., N.Y., n.d.).

[39] In *The Physical Basis of Mind*, ed. by P. Laslett (Blackwell, Oxford, 1950).

feelings, reasoning, and so on', namely concepts that are 'difficult to bring into the class of physical things'. If one eliminates the ambiguities from this definition by the qualification that all the aspects of mind referred to by *Sherrington* must be conscious, that is, occur as events in a private perceptual space–time system in order to be subsumed under the concept mind, then mind becomes entirely and completely synonymous with consciousness. This, of course, is the procedure which I have adopted, and, I believe, consistently followed in my writings on the topic under consideration. Under these premisses, I would be inclined to agree with one of *Sherrington*'s conclusions, [40] namely: 'Most life is, I imagine, mindless'.

3. *The 'Biological Significance' of Consciousness, or: Why does Consciousness exist at all?* In agreement with the results obtained by the most advanced and sophisticated logicians, such as *Wittgenstein*, [41] *Gödel* [42] and others, it seems permissible to reach the conclusion that when a formulation is no longer questionable, it becomes a mere tautology. *Ayer's* concept of '*a priori*' [43] is essentially identical with the notion of tautology. Yet, as I have attempted to show elsewhere, [44] several different meanings of '*a priori*' can be defined and employed.

However, this unfortunate limitation of human thought will only lead to what I consider to be the vacuousness or to the sophisticated trivialities of behaviourism, logical positivism and operationalism (operationism), if the actuality of consciousness with its *qualités pures* is repressed. On the other hand, if we clearly recognize the significant difference between a logical thought-model and the actuality of experience, in the sense of *Hume*'s 'mental geography', then we may be *Humean* sceptics, and still, making use of the many valid aspects of behaviourism, logical positivism and operationalism, work with 'reasonable probabilities'. We may successfully operate with such concepts reaching not an impossible logical certainty, but a reasonable degree of

[40] In *The Physical Basis of Mind*, ed. by P. Laslett (Blackwell, Oxford, 1950).
[41] *Tractatus Logico–Philosophicus* (Kegan Paul, London, 1922).
[42] 'Ueber formal unentscheidbare Sätze der Principia Mathematica und verwandter Systeme' (*M. H. Math. Phys.* **38**: 173–98, 1931).
[43] In *Language, Truth and Logic* (Dover, N.Y., 1946) and *The Problem of Knowledge* (Penguin Books, Harmondsworth, 1956).
[44] *Op. cit.*, 1961.

certainty, and obtain a workable and fairly satisfactory theoretical formulation, adapted to actuality.

The distinction between a describable phenomenological reality in the second sense, and a non-describable metaphysical reality in the first sense, 'beyond' the 'limit' of actual, describable consciousness phenomena (namely sensory percepts, abstract thoughts, affectivity and emotion), may be interpreted to fulfill *Wittgenstein*'s requirement that, in order to draw a limit, we should have to think both sides of this limit. Moreover, this requirement, based on the impeccable and rigorous mathematical concept of a limit, elaborated by *Cauchy* and others, might be evaluated as 'conceptually' valid, but not applying to perceptual actuality.

From an empiricistic viewpoint, it appears permissible to assume that a suitable concept of an actual private perceptual space–time as distinguished from a postulated public physical space–time is the key to an adequate formulation of the brain-consciousness problem. In addition, mathematical aspects of neural coding as well as the neurological aspects of mathematics must be considered, insofar as the resulting models fit the special boundary conditions obtaining in the particular aspects of the actual problem. All ambiguities should be eliminated to the limit of the possible. This last requirement is evidently very difficult, if not intrinsically 'impossible', since we cannot dispense with the use of language.

We may take the position that, since only one's own consciousness-manifold is directly observable, consciousness has no place whatsoever in the thought-model of biology conceived as a natural science in terms of events in public physical space–time. In medicine and psychology, which are related to biology, or can be included in biology, consciousness is, however, very important. Yet, in this respect, consciousness remains either an 'epiphenomenon' or a parallel, not 'causally' involved phenomenon. The difference between the two concepts can be regarded as merely one of emphasis. The term 'epiphenomenon' stresses the 'vectorial' or one-way, open transformation from public physical space–time into private perceptual space–time, such that the physical events remain entirely independent of the mental events, which latter, however, are dependent variables of the former. Or, in other words, the complete lack of feedback is emphasized.

The concept of parallelism stresses the non-causal relationship between the series of isomorphic (or, in this case more pedantically, homomorphic) events occurring in their respective space–time systems. It is here implied that causality means no more (and no less) than 'consistent' or 'necessary', conceptual or perceptual 'material' change, separable by an arbitrary cut into cause and effect, and comprising the postulates of contiguity, continuity and succession. These postulates restrict causal events to one and the same space–time system. Clearly, if two non-connected space–time systems are involved, the concepts of contiguity, continuity and succession (as well as precedence and simultaneity) become meaningless. However, 'causality' is merely a word, to which any meaning can be arbitrarily assigned. It should be clear, nevertheless, that, if *Broad*, or *Smythies*[45] on one hand, and myself, on the other hand, talk about 'causality', we are not talking about the same 'thing', although both *Smythies'* and my (i.e. *Hume*'s and *Schopenhauer*'s) 'causality' concepts have for referent a 'relationship'. Thus, if one would use the term '*Euclidean*' as applying to three-dimensional geometric relationships in general, regardless of postulates, then some *non-Euclidean* geometries become evidently *Euclidean* geometries. Again, in constructing a conceptual model, we are obviously free to choose whatever postulates we wish to adopt, and I shall make no foolish attempt to argue about unprovable as well as undisprovable arbitrary postulates. Causality, as here adopted, represents such postulate, and I merely assert that said postulate appears to me the most suitable in the aspect, or for the model, under consideration.

Now, if all biologic phenomena could occur as pure mechanisms, and if we are, in this model, or in this sense, automata, one might, of course, legitimately ask the question: why does consciousness 'exist' at all? One could also, if one prefers, subsume this question as one of the meanings of *Brain*'s question:[46] namely, what is the 'metaphysical' status of consciousness? Since I am very wary and sceptical about 'metaphysics' in rational discussions, I have interpreted that question in 'non-metaphysical' terms.

Now, as regards the question 'why does consciousness exist?', one might evidently say that the question itself is not legitimate,

[45] Review: 'Brain and Consciousness' (*Brit. J. Phil. Sci.* 10: 341–44, 1960).

[46] 'The Physiological Basis of Consciousness. A Critical Review' (*Brain* 81: 426–55, 1958).

and *Deussen*'s criticism of the question 'what becomes of us after we are dead?' can here be applied *mutatis mutandis*.[47]

It seems permissible or justifiable (although, of course, not 'logically' necessary) to assume that consciousness is a function of central nervous activity, with the qualification that not all, but only some nervous functions are correlated with phenomena of consciousness, while all other neural and biological, as well as physico-chemical activities are unconscious. Moreover, it may be postulated (but cannot be proved or disproved) that consciousness does not occur, or has no independent existence, apart from being an aspect of brain (or C.N.S.) function.

If, as has been claimed, all events whatsoever occurring in the postulated public physical space–time system, that is, in the world of physics, chemistry, biology, including ecology and behaviouristic sociology as well as linguistics[48] can take place without the requirement of consciousness, and, moreover, can be performed or imitated by hardware, then, of course, consciousness is superfluous, and we might again revert to, and emphasize, the question: why does consciousness exist at all?, or: what is the 'biologic', or, if we wish: what is the 'metaphysical' 'significance' of consciousness? This, then, is indeed a puzzling question. Unless, of course, we evade it by denying that we are conscious.

The phenomenology of our world, that is, of the world experienced by a conscious, sentient being such as man, does not, however, represent a 'system of undefined elements', nor a system of events characterized by abstract moving magnitudes and magnitudes of motion. 'My world' consists of coloured shapes, of hard or soft, hot or cold, and variously configured objects or masses, of multitudinous sounds, odours, and tastes, of pleasant, neutral, unpleasant or painful body sensations, of thoughts, and a wide variety of emotions.

Evidently, since this is the nature of experience, i.e. of consciousness, we may express this fact tautologically and state that consciousness is the *conditio sine qua non* for the occurrence of these phenomena. Clearly, 'consciousness' is merely the collective or abstract term for the cited events, occurring in a private per-

[47] H. Kuhlenbeck, *op. cit.*, 1961, p. 496.
[48] E.g. L. Bloomfield, 'Linguistic Aspects of Science', *Internat. Encyclop. of Unified Science*, Vol. I: 216–76 (Univ. of Chicago Press, 1955).

ceptual space–time system, and it appears, from this viewpoint, ludicrous to deny consciousness, or to claim that consciousness is 'a venerable hypothesis'. At most, we might say that consciousness is a 'venerable word or abstraction', which, however, appears fully justified since it possesses the primordially ostensible, in part even truly palpable referents. This abstraction would indeed become meaningless, if it were the abstraction for 'everything whatsoever'. But this would only be the case if one should insist upon dogmatic solipsism. If it is allowed that other similar, and therefore, by inference, describable private perceptual space–time systems exist, and that an independent reality in the first sense exists, namely a something that is not consciousness, then the concept of consciousness does not indifferently include 'everything', and is a useful descriptive term, subsuming the above-mentioned events as occurring in a private perceptual space–time system, which is regarded as 'similar' to a multitude of other such systems.

Thus, to repeat, since the occurrence of a private perceptual space–time system is the 'logical' prerequisite for the occurrence of its phenomenologic manifestations, which are experienced facts, consciousness is a logical necessity. This, then, is the unavoidably tautologic answer to the question 'why does consciousness exist?'

This rather unsatisfactory answer, on the other hand, in no way affects the operational validity of the term 'consciousness' in neurology. The questions (1) whether a person is conscious or not conscious, and (2) which brain events are related to consciousness, although not rigorously answerable, remain reasonably well answerable to various degrees of 'approximation', and, in my opinion, fully retain their validity.

Strangely enough, two philosophers who can be regarded as having little in common, namely *J. G. Fichte* (1762–1814) and the contemporary Zen-scholar *D. T. Suzuki*, made, nevertheless, almost identical statements, which, again, closely correspond to the here given tautologic and unsatisfactory 'logical' answer.[49] *Fichte* remarked: the World is because it is; and it is as it is, because it is so. *Suzuki*,[50] emphasizing the mystical concept of 'suchness', formulates, as one of the four 'ground-principles'

[49] Cf. H. Kuhlenbeck, *op. cit.*, 1957, p. 301, f.n. 67.
[50] *Outlines of Mahâyâna Buddhism* (Luzac, London, 1907).

of his *Buddhist* philosophy, the proposition: 'All is such as it is.'

A sudden emotional flash correlated with this 'insight' may, in my interpretation, be involved in at least some instances of the much discussed and disputed peculiar 'ecstatic' Zen-experiences designated as '*satori*'. We have here phenomena that can be subsumed under 'modified and pathologic states of consciousness' ('and' stands here not for 'conjunction' but for 'inclusive disjunction'), without thereby necessarily implying their discrimination as 'pathologic'.

As regards the various interesting neuropsychiatric implications of Zen, I have elaborated on these aspects in my monograph on 'Brain and Consciousness' (1957). I might here add that my comments referring to these topics are entirely based on first-hand acquaintance with the subject matter. In 1934 I spent some time as observer in the Zen-monastery Empuku-ji near Kyôto, where I was a personal guest of the Abbot and Zen-Master *Kôzuki Tesshû*. I had thus the opportunity to scrutinize Zen in action, and to discuss, with an authority on the subject, a number of relevant problems.

Although I stand quite close to *Mahâyâna Buddhism*, of course not as a devotee, but as *amicus curiae*, I have remained somewhat sceptical in my appraisal of Zen. A recent field trip, in 1961, to the large and important monastery Ei-hei-ji near Fukui, which represents the headquarters of the Sôtô-Branch of Zen in Japan, has increased rather than diminished my scepticism.

COMMENTS BY J. R. SMYTHIES

Whereas I am in full agreement with much that Professor Kuhlenbeck says, we differ on some points of detail. On page 157 he states that the concept of causality implies 'contiguity, continuity and succession' between its elements and he goes on to conclude that 'these postulates restrict causal events to one and the same space–time system'. However, I do not see that the concept of causality implies this and I would agree with Professor Price that there is no *a priori* reason why events in space A should not be causally related to events in space B. And, of course, in Broad's version of non-Cartesian dualism (in which the mental spaces belonging to different individuals and physical space from one *n*-dimensional manifold)—mental events and brain events maintain direct spatial relations with each other. Here causality is associated with spatial continuity and contiguity across a dimensional interface.

Some people have held that private perceptual space is located *in* the physical brain. Price's theory, of course, is radically different and locates the space of images outside the brain—images are in a space of their own. Kuhlenbeck however adds the following to clarify his position on this point:

> In my formulation, a private perceptual space–time manifold has no dimensions whatsoever in common (*a*) with any other such manifold, and (*b*) with the public space–time manifold (regardless whether this manifold is purely fictional, as I am inclined to assume, or is 'real' in the first sense, as I rather doubt, but, of course, cannot 'know'). Therefore I would most emphatically reject the notion 'that private perceptual space is located *in* the physical brain' (whatever the 'physical brain' is considered to be). Thus, far from having, in this matter, an opinion radically different from that of Price's theory, I fully agree with the assumption that 'images' (I assume that 'percepts' or 'perceptions' are meant) 'are in a space of their own'. The term 'outside' the 'physical brain' is perhaps somewhat awkward. The perceptual space, in my formulation, is neither 'outside', nor 'inside' the 'physical brain', but has no spatial relationship whatsoever to the 'physical space' in which the 'physical brain' is located.

FROM MECHANISM TO MIND
Donald M. MacKay

THIS paper discusses an aspect of the classical problem of relating mental and physical descriptions of human thought-processes which has acquired new prominence from the development of mechanisms with mind-like behaviour. A factual account of possibilities inherent in mechanisms now known leads to the conclusion (elaborated elsewhere) that any test for 'mentality' in terms of the information-processing activity of an artificial organism can in principle be met.

The suggestion is not that mentality is thereby guaranteed to such organisms, but that some traditional ways of posing the problem are inadequate and based on wrong assumptions. It is suggested that these developments are in no way inimical to the Christian doctrine of Man, but rather illuminate it by suggesting a possible synthesis between complementary ways of describing his powers.

1. *A new twist to the classical debate*

1.1. Debate as to the possibility of explaining mental phenomena on a mechanistic basis is as old as the Greeks. Between their subjectively known decisions and the appropriate bodily outcome, men observed a regular relationship of dependence. Between certain physical events in the external world, termed causes, and others, termed their effects, they also observed a relationship of dependence. What more natural than that both relationships should receive the same name of 'causality'? The impact of a rolling stone on a stationary one is termed the 'cause' of the movement of the other. The decision to move my finger must naturally then be termed the 'cause' of the motion observed.

Physical science progressed. Physical 'causes' proved to be reducible to a small and apparently exclusive number, in the sense that chains and interlocking patterns of a few causal relationships, interpreted as the manifestation of certain 'forces', seemed likely to represent adequately all observed sequences of physical events. Physiological science progressed. Causal links between bodily movements and events in the nervous system were discovered in increasing numbers. Any event simple enough to be chosen for study seemed to have a causal physical antecedent.

And, of course, the question arose, where do my decisions fit into the causal chain? Is any room going to be left for the Mind as controller of these events, if the network of physical cause-and-effect should prove to be complete? Further, if I accept the undoubtable dependence of voluntary movement on my decisions (and call the dependence 'causal'), what analogue of physical 'force' can be postulated as the link between the two? In short, how can Mind control Matter?

1.2. The problem, as thus formulated, was sharpened by further and complementary knowledge. It had always been known that physical violence could derange mental activity, and that the taking of drugs could distort the experience and character of the subject. Gradually, however, it became clearer that not only adventitious but fundamental features of personality and mental life were linked with biochemical, electrical and other features of bodily structure and activity. Here was evidence of a significant dependence in the reverse direction. Not only was there a problem of accounting for the action of autonomous Mind on servile Matter, but also one of explaining an apparently comparable action of material agencies on the very springs of mental activity. It began to be whispered, indeed, that we now had scientific proof that Mind was after all a 'mere epiphenomenon' of the motions of Matter: that Man was a 'mere automaton', driven by 'blind forces'—and so, of course, in no way responsible for his actions. But to the logic of this conclusion we return.

1.3. Naturally concomitant with these developments were speculations on converse lines. If the human brain and nervous system were in some sense a physical mechanism—or even if it were not—might it not be possible in principle to construct an artificial mechanism or 'artefact' which should behave as if it had a mind? For a long time the question had scarcely an academic interest, for technology could hardly point the way to equip an 'artificial man' with human powers of locomotion and action let alone of thought and dialogue. Even when the age of the machine came to render trivial the problems of motor activity, it was easy to ridicule the mental limitations of any foreseeable artefact—chiefly in respect of its inability to modify its responses or carry out any trains of reasoning comparable with those of human minds. 'Machine' indeed came to mean only a servile mechanism, capable perhaps of executing more quickly or more powerfully the purposes of its designer, but (more or less by definition) without any power of forming or adopting purposes of its own.

It is to avoid begging the question in this way that I prefer to use the neutral term 'artefact' (in the sense of artificial construct) for the class of mechanism that we shall here consider.

1.4. The nineteenth century saw the growth of two independent developments that eventually revolutionized the prospects of synthesizing mind-like behaviour in an artefact. Both had their seeds in earlier work. The first was the development of self-adjusting control systems, typified by James Watt's famous steam-governor. The second was the development of symbolic logic, in which George Boole played a classical part, making it possible for arithmetical calculating machines symbolically to carry out trains of logical reasoning. The advent of electronics multiplied the complexity and speed of devices embodying these developments, without introducing any essentially new principle. Indeed in the 1830s Charles Babbage designed an 'analytical engine' which in principle had all the powers of modern electronic computors, and brought upon him a spirited debate with those who saw in its imitation of human faculties a threat to the dignity of man.

But it was the advent of high-speed computors, using thousands of electronic valves, and capable of solving in seconds problems on which men spend months, that in the last two decades brought sudden popular attention to our question. Regrettably dubbed 'electronic brains', these devices acquired a reputation for mental power that seemed to put the human brain itself in the shade. The inevitable reaction has followed. It was never anything but absurd to suggest that present day 'digital' computors provide a good model of the brain, or to take seriously the analogies between their disorders and mental diease. But the question has at last arisen in realistic terms: how far could we go if we *wanted* to make, not a computor, but an artefact with characteristics that in a human being we should regard as evidence of mentality? What are the differences between present-day computors and human brains, and could they be eliminated—in principle—if we wished to do so? The answer is largely a matter of fact, and it is chiefly towards clarifying some of the facts that this paper is directed. For good or ill, the classical debate has taken a new twist. Factual developments make it no longer derisory to ask: could an artificial mechanism be said to have a mind?

2. *Towards the 'vitalization' of artefacts*

The author has elsewhere[1] discussed the technicalities of securing mind-like behaviour in artefacts, but a brief explanation of some of the principles on which present possibilities rest may help to place these in perspective.

2.1. What is perhaps the basic principle is illustrated by such familiar devices as the thermostat. An electric heater warms a room. When the thermometer rises to some preset level, the mercury pushes open a switch that cuts off the heat. When the room cools a little below that temperature, the mercury falls and closes the switch—and so on. The system behaves as if it were *trying to resist* changes in temperature. If the preset level is raised, the heater at once comes on until the room settles down at the new temperature. The system's basic 'goal' is the matching of the level of the mercury to the preset level, wherever that may be. Any discrepancy between the two levels occasions activity (heating or cooling) calculated to *reduce* the discrepancy.

The activity of the heater is here controlled by signals 'fed back', as we say, from its field of action. Such a system is called a 'goal-seeking' system because these so-called 'feedback' signals drive it in a way calculated to minimize the discrepancy between its actual state and the present state or 'goal', against any opposing influences (within limits).

The 'feedback principle' so illustrated can be applied in any situation in which a mechanism is required to pursue a goal or

[1] *Brit. J. for Phil. of Sci.*, **2**, 105, 1951, referred to below as 'M.B.A.'. Some of the author's later papers are listed at the end of this chapter.

maintain a norm. It need only be provided with appropriate receptors of the necessary information as to its separation from its goal—i.e. as to the success of its activity—and means of calculating from this information the next step to try in order to reduce that separation. If the output of the calculator is used to steer the mechanism, it will then automatically pursue its goal to the limit of its powers. Examples now realized include self-optimizing factory process-controllers, and the various self-guided missiles that can detect and pursue targets in spite of all evasive action.

2.2. It may be as well here to guard against a common misunderstanding. In judging a system to be goal-directed it is not the *observable end-results* of activity, but rather the internal process by which activity is *selected*, that affords the crucial evidence. As R. J. Spilsbury has pointed out,[2] a habitual criminal may in practice minimize the average interval separating him from prison, without having this as his goal! If x is the interval $(x_1 - x_2)$ between the actual state of a system (represented by x_1) and its goal (x_2) the diagnostic test would be to try to vary x. If one is in doubt whether x_2 is the goal, and is denied access to the inner workings of the system, the best test is to move x_2. (Try *offering* your criminal a prison sentence!)

2.3. The term 'goal-directed' can have either (i) the passive sense of 'goal-oriented' or (ii) the active sense of 'goal-guided'. Our variational test covers activity which is goal-directed in either sense (although in M.B.A. only sense (ii) was considered), and a pair of illustrations may serve to clarify the important distinction otherwise (and often) overlaid.

(*a*) Water, as we say, 'seeks its own level'. A certain river is blocked by a landslide. It rises until it overflows the barrier, and so continues on its way. Its activity, at a pinch, could be called goal-directed, but only in sense (i).

(*b*) Another river is blocked, but this time a water-level indicator transmits a control-signal that opens sluices and so arrests the rise in level. Here the activity of the system *as a whole* (not just the river) is goal-directed in sense (ii), because there is a distinguishable process of *control*.

Why can we not say in the same sense that the rise of level in (*a*) 'controlled' the release of the water? The reason, I think, is that to speak of A as 'controlling the corrective reaction R to a

[2] Symposium 'Men and Machines' (*Aristot. Soc. Suppl.*, XXVI, 1952).

situation S' implies that A reacted thus because he (or it) had received *information* as to S; this, in turn, suggests that if information had *not* been received, the reaction R need not have occurred. 'Control' not only implies corrective reaction, but the conceptual possibility of its *absence owing to lack of information*. Unless there is a separate information-path which could conceivably be interrupted, the concept of control is inapplicable and the reaction could perhaps best be described as 'Newtonian'. Where it makes sense to ask: 'What if information as to S failed to reach the control?'—then the reaction can be goal-directed in sense (ii). Where a corrective mechanism is such that the cause of reaction can in principle be removed only by removing its problem, its activity cannot be so described. In short (cf. M.B.A., p. 106), the *circulation of information* is an essential prerequisite (though not alone definitive) of goal-directed activity in sense (ii). We shall henceforward use the latter term exclusively in this sense.

2.4. So far we have avoided the use of the term 'purpose'. We may note by way of dismissal that 'purpose', like 'directed', has both an active and a passive sense. In the passive sense of 'function' it can be predicated of almost anything, and its use sometimes leads to confusion, as when pontifical statements are made that 'the only purposes a machine can have are the purposes of its designer'. Here we use it in its active sense of 'intention'.

In the Symposium already cited, Mr. Spilsbury suggested that one would be entitled to describe A's activity as 'purposeful' only if it made sense to ask whether X was A's 'real' goal. We have seen that one possible cause of ambiguity is an inadequate variational test; but there may be others. Let us consider, for example, a man pursuing an agile insect. If we give the insect a small displacement in the approved variational manner, we shall doubtless observe evidence that the man's goal is 'contact between his hand and the insect'. But if I accidentally tread on the insect he will probably cease his pursuit. What was his 'real' goal?

Here we uncover a subtle point. The variational criterion tells us only how to test whether some given thing is a goal. It gives us no help in discovering which thing to test. It tells us correctly that 'insect-contact' was a goal for the man until I trod on the insect; but only our ingenuity in framing hypotheses (aided, of course, by conversational or other clues) could lead us to apply the variational test to the goal of 'freedom from insect-bite'. There is no systematic procedure for discovering a man's 'real' goal—unless perhaps *asking* him.

This disadvantage is common to all 'definitions by test'. 'X is the man who wears yellow braces' defines X uniquely (assuming that no one else in the crowd wears yellow braces) but it leaves us to find our own reasons for picking our examinees.

Discovering a man's 'real' goal is thus an inductive activity which may never lead to certainty, and we must accept the same limitation in the study of our artefact, as long as we are restricted to external evidence. We can with normal luck spot a man's *immediate* goal and apply our variational test to it; and we can eliminate any number of pseudo-goals by the same test. But his immediate goal may itself be a means to a higher-order goal, to which observation could give a clue only over a much longer period. In general, in fact, we must recognize that human purposes are normally *hierarchically ordered*; so that just as in a simple case *activity* is abandoned when the goal is achieved, so in a hierarchy the lower-order *goals* are abandoned when a higher-order goal is achieved. Goals may be modified in response to information on their success as means to higher-order ends, in just the same way as actions are modified in the simple case.

There is no difficulty in arranging a similar hierarchical ordering of goals in an artefact. We require only to allow higher-order feedbacks to control selective mechanisms operating on the range of lower-order goals within the scope of the artefact.

2.5. We should expect that most higher-order goals would be defined in abstract terms rather than by physical objects. A man or artefact seeking to prove a geometrical theorem, for example, is kept in activity by recurrent evidence from his test-procedure that his latest method does not work: his response to the feedback of this information (as to the discrepancy between 'the outcome of my present method' and 'the required conclusion') is to try new methods—to adopt new subsidiary purposes.

I think it is clear that feedback (strictly, negative feedback) is essential for all such purposive behaviour, even when goals are abstractions without space–time location. If our man should hit on a successful method of deriving a theorem, we should doubt that he really had this as his goal unless its attainment made some difference to his activity—either halting his efforts or at least arresting his normal reach for the wastebasket.

It is less certain that the presence of such feedback is *sufficient* to ensure that behaviour will merit the adjective 'purposeful' in its human sense. A case might be made for attributing 'purpose' only to an artefact sufficiently complex to have hierarchically-ordered goals, and able to behave in ways more characteristic of human intelligent goal-seeking than the behaviour of a self-guided missile. I do not feel that the linguistic convention is here of vital importance, provided that organism and artefact are submitted to the same tests and judged by the same criteria.

2.6. In mechanisms such as these the various quantities such as distances and speeds entering into the calculations are represented in the calculating device by electrical or other physical magnitudes. The representation of features of the field of action by internal configurations of the mechanism in this way is a very general principle, which can readily be extended to the field of abstract ideas.

In one possible method every fact to be represented is given a code-number, such that each digit in the number is either 1 or 0, representing the answer (yes or no) to one of a set of standard identifying questions—as in the popular game of 'twenty questions'. Making deductions from facts coded in this way then amounts to doing arithmetic (in the scale of 2) with the numbers representing them, and standard calculating-machine technique can be used to mechanize processes of reasoning in principle as complex as desired.

A code-system of this kind is ideal for handling exact information of limited variety. It can enable an artefact in principle to engage in active, responsive and apparently purposive interaction with any field of activity capable of representation in such a code, including dialogue with a human interlocutor on suitable subject[3]. But such an artefact, despite the flexibility and complexity of its responses, which may render it quite *unpredictable* in practice, is still deterministic in its function. It may be judged to be so by a simple 'gedanken experiment': two such identical artefacts supplied with identical information would at all times be found acting in exactly the same way.

[3] Such as chess, for example: see Shannon (*Phil. Mag.*, **41**, 256, 1950).

3. *Spontaneity*

3.1. The reader may have his own views as to the extent to which the above statement would also be true of human beings, but it is at least commonly supposed to be false, and it is certainly not necessarily true of all conceivable artefacts. There are many ways in which a limited amount of indeterminacy could be introduced into the functioning of even such an artefact as we have discussed, so as to enhance its resemblance to a normal imaginative human being.[4]

3.2. There is, however, an opposite approach. Instead of introducing indeterminacy into the functions of a deterministic artefact, we might begin at the other end, as it were, and consider the possibility of approximating to intelligent behaviour by disciplining and organizing an artefact designed from the outset to be spontaneously active. As it seems not unlikely that the human brain itself is a mechanism of this latter type, it may be expected that resemblances to human behaviour would more readily emerge (rather than have to be contrived *ad hoc*) in such an artefact.[5]

3.3. Consider then an artefact comprising a very large interlocked population of elementary units (*elements*), each capable of sending out a signal (excitation) in response to a sufficient *stimulus*. Let us suppose that each element possesses a controllable '*threshold*' (roughly, has a variable resistance) to stimulation, such that the larger the total stimulus is in relation to the effective threshold, the greater is the *probability* of response by the element. A given element may have many input-paths for stimuli, and as many effective thresholds, which we will suppose to be individually controllable. Some elements may be spontaneously active, others not; others again may respond by altering only thresholds in their topological neighbourhood.

The behaviour of an element is thus only *statistically* predictable. This must not, however, be interpreted to imply the possibility of observing predictable frequencies in a *time-series*, for the probabilities of excitation are adjustable from moment to moment, and may change significantly during an interval in which

[4] D. M. MacKay, *The Christian Graduate*, September 1949; A. M. Turing, *Mind*, **59**, 433, 1950.

[5] Readers not interested in technicalities may prefer to skip to Section 5. *Author.*

no excitation occurs. 'Probability' here, as in statistical mechanics, may be interpreted as *frequency in an ensemble* of similar systems' but not as 'frequency in the time-series of the given system'.

When we describe the activity of such a system as statistically predictable, therefore, we mean that the *probability-distributions* governing it undergo transformations which are predictable in principle—not that we shall necessarily observe any sequences with significantly predictable frequency. To take a homely illustration, the probability that a given balloon will burst may depend in quite a calculable way on the pressure inside it; but we do not need to suppose, as a naïve 'frequency' theory of probability might suggest, that the change in probability occasioned by a change in pressure is meaningless unless we can observe a change in a 'frequency of explosion'.

Let us not go too far, however; by claiming that a system is statistically predictable we do mean that *if identical situations* (identical in all important respects both as to the system and its environment) *recur* often enough, we should be able to predict, with greater or less precision, the relative frequencies of responses. This, in fact, seems to be part of what we mean by saying: 'A *tends* to react thus in situation S.' We shall not be incredulous if A does not, but we expect a majority of A's reactions to be of the stated kind in a series of similar situations S.

The factor of learning or taking experience into account comes in precisely at this point. Operationally it implies that the relative probabilities of possible responses depend, *inter alia*, on the results of previous responses.

3.4. Returning to our artefact, we may suppose it equipped with a variety of artificial sense-organs, capable of receiving data from some field or fields in which it can carry out a variety of activities. Thus information as to the results of its activities is fed back to it, and if the information is in a suitable form for assimilation the artefact can be designed to engage in goal-directed activity in those fields.

Feedback has two possible ways of controlling activity here— by making corrective additions to the *input*, or by adjusting *thresholds* and so governing the relative probabilities of different courses of action. As this second process provides one of the main conceptual building-bricks that we shall use, a simple mechanical illustration may be forgiven.

Picture a long, straight, sloping runway, whose lower end loses its side-walls and tapers in width to a long knife-edge. Imagine a succession of small balls rolled down the runway. At the end they must eventually fall off the knife-edge, falling to right or left more or less at random if the transverse axis of the runway is horizontal and so forth. If, however, we slightly tilt the transverse axis one way, the probability will increase that a ball will drop to the left; if the other way, to the right. The tilt of the axis can in fact be considered as an operational token of the corresponding probability.

On each side of the knife-edge imagine a beam-balance, each normally collecting all the balls falling on its side in one of its pans, P_1 say. Then, as balls roll down the runway and out on to the knife-edge and off to left or right, the pans P_1 on both balances would normally descend steadily. Suppose, however, that on one side, say the left, we place a target T, in the form of a funnel which deflects all balls falling left into the other pan P_2 of the left-hand balance. P_2 on the left will now begin to descend steadily. We can say in fact that when T is on the left, P_2 on the left descends; when T is not on the left, P_2 on the left rises. The movement of each balance *evaluates the success* of the balls that fall on its own side, in striking the target T.

Let us now introduce evaluative *feedback*, by linking each P_2 mechanically to the corresponding side of the runway. Thus, if P_2 of the left-hand balance descends, it slightly lowers the left-hand edge of the runway so as to *increase the probability that the next ball will fall on the left*, and conversely. Evidently each time the target is hit, the probability is now increased that it will be hit again unless it moves. After a (controllable) number of trials the mechanism will in fact concentrate solely on the left-hand side where the target is. If now the target T moves to the right-hand side, the device will clearly in time readjust its 'thresholds' so as to drop balls on the right. More generally, if T divides its time between left and right in certain proportions, the arrangement can be such that the probabilities of falling left or right are automatically adjusted to match the relative frequencies of the movements of T. The principle is readily generalized for any number of alternatives. I think it can be shown, in fact, that evaluative feedback on thresholds suffices in a *hierarchically* ordered system to reproduce the features of all common types of learning.

3.5. It is perhaps unnecessary now to point out that the commonly discussed problem of 'producing new types of behaviour' is in our artefact the reverse of the actual one, which is to restrain its propensity for spontaneously producing new types of behaviour. Among its modes of internal activity (M.B.A., p. 116) is 'the alteration of the mechanism controlling response'. Our care in design would need to be exercised chiefly to preserve those minimal consistencies that can define a rational personality.

4. Representation of the field of action.

4.1. How then can such an artefact handle ideas, and represent the world in which it acts? In what physical form—by what kinds of internal symbols—could abstract concepts be represented, and how could we give meaning to any assertion as to what the artefact *believes*? Even more important, how far can we go towards rendering it (for its interpretation of data) independent of prior instruction and built-in categories? Can it abstract for itself significant features of its flux of data, and so *form* as well as *handle* concepts?

The physical representation of concepts which I think can most readily meet such requirements, and at the same time match such few data as we have on the human psycho–physiological side, is very different from that used in digital computers. Its essential features were described in principle in M.B.A. (on p. 114). Perception of a particular feature of incoming stimuli is regarded as an act of internal response—specifically, a self-guided adjustment of the internal organization to 'match' that feature, so that the artefact is made ready to take account of it in any relevant action. In the internal workings of the artefact, the combination of control settings whereby a feature is 'matched'[6] is ideally suited to function as its internal representative or symbolic correlate.

4.2 But we have not finished. In general a variety of internal combinations could match a given input-pattern of stimuli sufficiently well to meet a test having limited discriminative power. In fact, we may envisage a fairly low discrimination in the esti-

---

[6] Perhaps a less confusing term than 'replicated' (M.B.A., *loc. cit.*). It should be remembered that the matching procedure must be such that transformations under which the percept is invariant shall not affect its success. A simple example was given in M.B.A.

mator of 'mismatch'; we may also suppose that many different attempted adjustments may be evoked in parallel among different sub-groups of the population so that in our statistical mechanism the same input-pattern will not necessarily evoke identical matching-responses on successive occasions. Its perceptual activity is selective and may single out different abstractions from the input at different times.

How, then, can we imagine such a process leading automatically to the association of a unique physical correlate with a significantly invariant feature of the field of action?

Here again, 'evaluative feedback on thresholds' provides the key. By arranging that (roughly speaking) the chances of evocation of particular adjustments are controlled by their past success in 'matching', we can obviously ensure that those which have in the statistical scramble scored a greater frequency of success as matching-responses will become differentially more likely to be evoked. In fact, they will acquire permanent physical representation, each being represented by the *whole configuration of thresholds* or 'favoured paths' which contribute to its probability of evocation.

Now a high frequency of success implies normally a high frequency of past recurrence of the corresponding feature. Hence our artefact's repertoire of matching-responses—its internal symbolic vocabulary—will tend to contain mainly representations of most-frequently occurring percepts. In other words, it concentrates on things likely to be worth representing.[7]

4.3. Taking stock at this point we note that in the artefact, as in man, perception is distinguished from reception by something akin to *attention*. I receive a myriad data through eyes, ears, and other organs; I perceive only a changing selection of these—those by which my attention is momentarily attracted, as we say. The same selective action occurs in our artefact, which 'attends' only to the features it is currently matching. Now a percept becomes a datum for current thought; its perception has altered the totality of 'what I *believe* to be the case'. When I have once perceived X, my thinking cannot in every respect be as if I had not.

---

[7] Frequency of recurrence can, of course, be supplemented by other criteria of significance, so that an important thing perceived only in a single glimpse could acquire permanent representation in this way. We are only skimming the surface of the technicalities.

In our artefact likewise we must ensure that perception is followed by the consequences of perception, internal or external. In other words, we must have *coupling* between perceptual activity and all other relevant responsive activity if the artefact is to act as if it believes what it has perceived; and without going into detail, I think it is evident that the same type of self-guiding statistical process can supplement whatever degree of deterministic coupling we wish to introduce, so as to give the plasticity and adaptiveness that characterize the link between perception and action (mental or physical) in human thought.

In short, since our artefact's acts of perception are of a piece with its other acts, the probabilities of transition from an act of perception to one of its possible consequences can be developed and moulded by a mechanism similar to that by which any learned sequence of responses can be built up. The total of what the artefact 'believes' could be formally determined by the total set of 'conditional probabilities' that specify statistically its readiness to react internally or externally in all relevant circumstances.

4.4. To make the physical representation or internal symbol[8] for a percept the internal matching adjustment evoked thereby, eases several of the problems which philosophers have raised in recent debates (see for example the symposium cited on 'Men and Machines'). But before we turn to consider these, we may note that it also finds an encouraging consonance with a great mass of data on causes of aphasia and kindred disorders of concept-handling in human beings, and with some suggestive observations on the development of concept-handling in children. This kind of evidence, coupled with the fact that the artefact, like a child, learns as much by discrimination and negation (dissolution of connections, or diminution of transition-probabilities) as by the complementary process, is perhaps valid ground for speculation on actual cerebral analogues; but we are not here interested in speculation but in factual deduction. I believe it to be a fact that an artefact can perform these functions. It is only an encouraging bonus for our efforts that we seem to be developing an artefact

---

[8] 'Symbol' here means simply the physical representation of the corresponding concept, essential for its entry into the artefact's 'train of thought'. Whether perceiving is a 'symbolic activity' in any other sense does not now concern us.

that can not only function to some extent like the brain, but can also develop and go wrong in comparable ways.

5. Tests for mentality

5.1. In his essay in the symposium 'Men and Machines'[9] J. O. Wisdom drew an important distinction between the mere *imitation* of personal behaviour, and the *expression* of it. It is possible for a man to *feign* emotion by his observable behaviour. Does any analogous possibility—any corresponding distinction between feigned and real mental activity—exist in our artefact? If it did not, we might legitimately doubt whether the whole performance of the artefact, however good as an imitation, was not empty of any personal significance.

If the internal symbols for concepts were arbitrary configurations of elements (as in a digital computer for example), the distinction between simulation and expression might be hard to draw. In this and the following section, however, I shall try to show that the same distinction emerges naturally when we allow the internal symbols to evolve in the way we have sketched, as 'organizers' of the artefact's 'readiness' for the entities or states of affairs conceptualized.

5.2. Let us take first the contrast mentioned by Wisdom, between frowning and mere wrinkling of the forehead. In a human being, there are clearly three possibilities to consider:

(*a*) we can have wrinkling of forehead that does not look like or represent a frown;

(*b*) we can have wrinkling indistinguishable in appearance from that in genuine frowning but without the concomitant emotion;

(*c*) we can have wrinkling expressive of that emotion, and deserving to be called frowning.

Now our artefact can certainly in principle rise to (*a*) and (*b*). But what could we mean by describing its wrinkling as *expressive* and calling it *frowning*? Is it not simply that such wrinkling must be representational activity, the spontaneous outcome or concomitant of internal activity which has all the dispositional consequences we attach to displeasure, concentration, or whatever we

[9] *Loc. cit.*

take the frowning to betoken? If the internal process going on (e.g.) in anger *requires* the employment of elements having strong coupling to (high probability of exciting) wrinkling-muscles, then the resultant wrinkling *is*, I think, what we call frowning.

5.3. I cannot, however, introduce here the whole question of emotional expression, and will content myself with the undogmatic assertion that I have not so far been shown or thought of any case that cannot find an analogue in a concept-handling artefact which uses its internal organizing system—including (e.g.) the equivalents of visceral controls in the human being—as potential component-symbols for its representational activity. I think that anyone with one eye on the mechanisms which the human body uses to mediate emotional experience can scarcely fail to have the broad principles of its expression in such an artefact suggested to him.

5.4. There is however a more searching test, discussed more fully by Spilsbury.[10] Perhaps most characteristic of human mentality is the power to *imagine* states of affairs not currently presented to the senses. Once again we may readily suppose that an artefact could be programmed *ad hoc* to simulate the external signs of such activity; but could this behaviour *mean* what it does in a human being? What could it mean for an artefact to imagine itself in another place, or in the place of another individual?[11]

Once again, our answer would be that if the activity in question can be shown to arise naturally (rather than having to be synthesised *ad hoc*) in the appropriate relationship to other internal activity, then we can distinguish it in principle from mere imitation. In short our aim must be to reproduce not the *product* but the *process* of imagination.

6. Imagination

6.1. Let us then see how far—as a matter of demonstrable fact—our statistical artefact can go towards functioning imaginatively. Its normal perceptual activity, it will be remembered, consists in self-moulding matching-responses, by groups of elements in a restless population, to whatever features in its incoming stimuli 'catch their attention'. With time and experience, it builds up a repertoire of complex matching-responses that have found

[10] *Loc. cit.*   [11] R. J. Spilsbury. *loc. cit.*

application long or often enough to acquire relatively high prob-abilities of evocation as complete patterns. These patterns, or portions of them, could therefore under suitable conditions be evoked in the *absence* of the corresponding input—either as an occasional spontaneous outcome of the restlessness of the con-stituent population, or in response to internal stimuli. Such image-generation—the appearance of internal representational activity in the absence of corresponding input—will affect both the internal and external behaviour of the artefact as if it were *imagin-ing* the corresponding percept. Several possibilities emerge as consequences of different modes of evocation. These can hardly be discussed exhaustively, but we can make a start by distinguish-ing between *illusion, hallucination* and *normal imagination,* and con-sidering the analogous distinctions in our artefact.

(*a*) In *illusion* a real input evokes a false percept (e.g. optical illusions).

(*b*) In *hallucination* a synthetic percept appears to have qualities of reality (e.g. 'hearing voices').

(*c*) In *normal imagination* qualities of reality are absent, and images are evoked by conscious effort or consent.

Direct analogues of all three can be found in the artefact.

(*a*) 'Illusion' arises when the resolving-power of the estimator of mismatch is insufficient to cause rejection of the wrong match-ing-response; or if the data are too crude or ambiguous to decide between alternative candidates; or, of course, if some systematic error in the input channels or the estimator induces a false matching-response. It is easy to see, for example, how the artefact could be deceived by optical illusions.

(*b*) 'Hallucination' would arise if the spontaneous occurrence of a matching-response, without corresponding input, were not accompanied and checked by a resulting signal of mismatch. This could be caused by interruption of the evaluative feedback path or masking of the signal by 'noise'—two factors with interesting differences in resulting pathology which we cannot now pursue.

(*c*) 'Normal imagination' is our main subject and requires more detailed study. Let us first notice the phenomenon[12] of the ex-clusive 'competition' between observation and imagination. In our artefact this finds an immediate and necessary analogue. Observation of a particular scene here ousts imagination of it,

[12] Clearly brought out by R. J. Spilsbury, *loc. cit.*

not indeed because they compete for common *pathways*, but because imagination in the artefact takes the form of internal excitation of the matching-response mechanism, and this is *already* excited if it is engaged in observation of the same thing. Imagination is not 'blocked'; it simply finds nothing more to do.[13]

6.2. It has been suggested that special difficulty arises over *imaginative place-changing*. (Mr. Spilsbury[14] regarded as absurd the question whether any conceivable artefact could imagine itself in the position of another). I hope to show that the analogue of imaginative place-changing in our artefact requires no special technical complexities, and, in fact, is not qualitatively different from any other imaginative activity.

7. *The significance of concepts to an artefact*

7.1. It will help if we first consider, all too briefly, the *semantic* problem as our artefact deals with it. We have seen that it represents a given concept internally by the invariant control pattern wherewith it matches the received data exemplifying the concept. 'Triangularity' in a visual pattern is represented by the combination of control-signals whereby the internal response-mechanism is induced to match the definitive features of a triangle. 'Triangle' means 'something which evokes this . . . (a particular internal response-pattern)'. 'Imagine a triangle' means 'set up the (appropriate) internal response-pattern'. Now it is important to recognize that this response-pattern may in general include the *setting of thresholds* (altering the distributions of favoured paths) as well as the generation or modification of internal *activity*. The meaning of a concept, so defined, includes its statistical *associations*. 'Triangle' comes to mean not only 'that which requires internal activity X to match it' but also (e.g.) 'that which has probabilities $p_1, p_2 \ldots$ of requiring activities $X_1, X_2 \ldots$ to accompany or follow X.'

7.2. This may sound highly technical, but the basic notion is simple. Let us survey the argument: Our artefact is designed so

[13] To avoid misunderstanding, may I repeat that this also is *not* a speculation on the mechanism of the human brain, but a deduction of possibilities inherent in the activity of an artefact design to have a 'restless urge to make symbols'. Neurological speculation has its proper place elsewhere.

[14] *Loc. cit.*

that it will automatically tend to minimize some estimate of (mean) mismatch between its input and its total organization for action. Among its modes of response is that of internal symbolic representation, by internal activity, of 'that which is the case' in its field of activity. As component-symbols of its internal representations it comes to use selections among certain standard internal adjustments that have acquired special statistical status through frequent success as matching-response-components in the past. These standard patterns represent the elementary *concepts* of its field of discourse—the basic internal symbols which in appropriate patterns and sequences constitute its internal *descriptions*[15] of 'that which is the case'. In the course of its activity (which can include dialogue), however, it will gradually discover also statistical linkages between concepts, if the abstractive process described in M.B.A. (p. 116) goes on, whereby the artefact perceives patterns in (abstracts regularities from) its *own* perceptual activity as evoked by the flux of stimuli. Evaluative feedback can then be introduced to control also the probabilities of transition from one response-pattern to others. This will mean that in the course of time each response-pattern (representing a concept) will tend to be accompanied by an adjustment of thresholds (probabilities of transition) in favour of whatever activities have in the past been most often evoked next, and so on, with no fundamental limit to complexity. This highly-complex configuration of thresholds, conceivably practicable only in a self-organizing population such as we envisage, defines what we have called the artefact's state of readiness, and its ramifications define the richness of the corresponding concept. It is worth noting that this whole process of formation of concepts and their associations can in principle take place from scratch with a statistical *tabula rasa*, though, of course, it can be greatly accelerated by even small determining factors in design and by normal educative processes such as are used with children.

7.3. We are now in a position to visualize the process of imagination in the artefact in more detail. 'Imagine X' means 'evoke the internal representation of X'. This representation, as we have seen, includes a threshold configuration rendering highly-probable a transition to some state frequently associated with X

[15] To itself primarily, though, of course, we take for granted the easy step of linking these to communicative activity such as speech.

in the past. Hence imagining X is normally the starting-point of a *train* of representational activity, previously evoked in association with X, or for some other reason rendered highly probable.

Thus one of the best ways the artefact has of *trying* to imagine a concept, Y, say, is to evoke imagination of some 'X' with which it is strongly associated. Normally, of course, perception of the word used to define a concept is adequate as a stimulus to such a train of activity. More generally, 'an effort to imagine Y' amounts to setting as many thresholds as possible (preparing a state of readiness) so as to maximize the probability of excitation of representational activity corresponding to Y. The artefact does all that it can, as it were, and then awaits the spontaneous outcome. (It can, of course, have means of increasing the overall frequency of spontaneous transitions, as well as of guiding their directions).

7.4. Imagining some *familiar* scene therefore requires only re-evocation in the artefact of internal matching-responses previously characteristic of its experience there, and linked among themselves by high probabilities of transition. The word 'imagine' implies the temporary *diversion* of the evaluative signal which would normally force the internal activity to match the current input. It does not, however, imply the *absence* of all internal evidence of mismatch. Evidence of the unreality of the experience imagined is still provided by the presence of the diverted signal.

It will be apparent by now that the condition that our artefact should imagine *itself* at a familiar place P is simply that its representations of the familiar percepts of P should include those characteristic of its own presence, especially states of readiness to react as if present.

7.5. Imagining an *unfamiliar* scene differs only in that the components of the representation must be evoked in response to description, or else taken from past experiences believed typical. I have never seen the Square in Vladivostock, but when I try to imagine myself in it I find myself constructing a pastiche of elements of my experience of Squares. Any such activity could find a precise parallel in our artefact. Imaginative *time*-changing raises, I think, no different problems from imaginative *place*-changing.

There is, of course, another sense in which I could imagine myself in a place P (whether familiar or otherwise), namely as one of the features of the imagined scene. This is less important, for in this case 'I' am represented by an imagined object on the same footing as all others in the image. No new difficulty is introduced in imagining a scene in which 'the fourth black dot from the left' is myself instead of someone else.

7.6. We come lastly to the test case proposed by Mr. Spilsbury.[16] How could our artefact A imagine itself not only in another place, but in the place of another person or artefact B?

Let us first decide what we shall accept as evidence of success in such imagining. Were I, for example, to try to imagine myself in the place of a sceptical opponent, I should begin by lecturing myself on the absurdity of predicating 'mentality' of artefacts. I should go on to try, in all respects on which I have evidence, to 'think myself into his state of mind' by assuming a disposition as close as possible to what I infer to be his own. If I knew his life story I should endeavour to relive as much as I could in imagination, retaining whatever attitudinal 'set' my imaginings had induced—and so forth.

What am I doing? Clearly I am not concerned with imitation of what my opponent is *doing* now. What I am trying to set up in myself is a complex state of *readiness* sufficiently similar to his to enable me to *experience* (I hope) *similar reactions* to his own in given situations. I judge my success in imagining myself in his place according as I am able to feel within myself the rise and fall of the same emotions and other inner experiences of which he gives evidence as he meets the same course of events. Normally, of course, we do not meet the same events, so that if I am watching him and trying to imagine myself in his place I have also to imagine (in the way we have discussed) myself as experiencing these events, in an artificial state of readiness bearing the maximum of resemblance to his.

The reader can doubtless now anticipate the way in which our artefact A would meet this test. In an analogous manner, it can first evoke internal representational activity to develop within itself a configuration of thresholds calculated to represent the 'attitudinal set' of B with respect to relevant inputs. (This assumes some degree of similarity of conceptual frameworks in A and B, as Mr. Spilsbury has noted in the case of human place-changing.) In this state of readiness it imagines itself in the circumstances of B by setting up an internal-matching response to what it sees

[16] *Loc. cit.*

or considers B to be receiving. By virtue of A's 'state of readiness', this results in the evocation of a train of further internal responses normally 'uncoupled' from overt action, representing what A imagines to be B's reactions in those circumstances.

7.7. One could of course elaborate in endless detail, but I can think of no example of human imagination that cannot be paralleled in principle along these lines. To imagine oneself in the place of someone now dead, or in a place not visible, for example, requires only a combination of the processes already discussed. Whether in imaginative place-changing or time-changing, no question of 'duplication'[17] arises, because when I imagine myself elsewhere—or when the artefact does—I and it remain just where we are, and only induce internal activity in ourselves as if we were elsewhere.

8. *The personality of an artefact*

8.1. Does such an artefact then have a mind? Is it conscious of what it is doing? Does it really feel and not merely simulate emotion? Such are currently popular questions. One might join in ridiculing the suggestion 'that a mass of wireless valves could ever fall in love'.

But to consider the suggestion in this form is, of course, to commit a vulgar error. In the analogous case of a human being, it is not the mass of nerve-cells inside the skull that has fallen in love. To say so would be a misuse of language. It is the *person* who has fallen in love; and to assert—or even to deny—that the nerve-cells of his brain are in love would be to show ignorance of the proper uses of the terms. (Ref. 13)

It would therefore be but a perverse distortion of the issue to ask whether an artefact could be angry or affectionate, if by 'artefact' we meant 'some box of wires and valves'. If we are interested in evaluating the true parallel, we must compare the box of wires and valves with the sight that a brain surgeon sees on an operating table; it is only the *personality* mediated by the box of wires and valves that we can compare with the human personality.

We are accustomed to the unconscious process that can hear a declaration of love in the noisy wobbling of the red-and-pink protoplasm we call a face. We choose to use *personal* language in

[17] J. O. Wisdom, *loc. cit.*

describing such an encounter, because it makes more sense to do so. It may require much mental discipline to bring ourselves to the corresponding abstractive effort with our artefact. One could perhaps be helped by imagining the artefact as a correspondent, or as decently clothed in some fashion! But it is only when this effort has successfully been made that we are in a position to face the philosophical question. In its original form the problem is quite overlaid by what amounts to the humour of buffoonery.

8.2. Our first question is therefore: could personal language consistently be used to describe the encounter with such an artificial personality? I believe that it could, for the simple reason that any deficiencies in the 'personal' features of the activity can in principle be remedied as soon as they can be specified.

But in the last phrase there is a rub. It is easy enough to specify enough characteristics to make the artificial personality a tolerably intelligent and interesting and even emotionally-motivated interlocutor. To that extent personal language would indeed seem to be not only justified, but the only sensible language to use, just as in the case of a human being. But it is by no means obvious whether now or at any time or even in principle it would be possible for human beings to understand enough of the depths of human personality to be able to specify adequately *all* the deficiencies remaining unremedied.

8.3. To the second question therefore as to whether such a personality could ever be fully human, we must return the old Scots answer of 'Not proven'. The one thing that seems safe to assert is that the barrier, if barrier in principle there be, will be conceptual rather than physical, resting on limitations to our psychological rather than our mechanical knowledge.

In short it is worse than folly to consume energy in searching for behaviour that 'you'll never be able to reproduce in a machine'. To do so is to accept a misconstruction of the real issue, which concerns the extent to which man can understand his own nature well enough to specify the information-processing requirements for an artificial human personality.

8.4. What then of consciousness and mind? I should be prepared to defend the thesis that *as far as we can find words for tests* for these attributes, it is possible for an artefact to meet those tests. But if we were to leap the ditch that is deductively unbridgeable, and say that an artefact that behaves in every way as if it were conscious *is* conscious—what then? Conversely, what would we think we were denying if we say it is not? As I have pointed out elsewhere (Ref. 13), this is no rhetorical question. Consciousness is for each of us a matter of fact, not of convention. But the temptation to suppose that it admits of behavioural demonstration with certainty (either way) must be resisted. We are in fact facing a problem quite similar to the classical one of deciding whether anyone is conscious but ourselves; the reader who would venture to frame a deductive behavioural test for the artefact had better walk warily, lest he deprive himself also of consciousness (in the eyes of all others) by the same stroke.

8.5. More seriously it may be asked whether there are any grounds in Christian revelation for pontification here where deduction fails. Is not the production of an artificial human being theologically impossible, as usurping the Divine prerogative?

Accepting fully as I do the authority of Christian revelation, I fail to see any cogency in this argument. Man is already licensed by God to grow new personalities by natural procreation. His doing so by other means, in other materials, may well be insuperably hindered by practical obstacles, as we have seen; but I know of no prior objection to the possibility on biblical grounds. My suggestion would be that in the face of our patent ignorance, and even doubt as to the meaning of the question, the Christian's attitude has to be one of 'reverent agnosticism'—reverent because personality, even an imitation of our own, is a great mystery; and agnostic because plain honesty thus best describes the position.

9. *Implications*

9.1. We began by considering without comment the traditional view that the relationship between my decisions and my bodily movements was one of causality. We saw that this view implied, but did not suggest the nature of some mechanism of interaction between an entity termed my mind and my body. We saw how physical causation has gradually spread through the bodily picture, steadily diminishing the area on which 'mind' might be able to lay causal hands. We saw that in this language, mind itself seemed subject to the action of physical causes.

And then from the opposite direction we have followed a new twist in the story. It has appeared that those features of behaviour which we most commonly attribute to the 'causal action of Mind' can be quite naturally and well reproduced in a mechanism functioning throughout according to ordinary physical principles.

9.2. Squeezed out in one direction, never admitted in the other, it might seem as if Mind should soon find no place in our view of Man. But of course it is not so. What we are being forced to realize, I suggest, is rather that 'Mind' is a word which belongs to a different logical vocabulary from words describing physical causes, in the sense that words of an algebra problem belong to a different logical vocabulary from words describing the ink that delineates it. 'What is on the paper' can be described completely in terms of algebra or in terms of ink, but the two descriptions do not mix. They are correlates, but not translations of one another, for although they both point to the same situation, they are not talking about the same aspects of it. In the same way our suggestion is that the 'mental' or personal description of a human activity does not rival but is complementary to a description in physical terms. It is not the descriptions which are mutually exclusive, but the logical backgrounds in which the respective terms are defined (Refs. 7, 10).

9.3. What then is our alternative to the classical account? Between my decision and my *responsibility* it would seem proper to posit a causal relationship. Between the physical events in my brain concomitant with my decision, and the appropriate bodily motions it is also proper to posit a causal relationship. But to attempt to use an identical relationship of causality as a link between my decisions and their physical expression appears to be an error. If we must call the link 'causal', we should logically use some distinguishing adjective to prevent our habit from leading to nonsense.

For what we call our 'decision' may from the physical observer's standpoint be the concomitant of a whole sequence or pattern of physical brain events whose causal linkages, even if not complete and unbroken, may extend backwards and forwards considerably in the time of the observer. Not even temporal priority could therefore be guaranteed to what we wish to term the mental 'cause' of our action, and it seems not unlikely that in the physical picture the room available for a causal antecedent would too often be almost completely occupied by well-knit chains of physical events.

9.4. But why should we wish at all to use this language of quasi-physical causality? Perhaps the commonest reason is the belief that unless I can call my decisions the (quasi-physical) causes of my actions, I am not responsible for those actions. We cannot here discuss this view adequately; but I believe that it is fallacious. If I find my body jerking in activity *against* my will, then I may fairly disclaim responsibility. But the reason is not that there was a physical cause of my action and therefore no mental cause, but that if I am asked 'Was this of your will?' I know directly what is meant and can answer 'No'. If, however, I choose deliberately to take some action, my answer to the same question is 'Yes' and I cannot evade responsibility; for the physical description of what went on in my brain, however causally enchained, is but a complementary account of the physical aspect of my deliberate choice. In short, our suggestion is that responsibility is to be judged not by the question: 'had the act a non-physical cause?' but rather: 'was the act the outcome of a decision?'[18] The language of the actor, rather than the complementary language of the observer, is the group in terms of which the calculus of responsibility is framed. And in the last analysis it is neither acts nor consequences that Christianity at least declares to be the first objects of moral appraisal, but attitudes, in the most fundamental sense of the term.

9.5. At the same time we may note that current physiology in any case gives little encouragement to the view that the physical course of a human brain should be predictable—even in principle—over any appreciable length of time. And we have seen that an artefact could show an enhanced resemblance to a human being in the domain of originality and choice if it incorporated a measure of indeterminacy in its mode of operation. The significance of this indeterminacy is yet another of the problems to which these developments direct attention, but which we cannot now discuss.[19]

9.6. It may seem disturbing to some to be invited to modify

[18] See references 8 and 11 for a further development of this argument in terms of 'logical indeterminacy.'

[19] I have discussed it and argued for its irrelevance to human responsibility in references 8 and 11.

a thought-model so traditionally wedded to Christian apologetic. To those accustomed to think of Mind as a kind of 'stuff' inhabiting the body and exerting occult forces on its movements, it may seem heretical to suggest that an artificial organism could show the behaviour which has always been interpreted as evidence of these forces.

But is that currently 'traditional' view—or habit of speech—in fact Biblical? It would seem that for the Hebrews at least a debate in these terms could scarcely have been formulated, for their view of Nature entertained no such concept as 'mere matter obeying mechanical laws'. The main Biblical distinction would seem to be between 'spirit' on the one hand, and 'mind–body' or 'organism' on the other. *Spiritual* life is declared to be something not automatically present in a human being, but having to be received in repentance as the gift of God; it is eternal, and not limited to the spatio-temporal phase of the human organism.

The concepts of *mental* life on the other hand find no Biblical mention apart from a body of some sort. The doctrine of the resurrection of the body indeed lends weight to the suggestion that Biblically mind and body constitute two aspects of a concrete unity (14). This is not to say that the perishing of the present body is the end of the personality it mediated: for the person concerned it need not necessarily be even an interruption. (Even in the case of an artefact a complete knowledge of its momentary state before destruction could enable its personality to be reproduced and to 'take up where it left off' in a new mechanism, not necessarily built of the same material.) The continuity that matters is not a continuity of material but of memories and relationships, past and present, above all with God Himself.

Nor do we imply that 'spiritual life' and 'mental life' are two varieties of the same thing. Rather might we say that spiritual life is mediated or expressed by our psychological activity in something of the way that mental life is mediated or expressed by our bodily activity (14). But here the water is deep, and speculation finds few landmarks in revelation. It is evident that no linguistic distinction that one might wish to draw has any parallel in common usage, even in translations of the Bible, where 'spirit', 'soul' and 'mind' are often interchanged. But conceptually the distinction seems clear and necessary, and might perhaps be followed up with profit by those more competent to do so.

189

9.7. Underlying our whole approach has been the conviction that either to assert or to deny that mind is 'nothing but' a by-product of mechanism, is to lend countenance to a false formulation of the problem. The phrase 'nothing but' begs the question here as in other debates, and typifies what one might call 'nothing buttery' or 'reductionist' thinking.

Reductionism is properly attacked not by disputing the *exhaustiveness* of a given reduction—say to mechanical terms—but by challenging the implicit and undefended assumption of *exclusiveness*.

It is a simple *non sequitur* to argue that mechanical explanation of the embodiment of mind need in any way affect the reality and responsibility of the personality so mediated.

10. *Conclusion*

The foregoing inadequate discussion has had one limited objective. It is not contended that artefacts constructed along these lines *must* in principle be admitted to have 'mentality'.

Our suggestion is merely that the contrary is not proven, and that any attempt to 'maintain the dignity of man' by searching for limits to the information-processing powers of artefacts is misguided and foredoomed. This is no prophecy, but a deduction from the demonstrable fact that to specify exactly a behavioural test of information-processing capability amounts in principle to specifying a mechanism that can meet it.

We have left open the question whether we could ever enunciate an adequate test for mentality in the full human sense. Indeed our plea would be for more open-mindedness in facing an issue on which it is difficult to conceive of the kind of evidence that would be adequate. The view here offered is that these developments only illuminate and in no way controvert the Christian doctrine of Man.

Postscript. The papers conflated to form this chapter were both written in 1952 and first published as follows:

1. 'Mentality in Machines', *Proc. Aristot. Soc. Suppt.*, 1952, Vol. XXVI, 61–86.
2. 'From Mechanism to Mind', *Trans. Vict. Inst.*, 1953, **85**, 17–32.

Since then the author has amplified a number of the arguments sketched here, and the following papers give developing statements of his position:

3. 'Operational Aspects of Some Fundamental Concepts of Human Communication', *Synthese*, 1954, **9**, 182–98.
4. 'On Comparing the Brain with Machines', *The Advancement of Science*, **40**, (March 1954), 402–6; also *American Scientist*, 1954, **42**, 261–8; and *Ann. Report of Smithsonian Inst.*, 1954, 231–40.
5. 'The Epistemological Problem for Automata', *Automata Studies*, Princeton University Press, 1955, pp. 235–51.
6. 'Towards an Information-Flow Model of Human Behaviour', *Brit. J. Psychol.*, 1956, **47**, 30–43.
7. 'Complementary Descriptions', *Mind*, 1957, **66**, 390–4.
8. 'Brain and Will', *The Listener*, May 9 and 16, 1957; also (revised) in *Body and Mind*, (G. N. A. Vesey, Ed.), Allen & Unwin, 1964, pp. 392–402.
9. 'Information Theory and Human Information Systems', *Impact of Science on Society*, 1957, **8**, 86–101.
10. 'Complementarity II', *Proc. Arist. Soc. Suppt.*, 1958, **32**, 105–22.
11. 'On the Logical Indeterminacy of a Free Choice', *Proc. XIIth Int. Congress of Philosophy, Venice*, Sept. 1958. Vol. III. 249–56, and (revised) *Mind*, **69**, 31–40 (1960).
12. 'Operational Aspects of Intellect', *Proc. N.P.L. Conf. on 'Mechanization of Thought Processes'*, Nov. 1958, 37–52 (H.M.S.O. 1959).
13. 'The Use of Behavioural Language to Refer to Mechanical Processes', *Brit. J. Phil. of Sci.*, XIII, 89–103, 1962.
14. 'Man as a Mechanism', *Faith & Thought*, **91**, 145–57, 1960; also (revised) in *Christianity in a Mechanistic Universe*, edited by D. M. MacKay, Tyndale Press, 1965.
15. 'Communication and Meaning—a functional approach' in *Cross-Cultural Understanding: Epistemology in Anthropology*, edited by F. S. C. Northrop and Helen Livingston, Harper and Row, 1964, 162–79.
16. 'Freewill and Causal Prediction', *Op. Cit.* ref. 15, 356–64.
17. 'Information and Prediction in Human Sciences' in *Information and Prediction in Science*, edited by S. Dockx and P. Bernays, (Symposium of Int. Acad. for Phil. of Science, 1962), Academic Press, New York, 1965.
18. 'A Mind's-Eye View of the Brain', in *Progress in Brain Research*, *1965*, edited by J. Schadé. In Press.

In the course of a most thought-provoking paper Professor MacKay has advanced a number of important theses of which the following I take to be crucial for his position:

(*a*) Any type of behaviour found in living organisms which can be described precisely and unambiguously can, *ipso facto*, be simulated by a suitably programmed automaton.

(*b*) All human behaviour could in principle be so simulated, even if in practice some kinds of behaviour are too complex ever to allow for the requisite specification.

(*c*) An automaton capable of simulating human behaviour to an unlimited degree of success would qualify a being endowed with a *mind*, in any meaningful sense of that word.

(*d*) It follows that to talk of mind as an incorporeal or extraphysical factor in human personality interacting with the body-mechanisms is to talk gratuitous nonsense.

(*e*) The aforegoing theses are in no sense incompatible with certain traditional ethico-religious conceptions of human personality.

Now, with respect to these theses I fully accept (*a*) but for the rest I regard (*b*) as problematic, (*c*) as demonstrably false, (*d*) as invalid and (*e*) as absurd. I want therefore to say a few words about each in turn so as to explain where, in my opinion, MacKay goes wrong.

So far as (*a*) is concerned, it is, I believe, now accepted as axiomatic by cyberneticians and computerologists. Indeed, if formulated with sufficient care and rigour, it would, I believe, stand revealed as tautologically true. But this is not to say it is no more than a trivial truth. On the contrary, it has already greatly contributed to our understanding of the essential meaning of behaviour and much of MacKay's paper can be regarded as illustrating this axiom and in a very illuminating way.

As regards (*b*), MacKay is quite frank about the reservations he himself feels in putting it forward. There may be, he admits, some kind of theoretical 'simulation-barrier' beyond which we could never hope to go, but he insists that 'the barrier, if barrier in principle there be, will be conceptual rather than physical resting on limitations to our psychological rather than our mechanical knowledge' (Section 8.3) and the unspoken implication here is that such limitations even if they do exist do not materially upset or even modify the basic machine-analogy which the remainder of the paper develops. At this point I suggest that a recent article by the American psychologist Ulric Neisser[20] on 'The

[20] See *Science*, **139**, January 18, 1963.

Imitation of Man by Machine' provides a useful supplement. Neisser recognizes the stimulus which computer-models can give to psychological research but he warns us against being misled by them. In particular, he stresses the multiple and inextricable bonds that exist in the human case between thought and feeling and adds that 'a multiplicity of motives is not a supplementary heuristic that can be readily incorporated into a problem-solving program to increase its effectiveness. In man it is a necessary consequence of the way his intellectual activity has grown in relation to his needs and feelings'. Just how far simulation can go, therefore, is still a matter of conjecture but, in the meanwhile, we ought to admit that the simulation-barrier may arise not just from our ignorance of the mechanics of human behaviour but from the possibility that human beings are not machines in the first place.

But it is with respect to (*c*) that MacKay first goes seriously astray. By Section 8 it has become abundantly clear that the implicit assumption of the entire paper is that an *operationist* analysis can be given for all mental concepts. Now, if this were so, (*c*) would indeed follow but I shall try to show that this cannot possibly be the case. It is significant that in discussing mind the author nowhere makes any allusion to those entities that, traditionally, have always been regarded as having a prior claim to the title of 'mental' or 'psychical' i.e. the immediately introspectible or inspectable contents of experience. Even when he is discussing perception he talks only about internal matching *responses*. Thus he evades any consideration of just those aspects of mind which form the point of departure for so many of his fellow symposiasts and which go to make up what is ordinarily associated with the term 'consciousness'. Here I shall mention just one argument (but that I consider a fatal one) against such a comprehensive operationism as MacKay proposes. One can easily satisfy oneself, on the basis of experience, that there are some facts we know directly and which require no further corroboration. Yet if we take seriously the operationist criteria of knowing then before I could claim that I know what, say, my intention is in a given case I would have to perform some test or experiment such as MacKay describes and observe my reactions, and if then I wanted to claim that I knew the outcome of these tests I would have to perform a further set of tests and so on indefinitely. Hence in order that we should know anything at all, in a sense that implies conscious awareness of what we know, some knowledge must be of this direct kind.

It is important to realize that the argument I have just given does not prove that an artefact cannot have a mind. It is certainly conceivable that the perfect simulator *does* know what it is doing, that it *can* introspect its cognitive processes, that it *is* conscious of what it perceives and so on, but none of this necessarily follows from the similarities on the performatory side. Indeed, Professor MacKay appears to recognize this since he himself points out, quite correctly (Section 8.4), that a perfect simulator if such a thing were possible would confront us once again with the classical 'other minds' problem. But he fails to realize how damaging is this admission for his entire position for he then blithely asks what we think we are denying of the artefact when we say it is not conscious. The implied answer to this question is 'nothing worth speaking of'; the correct answer is, of course 'mind'.

(d). Here, I fear, MacKay shows much less discernment than the late A. M. Turing who, in other respects, held very similar views on mind and mechanism. For, Turing[21] admitted that if ESP were a reality it would defy computer simulation (presumably because in ESP it is impossible, *ex hypothesi*, to furnish a physical specification of the input signals). Now, if the machine analogy that MacKay has been pursuing is, as I have taken it to be, an empirical thesis, and not something that is supposed to be analytically true, one would naturally assume that the author would show a lively interest in any empirical attempts that may have been made to refute his thesis. He may not admit, of course, that any such attempts have been successful and he may feel secure that no such attempts ever will succeed, but he could scarcely avoid mentioning them. Yet, not only does he do just this he states categorically that 'any attempts to "maintain the dignity of man" by searching for limits to the power of artefacts is misguided and foredoomed' (Section 10). Yet the only reason we are given for this strangely dogmatic pronouncement is that it is a deduction from the demonstrable fact that 'to specify exactly a behavioural test amounts in principle to specifying a mechanism that can meet it' or, in other words from thesis (a). But we have already seen that nothing follows from this axiom regarding the presence or absence of mind. I conclude, therefore, that no grounds have been given for rejecting out of hand the possibility of an interactionist solution of the mind–body problem and I would further point to Professor Ducasse's paper (q.v.) that such a solution can be plausibly defended.

(e). Having advanced what has, conventionally, been regarded as the 'mechanistic' or 'materialistic' interpretation of mind MacKay devotes Section 9 of his paper to reconciling his views with the Christian Doctrine of Man which he tells us he unreservedly accepts. Now, it would indeed be a presumption on the part of an agnostic like myself to challenge MacKay on points of Christian doctrine or biblical exegesis. If he assures me that Christianity is quite compatible with the truth of Mechanism or Materialism I am quite happy to take his word for it but he must not complain if he has increased my suspicion that Christianity (at least as professed by someone at MacKay's level of sophistication)

[21] See 'Computing Machinery and Intelligence' (*Mind*,, **59**, 1950, 433–60).

is compatible with anything at all. I may be mistaken in this, if so it would be most illuminating if MacKay would specify for us some state-of-affairs that would not be compatible with the truth of Christianity, but, if I am right, the reason is surely that we are dealing here not with a set of beliefs but rather with an attitude of mind,[22] and an attitude unlike a belief cannot be either true or false and hence cannot be contradicted by any empirical facts. A really resolute optimist may persist in his optimism even in the face of the most appalling catastrophes! Nevertheless certain beliefs are conducive to certain attitudes and I would predict on psychological grounds that if the belief were generally accepted that the differences between men and machines were trivial or incidental the Christian attitude would very quickly disappear.

MacKay, however, cannot be held responsible if most people are confused about these issues so before we have any right to dismiss his contention as absurd we must examine his own arguments for the consistency of his position. His main argument is based on the so-called 'two-language hypothesis' which linguistic philosophy has done so much to popularize in recent years. Briefly, that since statements about minds or persons belong to a different logical category from statements about physical causes and processes, nothing that is said in the one language undermines anything that may be said in the other language. This argument has already received some hard knocks at the hands of Flew (q.v.) so here I would like simply to pose a question: Why is a personalistic language necessary when talking about human behaviour? There was after all a time when mountains, rivers, trees, winds and so on were all deemed abundantly worthy of personification. Yet today, except perhaps for special poetic purposes, a description of natural phenomena in the language of classical mythology would rightly be regarded as ridiculous, and not because it is necessarily contradicted by the scientific account but simply because it has been rendered otiose and empty. Now, why should the same fate not overtake the personalistic account of human behaviour? At best it would be retained only as an understood shorthand substitute for the more complex physicalistic account. For the point is that the two languages are not, as MacKay suggests, complementary but equally valid alternatives; the physicalistic language, claiming as it does a universal application will always be theoretically superior to any alternative. That is, unless the alternative refers to some independent reality and that, of course, is precisely what MacKay wishes to deny in the case of 'mind-talk'.

[22] This suggestion has not been made with any disparaging intent. Indeed, some modern Christians I have spoken to, like the scientist-theologian Mr. John Wren-Lewis, have said as much themselves.

COMMENTS BY C. J. DUCASSE

The term 'mechanism', used again and again in the paper, is nowhere defined. The statement, p. 186, that the view 'that the relationship between my decisions and my bodily movements was one of causality ... implied, but did not suggest the nature of some mechanism of interaction between an entity termed my mind and my body': The term 'mechanism of interaction' is not defined, but seems intended to designate the 'how' of such causation. But the question 'how?', as to causation, has no other sense than 'through what intermediary causal steps?'; and is therefore congruous only to cases of *remote* causation; but incongruous, i.e. nonsensical, as regards cases of *proximate* causation, which is what causation as between brain and mind or mind and brain would be.

Occurrence of mechanical processes is not exclusively in the material world. Some mental processes too are wholly mechanical. This is evident, once the difference between mechanism and purposiveness has been precisely analysed.[23]

The causality relation is wholly neutral as to whether the cause-event and the effect-event are both material, or both mental, or either one material and the other mental. It requires only that the two be *events*.

Page 188: The distinction made there between 'activity *against* my will' (e.g. tics, or the knee-jerk reflex, etc.) and 'action deliberately chosen', is not enough. It leaves out the innumerable actions that are 'conditioned responses', but which, although they are not *willed*, are nevertheless 'voluntary' in the sense that deliberate *volition to inhibit* the response conditioned to occurrence of a certain stimulus (e.g. turning towards someone who calls out one's name) would have sufficed to cause non-occurrence of the response.

One is *morally responsible* not only for such of one's acts as are 'the outcome of a decision,' but *also* for those which, although they are not outcomes of decisions, are yet ones which a decision would have sufficed to prevent. Anyway, it is necessary to distinguish between (*a*) 'historical' responsibility for the effects of one's unintentional acts, (*b*) legal responsibility for some acts not one's own (e.g. acts of one's child, or of one's agents) and (*c*) moral responsibility, which concerns both willed acts, and acts 'voluntary' in the sense above; i.e., acts of omission, as well as acts of commission.

[23] See my address to the 1957 InterAmerican Congress of Philosophy, entitled 'Life, Telism, and Mechanism' (*Philosophy and Phenomenological Research*, Vol. XX, No. 1, September 1959), p. 22.

COMMENTS BY J. R. SMYTHIES

It should be clear that Professor MacKay and I are using mind in two quite different, although equally legitimate, senses. His discussion is based on 'mind' in the sense of 'mentality' and I would agree with most of what he says about this. I would suggest, however, that modern science presents an inadequate account of what constitutes the human organism. This may consist not only of the physical body (where the ankle-bone is) but the mind as well (as defined in the comment I made on Ducasse's essay) (including the somatic sensory field—where the pain is). Non-Cartesian dualism is a completely materialist and mechanist theory and merely claims that contemporary physics, cosmology and indeed geography have all overlooked the simple possibilities that there may be more than one space in the world of events (as in Price's theory) or that the events in the Universe may take place in an n-dimensional manifold and not in a 4-dimensional one (as in Broad's theory where 'dimension' is used in a *strictly* geometrical spatial sense and *not* in its wider logical sense).

In this case MacKay's attempts to reconcile physiology and Christian theory may become unnecessary since the current laws of physics are on this theory, only accounting for events in part of the Universe, whereas it should, I suppose, be the concern of physics and cosmology to give an account of the whole Universe. If non-Cartesian dualism is right the Ego may play some causal role in the determination of our actions—albeit only a small one, since, on any analysis, habit, instinct and unconscious motivations determine much of what we do and purely brain events likewise constrain our freedom to act; as clinical neurology and psychiatry amply demonstrate. Nevertheless, non-Cartesian dualism leaves open the possibility that the Ego may, by an act of will, make one decision rather than another—in some complex ethical situation perhaps. Non-Cartesian dualism also leaves open the possibility that this may not be the case, and that causal brain–mind relations may be entirely one way.

REPLY TO C. J. DUCASSE, J. R. SMYTHIES AND J. BELOFF
BY D. M. MACKAY

I am grateful to all discussants for their illuminating contributions. I agree with Ducasse that my passing reference to moral responsibility was inadequate; but in my later papers cited (refs. 8, 11, 13, 16, 17) and in my comment on Flew's paper, I have suggested a criterion which applies equally to acts of omission and commission. What matters, I think, is whether (or to what degree of precision) an advance prediction of the act exists which is binding upon the agent, whether he knows it or not, in the sense that he would be correct if he were to believe it, and incorrect if he did not.

The question begged by Ducasse is whether a brain event and its 'proximately causal' mental event are two events or one. If we say they are two events, and that the mental 'causes' the physical, we are in effect claiming that the physical pattern of 'intermediary causal steps' is not alone sufficient to determine the brain event in question: that exactly the same physical antecedents could have had a different consequence. This is all very well as speculation; but if it is to be distinguished from wishful thinking we are entitled to ask at what point in the physiologist's causal model of brain activity his mechanistic assumptions are being denied. This may be a difficult question; but I do not see it as 'nonsensical'.

My difficulty with Smythies' invocation of extra 'dimensions' is again to see how this can be scientifically disciplined. When England rises on the scale of national productivity, the 'economic dimension' or 'space' in which this motion takes place is extra-physical; yet it is hard to see what would be gained by adding it to the manifold of the cosmologist's world. Addition of economic or mental or any other dimensions to this manifold could be justified only by empirical evidence that the cosmologist's present enterprise could not succeed without them, and would succeed with them. On this point Smythies leaves me unconvinced.

As Beloff has presented a 'summary' of my paper which directly contradicts my own at the crucial point (compare his (*c*) with my summary and conclusions), I can only assume that the fault is mine, and take the opportunity to restate what I must have said badly. I am not sure that Beloff should accept (*a*) if he takes seriously some claims of parapsychology; but in relation to *information-processing* behaviour, I agree with him.

(*b*). My doubts (para. 8.2) whether we could ever complete a specification for human behaviour, even in principle, were based not merely on the complexity of the task, but on the *conceptual* difficulty (if not impossibility) for a human being to comprehend fully, and explicitly, what it is to be a human being. Hence even if all specified behaviour could be simulated, this gives no proof that 'all human behaviour' could be simulated. In our present ignorance of brain-processes, of course, anyone is free to imagine yet other barriers without fear of contradiction. What he cannot claim is that any pattern of information-processing behaviour once specified is impossible of simulation—even if it originated in a 'non-machine-like' brain.

Beloff's (*c*) is a complete misreading. My own position on this question was clearly described as agnostic, and I have elaborated in later papers my own rejection of performatory simulation as a *guarantee* of consciousness. The difficulty here is that an outsider with no axe to grind finds himself assailed on two fronts. My paper was originally written (refs. 1 and 2) as a reply to those who supposed (in 1952) that information-processing tests for 'mentality' could still be found which no artefact could meet. Having (I think) illustrated the lines on which such tests can be met, I contended that in any case the search for conclusive behavioural tests was as pointless here as in connection with the problem of 'other minds'.

On the other hand I have not the least interest in defending the absurdities of Beloff's 'operationist'. For me, my immediate experience is ontologically prior to any story about observable behaviour or a physical world. Operational criteria are relevant not to my *knowing* my intentions, etc., but to my (or anybody else's) attempts to relate these to what goes on in my brain. I cherish the hope that a one-to-one correlation exists between what I experience and what an observer might in principle detect as the activity of my brain—viewed, incidentally, not as a 'spongy mass' but as an information system. The problem is, of course, to find the right categories in terms of which to analyse the brain activity so that any correlates may be spotted. It is because the notion of 'operations on information' is one of the few generic concepts applicable at both the mental and the physical level that operational formulations of mental function are so vital to this enterprise. That they leave out the 'raw feel' of it is one of the reasons for the agnosticism I expressed on the issue of consciousness in artefacts; but it is no excuse for obscurantism.

(*d*). Beloff is right to point out that I ignored ESP. I have yet to find anyone who required a demonstration of ESP as evidence of consciousness or mind in others, and my purpose was to deal with 'postulates of impotence' of a less exotic sort. The 'powers' I was speaking of, as the context makes clear, were information-processing powers, and even physical, let alone para-physical, human capacities were not in question. In any case, neither Beloff nor I have any knowledge that a suitable artefact might not perform as well as a human being under ESP test conditions. The game of *'ignotus per ignotum'* is one that two can play.

Though my statement did not have ESP in view, however, I must add that it would seem strangely misguided to rest the dignity of man on anything as irrational and unreliable as ESP at its alleged best. All that it could demonstrate is that people (and/or people's brains) can influence one another remotely, in presently inexplicable ways. This does not come within miles of justifying an interactionist model of the mind–brain relationship in preference to any other. On all views it would be fascinating, if established, but in no way decisive. Beloff's plea to the contrary is a revealing *non sequitur*.

(*e*). I claim that there is no Biblical support for interactionism, in preference to a view of man as a (mysterious) unity with multiple aspects. Why is Beloff so angry? As I have argued elsewhere,[24] the claims of Christ are open to test in other and more deep-going respects if a man is ready to follow up the consequences of discovering their truth. Beloff's professed fears are therefore groundless, as well as irrelevant to the issue.

To state that a personalistic account of human behaviour would be rendered 'otiose and empty' by a physicalistic account is simply wrong. As I have shown elsewhere (refs. 13, 15, 16) any attempt to claim universal application for the physicalist language breaks down precisely where it matters most—not only in self-description, but also in dialogue. This is, I think, the right direction in which to find an answer to Beloff's question on the necessity of personalistic language. To talk as if theories of non-physical disturbance of brain function were the only justification for such language, psychological or logical is, I am afraid, a confusion of the issue and (to use Beloff's term) 'absurd'.

[24] *Science and Christian Faith Today*, Falcon Press, 1960 and 'Science and Religion' in *Science in its Context* ed. by J. K. Brierley (Heinemann, 1964).

MIND AND MATTER
Anthony Quinton

I

THE view that the mental and the physical have radically different kinds of existence is described by Professor Ryle as 'Descartes' Myth'. He goes on to admit that 'it would not be true to say that the official doctrine derives solely from Descartes' theories'. But whatever anticipations of it may be found in Plato, the Stoics or St. Augustine or even in the most primitive forms of language it is nowhere more simply, forcibly and comprehensively stated than in the writings of Descartes. Although the distinction has been of the first importance in all subsequent philosophy and has been taken by most philosophers to have almost self-evident validity, Descartes' way of formulating it has not been replaced or even substantially improved upon.

His version of the distinction can be given in two familiar quotations. 'Extension in length, breadth and depth constitutes the nature of corporeal substance; and thought the nature of thinking substance. For every other thing that can be attributed to body presupposes extension and is only some mode of an extended thing; as all the properties we discover in the mind are only diverse modes of thinking.'[1] 'Because on the one hand I have a clear and distinct idea of myself, in as far as I am only a thinking and unextended thing, and as on the other hand I possess a distinct idea of body in as far as it is only an extended and unthinking thing it is certain that I, that is my mind by which I am what I am, is entirely and truly distinct from my body and may exist without it.'[2]

---

[1] *Principles of Philosophy*, I, lii.   [2] *Meditations*, VI.

On this view the mental and the physical are exclusive of one another. Each is the possessor of a positive essential attribute. The mental is conscious and the physical is in space while the mental is not in space and the physical is not conscious. As far as temporal things go the two categories seem also to be exhaustive. Everything in time is either in space or not in space. If it is in space it is physical. If it is not in space then it is mental and therefore conscious.

Both sides of Descartes' contrast call for investigation. On the one hand many *prima facie* mental things are in some sense extended or spatial: pains and other bodily sensations, sense-impressions and dreams. With consciousness the problem is rather that of discovering what precisely is meant by saying that all and only the conscious is mental. Does it mean that the mental is essentially a subject, conscious of something, or that it is essentially an object of consciousness? It seems reasonable to say that minds, the most substantial of mental things, are by definition *subjects* of consciousness. Brentano, in holding that it is characteristic of mental facts to be intentional, to be awarenesses of objects, extends this idea from minds to the mental events of which they consist or in which they figure. But it can equally reasonably be held that the mental is an object of consciousness, at least of direct or immediate consciousness. Descartes himself favours this interpretation when he observes: 'By the word *thought* I understand all that which so takes place in us that we of ourselves are immediately conscious of it'.[3]

My object in examining Descartes' distinction is not only to test its correctness. I aim to see whether, in any form it may be given, it is an irreducible obstacle to the theory that there is a contingent identity between mental states and what are usually held to be corresponding but numerically distinct states of the brain. Before starting there are two preliminary matters to settle. First, I must consider the fashionable opinion that there is really nothing here to discuss. Secondly, I must establish my claim that Descartes' account of the distinction has not been substantially improved upon or superseded.

[3] *Principles*, I, ix.

2

In the present philosophical atmosphere there is an almost reflex hostility to inquiries of this kind into the nature of the traditional technical terms of philosophy. Why, it will be asked, do you assume that everything we can mention must be either mental or physical? Why, for that matter, do you assume that there is any one distinction or any clear distinction between them at all? In entering on this inquiry one is not in fact making either of these assumptions. To examine the distinction between the mental and the physical is not to be committed from the start to the position that there is one at all or that there is only one, let alone that it is an exhaustive distinction. The idea that there is a clear and exhaustive distinction between the two realms is the subject-matter and not the presupposition of the inquiry. It has been widely held by philosophers as a matter of explicit belief that there is such a distinction and something of the sort is taken for granted by ordinary men. Unless there is some such distinction, whether exhaustive or not, there can be no such thing as the mind–body problem and both dualism and the identity theory that opposes it must be equally confusions. Since there is a large measure of intuitive agreement as to what falls in each realm I take it to be fairly obvious that there is some distinction. No doubt the concepts of the mental and the physical have been much handled by philosophers. But they have either come to have or else retained a life of their own in common discourse. It would be generally agreed that mountains, clouds, snowflakes and protein molecules are physical and that a farmer's hope for rain, a man's image of Salisbury cathedral and someone's feeling of embarrassment are mental. But there are plenty of controversial cases. Such visual phenomena as the sky, shadows and rainbows are only insecurely physical. On the other hand pains and sense-data would not be universally agreed to be mental. It is by reference to this measure of intuitive agreement that the adequacy of any proposed account of the distinction must be tested. Critical instances for testing its adequacy must be drawn only from the area where there is intuitive agreement.

The intuitively mental is more varied in form than is generally allowed for in philosophical discussion. Philosophers tend to fasten on a particular kind of instance of mentality, on such momentary and rather noticeable happenings as a sudden fit of annoyance or pang of despair. But what we intuitively regard as mental is not all as granular or bitty as this propensity tends to suggest. As well as events there are what might be called states and traits. By a state I mean some such more or less persisting condition as a belief or the desire for a long-term end. Traits are such things as generosity, a good memory and the ability to speak a foreign language, all the more or less permanent property of their owners. Of all mental things traits are the most amenable to analysis as behavioural dispositions in the manner of Ryle. Their possessors either have no more privileged access to them than anyone else or are even less well situated than others for detecting them. States, on the other hand, although intimately connected with dispositions to behaviour are not so readily identifiable with them. Events are the most resistant of all. There is no hard and fast distinction between these three kinds of mental entity. It is enough that we should be aware of the variety that the classification reveals. Philosophers have been comparably selective in their treatment of physical things. Articles of domestic furniture have notoriously been the epistemologist's favourite object of study: visible and tangible things of the same general order of magnitude as the human body which, like the human body, are clearly separated from their physical environment by a definite boundary and retain their observable characteristics, in particular their shape, for longish periods. Many physical things are not at all like this. They can have much greater or smaller size and duration: consider continents and germs, atoms and lightning-flashes. They may have no definite shape at any time, like fogs, or fail to retain their shape through time, like puddles.

3

There is a most useful survey of alternative, non-Cartesian, ways of formulating the mind-matter distinction in Feigl's *The Mental and the Physical.*[4] He considers five possible criteria of the mental besides non-spatiality and consciousness in the two senses I have mentioned. These identify the mental with the qualitative, the purposive, the mnemic, the holistic and the emergent. Only the first two of these will detain us for any length of time.

[4] Minnesota Studies in the Philosophy of Science, Vol. 2.

(1) The idea that the mental is intrinsically non-quantitative, that it cannot be numerically measured, has much to recommend it. Ryle often conducts his polemic against inner mental entities by asking rhetorical questions about, for example, the number of acts of will or inferences one performed in the period between breakfast and lunch. Certainly some of the rhetoric dissolves on closer inspection. A business man who has been thinking about economies can, when he is asked what he has been doing for the last half hour, truly and intelligibly answer that he has been making four painful decisions. But would he be able to give a confident answer to the question whether these four were the *only* decisions he took in the period? The four he refers to are those he is now ready to pronounce and to stand by. But if he had been called on for a progress report during his reflective half hour he might well have announced decisions not in the final list. To some extent his confusion could be attributed to an insufficiency of data. At the end of the half hour he will not remember without effort much of the detail of his thinking. But even if he had been thinking aloud throughout into a tape-recorder the resulting monologue would have been hard to interpret. For how long does he have to embrace a possibility for it to count as a decision? And how firmly? The first difficulty about quantifying the mental, then, is that of identifying units for the purpose of enumeration.

It may be that the duration of such mental events as fits of bad temper can be measured but their non-temporal characteristics are more elusive. Yet, as Feigl points out, such features as the intensity of emotions can be ranged ordinally, though here too there are difficulties. In comparing the strength of my present desire for a holiday with the similar desire I had six months ago I cannot resurrect the earlier state for direct comparison with the present one. I have to rely on a kind of memory in which I may well feel little confidence. I am quite ready to have my comparative judgment overridden by others who base their opposite judgment on the physical volume of the self-pitying groans I emitted on the two occasions. For full-blooded cardinal measurement we need congruent units and these are not provided by the introspective awareness of our own mental states.

But this last consideration reminds us that, even if introspection yields quantitative information that is only of a rather flimsy enumerative and ordinal kind, the science of experimental

psychology is as resolutely quantitative as any. The study of reaction times, rates of forgetting and intelligence quotients has given
rise to a great deal of quantitatively expressed theory. Now it could
be objected that the psychologist's measurements are irrelevant
to the issue since they relate only to manifest behaviour. But this
objection cannot be sustained. For the behaviour observed must
either be identified with mental life, as by behaviourists of
various sorts, or else be regarded as in some way causally connected to it, as by both dualists and identity theorists. If the
behaviourist view is correct mental phenomena are directly
measurable in a quantitative way. If the causal view is correct
then mental phenomena can be indirectly measured through the
stimuli that give rise to them and the responses they produce.
But then many unquestionably physical phenomena can be
quantitatively measured only in this indirect causal way. We
measure the temperature of bodies of air, to take a familiar example, by considering the effects they have on columns of mercury. Only a dualist who held that mental phenomena varied
quite independently of behaviour, were not even parallel, let alone
causally connected to it, could hold that the measurement of
behaviour was not even an indirect way of measuring the correlated phenomena of mind.

4

(2) The next non-Cartesian criterion is purposiveness. It is often
held that the realm of the mental is distinguished by the fact that
teleological causation prevails within it while mechanical causation is confined to the realm of the physical. There are four points
to be made here. First, it cannot be convincingly maintained that
mechanical causation is wholly absent from the mental domain.
In the simplest cases of association of ideas the relation between
an idea and its associate, between the sight of a striped umbrella
and an image of buckets and spades, is not teleological but
mechanical. Secondly, if by purposiveness is meant the existence
of processes which can be rendered intelligible by interpreting
them as directed towards the achievement of a certain end-state
then the purposive is by no means confined to the domain of the
mental. If a man trying to discover the solution of a geometrical
problem is purposive so is a plant that turns its flowers towards

the sunlight or stretches its roots towards the water. It is only if purpose is understood, in what some would call a literal way, as conscious purpose, that the unquestionably physical is ruled out. But this amendment brings us back to Descartes again. No new criterion has been established. Thirdly, although purpose is exhibited in mental life it is not clear that all mental events fit into a teleological scheme. Common sense distinguishes between intentional mental processes and mere mental happenings, idle, capricious or passive elements in the stream of consciousness. Freud took issue with common sense in this matter. But his doctrine that dreams are the symbolic fulfilment of wishes is, and is put forward as, a contingent, empirical truth. His view is that more of mental life is in fact purposive than we had realized. He does not hold that purposiveness is a defining characteristic of the mental. Finally, it is no longer plausible to hold that teleological and mechanical causation exclude one another. Two large scientific developments of the last hundred years show how teleological processes can be analysed in mechanical terms. Evolutionary biology explains the way in which living matter adapts itself to its environment in terms of the mechanism of inheritance and chance variation. More recently the theory of servo-mechanisms has enabled us to understand and to construct teleological machines.

5

(3) Purposiveness provides an exemplary model for the treatment of other non-Cartesian criteria of mentality. For such criteria are generally exposed to a dilemma. Either they do not apply exclusively to the mental or they have to be amended by the insertion of Cartesian elements. It is not hard to find non-mental events that are mnemic, holistic and emergent in the originally intended sense of these terms. Take the case of mnemic causation, where there is a temporal gap between cause and effect. A bridge may collapse half an hour after a heavy lorry has been driven over it. It may be argued that this is not a proper example of mnemic causation since the temporally separate cause and effect are in fact linked by a sequence of unobserved structural goings-on in the bridge during the intervening period. But we can only rule out a similar linkage between my present hostile attitude to this

red-haired man and my dislike as a child of an unpleasant red-haired schoolmaster by limiting the set of admissible intermediaries to conscious events. And in that case we are back once more with Descartes.

6

We can now embark on our principal business: the investigation of Descartes' account of the distinction between the mental and the physical. To start with we may ask why it is held that the mental is not spatial, or, at any rate, not in space. It does not seem unreasonable to suppose that other people's experiences are where they, or perhaps we should say their bodies, are and where the behaviour that manifests them and their proximate physical causes are to be found. Furthermore we make spatial-sounding remarks about people's mental life. We say that there is a lot of imagination in that boy, that there is a streak of cruelty in that woman, that inside himself he is devoured by ambition. But these figures of speech cannot be taken very seriously. They can be paraphrased in ways that make no reference to space. That boy would show imagination if he were given the opportunity; that woman is occasionally cruel; he is very ambitious but he conceals the fact. Absurd results follow from taking these spatial locutions too seriously. How much room does his imagination take up? How long is her cruel streak? Is the ambition that is devouring him above or below his affection for his parents, to the left or the right of his spinal column? These embarrassing questions are variants of Hume's inquiry 'can anyone conceive of a passion of a yard in length, a foot in breadth or an inch in thickness?' They imply, as it does, that it is nonsense to ascribe spatial position in a literal sense to mental entities.

Feigl tries to resist this line of argument by accusing it of making the trivial point that abstract entities or universals, such as the feeling of motherly love, are not located anywhere. Even if it were relevant this rebuttal would not be obviously correct since in answer to the question 'where is redness' one might just as well answer 'here and here', pointing to a red flag and a tomato, as 'nowhere'. It is not relevant because particular instances of mental universals seem no more intelligibly locatable than the universals themselves. Mary's current feeling of motherly love for a particular child is as little the possessor of size, shape and position as the feeling of motherly love in general.

7

A reason that might be given for the view that the mental is not spatial is that the objects of direct, introspective awareness do not reveal any spatial characteristics. By introspection we can discover the temporal duration, the intensity, the mode and perhaps the object of a feeling but we do not discover anything about its spatial position. On the other hand there are two kinds of rather dubiously mental things which have spatial properties and spatial relations to other things. In the first place there are bodily sensations, on their own or as constituents of powerful emotions, which seem to be at or to pervade regions of the body. Secondly there are what may be generically described as impressions, the constituents of our dreams and more vivid imaginings and the visual and tactual data which are the most important of the supposed immediate objects of perception. These impressions have shape, and they have size and position relative to one another.

But the spatiality of both these kinds of thing is of a suspect, or at any rate marginal, kind. Consider the pain I claim to have in my right ankle. Is this claim rebutted if there is no injury to my right ankle or if I have no right ankle at all? If it is not then what I have claimed is that I have a pain and that it feels as if there were an injury to my right ankle. In this case the pain has only a courtesy position. It cannot have a real position since there may not be such a place as 'in my right ankle'. On the other hand if that I have a pain which feels as if my right ankle were injured is not what I *mean* when I say I have a pain in my right ankle but what I have to retreat to when it is shown that my right ankle is not injured or that I have no right ankle it follows that my unamended claim is partly about the location of something physical, namely my injury. But in neither case is the pain itself literally in my right ankle in the way that my right ankle-bone is.

Impressions are less convincingly spatial than bodily sensations. They can have shape but they have size and position only relative to one another. And their position relative to one another can only be stated for non-simultaneous cases by way of conventional points of reference in the visual field; its centre, top and bottom, left and right. There are two ways of taking such a statement about the spatial nature of an impression as 'there is a green patch in the middle of my visual field'. We can take it as it stands as a statement about a phenomenal object in a phenomenal space or we can take it as saying that there appears to be, or that it is as if there were, a green material object in ordinary, public space. In neither case does it imply that the green patch has a real spatial position. This applies even to the most spatial-looking of impressions: after-images. Even if we say that we cannot read the indicator on the bus because an after-image is in the way we do not suppose that it is somewhere out there in between us and the bus. Or if we do suppose this we are simply mistaken.

If the spatiality of impressions and bodily sensations is suspect so is the categorization of them as mental. Yet both are mental by the most favoured version of the consciousness criterion. Both are, as much as anything is, private to and directly known by their possessors. Of them, if anything, we have incorrigible knowledge and of them, if anything, is it true that *esse* is *percipi*. They are the most immediate objects of consciousness. The claim that if we believe them to exist they do and if they do exist we must be aware that they do is stronger in their case than any other. However, though both would appear to be objects of consciousness, even to be necessarily objects of infallible consciousness, it has often been denied, most notably by neutral monists like James and Russell, that they are mental. This view that they are the neutral elements out of which both mental and physical things are constructed will be examined later. There is more behind it than the somewhat marginal spatiality of impressions and bodily sensations. There is another version of the consciousness criterion which holds that only subjects or at any rate acts of consciousness are mental. If an infinite regress is to be avoided there must be terminal objects of consciousness which are not themselves consciousness of anything else. Until the consciousness criterion has been examined the marginal spatiality of impressions and bodily sensations cannot be invoked to show that some mental things are spatial, even if the marginal nature of their spatiality is ignored. So far it remains possible that all and only mental things are non-spatial and that all and only physical things are (strictly) spatial.

8

There is, however, a further reason for saying that mental states and events must have a real position. This is that unless experiences have a position in space they cannot be individuated. Suppose that two people, A and B, have qualitatively indistinguishable feelings of annoyance at a high whistling noise in their immediate neighbourhood, beginning at the same time and persisting for the same period. How in these circumstances are we to justify the belief we are very strongly inclined to hold that there are two experiences going on here and not just one? By hypothesis the experiences of A and B are not distinguishable from one another in respect of their temporal and introspectible characteristics. We cannot individuate them as 'the experience caused by the physical stimulus to A's hearing' and 'the experience caused by the physical stimulus to B's hearing'. For these two descriptions do not entail duality of reference. One and the same window can be broken by two different bricks hitting it simultaneously. Nor can we distinguish the two experiences as 'the experience causing A's report and behaviour' and 'the experience causing B's report and behaviour'. Two different bricks can be projected in different directions by a single explosion. It will be of no help to appeal to the supposed requirement that cause and effect must be spatially contiguous. For this principle can only be combined with the view that experiences are causally connected to the physical events that produce or express them, a view common to both dualists and identity-theorists, if it is admitted that experiences have a real spatial position.

The point can be more strikingly brought out by the supposition, which must be admissible to the dualist, that A and B are disembodied. Can the dualist attach any sense to the idea that two experiences of disembodied persons that are strictly contemporaneous and indistinguishable in introspective content are really distinct and not one and the same experience? In fact he will probably attach the experiences in question to some ghostly but really located surrogate, a shade or spectral voice, to carry out the indispensable positioning work ordinarily done by the body.

Could the dualist preserve the distinctness of such a pair of indiscriminable experiences by claiming that they are distinguished by their respective relations to different mental or spiritual substances? Even if we ignore the difficulty of making clear what more there is to saying that an experience is owned by a mental substance than that it is a member of a particular related series of experiences this is of no help. For how is it to be shown that a single experience cannot be owned by two such substances?

The dualist must admit that if experiences are radically non-spatial it is logically possible, whether or not it ever actually happens, that one and the same experience should occur in the history of two distinct selves. But if this is admitted then experiences can no longer be private in the most primitive sense of the term, that of being owned by one and only one person. And if they are not necessarily private in that sense then there is no reason to hold that they are necessarily private in any other, epistemologically more interesting, sense such as being necessarily known directly or authoritatively by one and only one person.

9

I suggest, then, that in our ordinary understanding of the matter an experience is where the body of the person who has it is. We already speak as if this were so and it is, of course, admitted by both kinds of behaviourist. Old-fashioned categorical or steam behaviourists, by identifying experiences with small movements of the larynx or other parts of the body, inevitably assign the unquestionable spatial position of the latter to the former. For dispositional behaviourists it is not necessary that the dispositions with which they identify mental states should issue in any public, physical manifestations. But a disposition cannot exist in a dis-embodied way. It must have a bearer even if it does not have to be manifested. The identity-theorist would go further and say that, here as elsewhere, a disposition must have an underlying explanatory structure as well as a bearer but he agrees with behaviourists that experiences must be located somewhere in the body.

What sort of position do mental entities have on this view? Is it *totum in toto* and *totum in qualibet parte*, which, Hume says, is much as if we should say that a thing is in a certain place and yet is not there? Hume's argument to prove that only what can be seen or touched is in space and thus that 'an object can exist but be nowhere' is unconvincing. Take the case of a smell. It can be literally present in a certain region of space without our knowing what visible or tangible object is its cause, indeed without its having any cause. A cellar can still smell after the dead cat that caused the smell has been removed and cremated. This smell, though hardly a material object, is still a physical thing. It should not be confused with the olfactory experiences of people who visit the cellar. The known fact that it is in the cellar will deter people from getting into a position where they have such experiences. Unlike standard material objects it has no definite shape and size. It will rather have a focus of maximum intensity and exist with diminishing force as the distance from this focus increases. It need not terminate in a definite surface though in the case of a well-sealed cellar it may be sharply bounded by the inner surface of the cellar. Perhaps we should not have any conception of space unless there were visible and tangible things but it does not follow from this that only the visible and the tangible is in space.

In this respect heat and noises are like smells. Common sense gives them a rough, indeterminate location in space. Scientific investigation then makes the findings of unassisted observation more precise. It shows that the roughly located thermal, auditory and olfactory entities of common observation are in fact rather complicated physical processes whose constituents have a definite position in space at any one time.

The situation is much the same with experiences as with these non-material physical things. Commonsense ascribes a rough position to them, one sufficient to distinguish them from qualitatively identical experiences that are strictly contemporaneous with them, by locating them in the bodies of their owners. The fact that their proximate causes and effects are in these bodies makes this the obvious thing to do. It is then up to neurophysiology to establish the precise position of the events or states within the region roughly assigned to them by common observation. It does not follow from the proposition that mental entities have a real, if indeterminate, position in space that the identity theory is correct. It might be that they are where the bodies of their owners are and nothing more. But then one could perversely take this line about noises and smells. However, our success in eliminating parallel indeterminacies of position gives us good inductive reason for thinking that we shall bring off the same improvement in this case.

10

Before concluding this part of the discussion there are two points to be made. First, even if the phenomenon of gravitational attraction leads us to admit action at a distance and abandon the principle that cause and effect are spatially contiguous this does not make the dualist belief in interaction between the spatial and the non-spatial any more attractive. By locating the mental causes of speech and behaviour in the body we at least locate both cause and effect somewhere in space and define a region within which a possible intermediary mechanism could be found.

Secondly, by locating experiences in the bodies of their owners we provide a more solid support for the Berkeleyan principle that every mental state must have an owner than the intuitive irresistibility which is the best that such defenders of it as McTaggart and Ayer have been able to provide.

Spatiality does not distinguish the physical from the mental. If it is argued that the spatiality accorded to the mental by the individuation argument is of a weak and suspect kind the criterion is not rescued. Many unquestionably physical things are spatial only in the weak sense which is all that the argument ascribes to the mental. Furthermore, the fact that noises and smells are weakly spatial in the way that experiences are does not rule out the discovery of their strongly spatial characteristics.

If it were necessary that mental entities should not be spatial, if the ascription of spatial characteristics to them were contradictory or nonsensical it would have been disastrous for the identity theory. For it claims that mental entities do have a precise location in the brain. But in fact there are good reasons for saying that mental entities have at least a rough position in space of a kind which here, as in other cases, scientific inquiry may render more precise. It is often asked what criterion is invoked by the identification of mind and brain. The answer is a rough spatio-temporal coincidence (which if perfect would, of course, be an entirely sufficient criterion of identity), supported by concomitant variation of properties. It is the same criterion that we employ when we identify a physical sound or smell with some state of the molecules in the region of the sound or smell in question.

II

We are left, then, with the other Cartesian criterion which identifies the mental with the conscious. I have already mentioned the
fact that it can be taken in two ways. Anderson[5] and Colling-
wood[6] have been particularly insistent on this duality which is
often politely noticed but seldom sufficiently taken account of.
To identify the mental with the conscious may be to say that the
mental, alone and always, is what is conscious of something, is a
subject or act of consciousness. It may, on the other hand, mean
that the mental, alone and always, is that which something is
conscious of. The criterion thus has an active form—all and only
consciousness is mental—and a passive form—all and only the
objects of consciousness are mental.

The active form of the criterion, as my formulation suggests,
can itself be understood in two different ways. It could be taken
to say that the only true mental things are the subjects of consciousness, in other words minds, or perhaps we should say
persons. The other possibility is that only acts of consciousness,
particular consciousnesses of things, are mental. We shall consider
this possibility later.

No one will dispute that all subjects of consciousness are
mental. But it is not obvious that they are mental in an exclusive
way, that they are not also physical. It is well known that Locke
toyed with this idea. It is, he wrote, 'impossible for us, by the
contemplation of our own ideas without revelation to discover
whether omnipotency has not given to some systems of matter,
fitly disposed, a power to perceive or think'.[7] And we do, after
all, ascribe consciousness to things that are, at least in part,
material: human beings and the higher animals. Indeed unless we
accept the findings of psychical researchers about spirit messages
and put a certain construction upon them, the only things for
whose consciousness we have direct empirical warrant are, at
least in part, material. The strict dualist will maintain that although all known subjects of consciousness have material *as-
sociates*, whose activities they influence and by whose processes

[5] *Studies in Empirical Philosophy*, Angus and Robertson, 1963, pp. 37–40,
69–70.
[6] *New Leviathan* (Oxford, 1942), p. 37.   [7] *Essay*, IV, 3.6.

they are influenced, these subjects are themselves entirely non-physical. Such purely mental subjects of consciousness have been conceived either as mental substances or as somehow systematically related bodies of experiences. Now even if it is admitted that all subjects of experience conceived in either of these two ways, are mental it would be odd to conclude that *only* such things are mental. Could a mental substance be mental unless the states of consciousness belonging to it were? Could a related body of experiences be mental unless the experiences comprising it were? Being a subject of consciousness is too stringent and exclusive as a necessary condition of mentality. To adopt it is to assert that while minds are mental the experiences they have, or of which they are composed, are not.

Something like this position is characteristic of neutral monism. For neutral monism experiences are the ultimate stuff of the world. The ultimate elements figure in two sorts of complex. They can be constituents of minds or of physical objects. Some experiences —the less arbitrary and subjective sense-impressions—will be present in complexes of both sorts. But some will be present only in minds: images, thoughts and emotions. Even the reductive enthusiasm of Russell's *Analysis Of Mind* leaves images in this position. But only if Russell's concept of the *sensibile*, the entity that resembles a sense-impression in everything but the fact of being sensed by some subject, is accepted, will there be anything that is present only in physical objects. So there is something spurious about the open-mindedness of the neutral monist about the categorial status of experiences. The only elements that are clearly non-mental are the *sensibilia* and it seems more natural to interpret them as hypothetical sense-impressions than as actual ingredients of physical objects. Furthermore, on the theory of mind most congenial to neutral monists, experiences are not literally parts of physical objects though they are literally parts of minds. Neutral monism does not abrogate physics. Physical things are literally composed of smaller physical things. They are logical constructions out of experiences and not wholes composed of them. Thus the supposedly altogether non-mental elements of the neutral monist ontology turn out on closer inspection to be hypothetical constituents of minds and minds are more closely related to the elements of which they are composed than physical objects are to the elements of which they are logically constructed. All the uniferred elements of the neutral monist system are mind-dependent to the extent that they figure in minds and many of them figure in minds without playing any part in the constitution of bodies. So the view that experiences are neutral is deprived of most of its force. All it comes to is that some literal constituents of mind, the ultimate stuff of the world, play a part in the logical construction of physical objects.

12

Still it might reasonably appear that nothing has a better claim to being described as mental than minds, the subjects of consciousness, conceived in the dualist fashion as distinct from the bodies that affect or are affected by them. It is also widely believed that every experience must belong to some mind. For McTaggart and Ayer this is as intuitively self-evident as the other Berkeleyan principle that an experience can belong to only one mind. A grudging respect for it underlies the misgivings about his theory of personal identity expressed in the appendix to Hume's *Treatise*.

> It seems to me [says McTaggart] that it is impossible that there should be any experience that is not part of a self. . . . That proposition seems to me evident, not as a part of the meaning of the term experience, but as a synthetic truth about experience. . . . But it seems to me beyond doubt. . . . Nothing that we know, so far as I can see, suggests the existence to us of impersonal experience. . . . It seems as impossible to me that such a state should belong to more than one self as it is that it should not belong to a self at all.[8]

Ayer is rather more explicit than McTaggart for whom these propositions are ultimate and not susceptible of proof. If the relations between experiences which constitute a mind are factual, he says, 'it is logically conceivable that there should be experiences which were not the experiences of any person'.[9] 'The suggestion that there are experiences which so exist I do find nonsensical; there would seem to be no conceivable way in which its truth or falsehood could be tested.'[10] He resolves the difficulty by saying that 'from the fact that an experience occurs it will follow, on this view, that there are some other experiences to which it bears the relations in question i.e. those constituting personal

---

[8] *The Nature of Existence* (Cambridge, 1927, Vol. II, c. 36, secs. 400–1).
[9] *The Problem of Knowledge* (Penguin Books, Harmondsworth, 1956), p. 217.
[10] *Ibid.*, p. 224.

identity. But the other experiences are not specified. Any statement to the effect that two given experiences are so related will
remain contingent'.[11]

Now if this principle of the logical dependence of experiences
on minds is accepted experiences do become a little insubstantial.
To say that an experience occurs is simply to say that a mind is
affected or active in a certain way. Supporters of the principle
would deny the status of mental things to experiences not so much
because they are not mental as because they are not things. They
are not non-mental things but mental non-things. Is it, as McTaggart and Ayer contend, really impossible to conceive of impersonal
experience, of experience without an owner? The empirically
most familiar type of mind or subject of experience has two
features which are not obviously definitive of mind however
strongly they are contingently implied by it. The minds we know
are, first, rather persistent through time and, secondly, associated
either with human bodies or at any rate with animal bodies in
which the head at least can be clearly discriminated from the rest.
Could we intelligibly ascribe experiences to a momentary thing or
to a thing that was headless and non-animal (even if not exactly
non-animate)?

Men hope to last seventy years and many of them do. But
mentality is not denied to a child that dies at the age of two. How
far can this process be continued? A tree that talked rationally and
manipulated its environment in accordance with stated intentions
would have to be regarded as a subject of consciousness if it
successfully passed the most rigorous tests for fraud. And if that
is allowed why not allow mentality to a conversational matchbox?
Suppose, now, that blowing soap-bubbles one day from a particularly artful solution I hear them talking appropriately in the
few seconds of existence that they have. 'Am I not lovely?' one
says. 'My beauty is all the more poignant because of its short
duration,' says another. A third observes, 'Do not look so sad.
There are more where I came from.' Stolid human observers
agree that these remarks have come from the bubbles and help
me to ensure that no trickery is involved. Would it be so absurd
to say in these circumstances that the bubbles had experienced
self-satisfaction or concern. If we do say this the experiences

[11] *The Problem of Knowledge* (Penguin Books, Harmondsworth, 1956), pp.
224–5.

ascribed still have owners even if they are not temporally persistent nor of a human or higher animal kind. But if we are to rely on the ordinary kind of evidence we have for the existence of experiences these must, it seems, be ascribed to some sort of physically-located owner.

But now suppose that I have a telepathic power. From time to time I find myself firmly convinced, with nothing better to go on than the strength of the conviction, that a particular person is having a particular experience. Checked against the findings of ordinary observation my convictions invariably turn out to be correct. Suppose now that I become convinced that a person whose body I know to have been destroyed is displeased by his wife's remarriage. It would seem possible to accept this, at least as an intelligible conjecture, on the basis of my tested successes.

Can we put these two fantasies together to arrive at the idea of an unlocated subject with only one experience. The two examples suggest that there are two kinds of poverty that an owner of experiences can be conceived to have, as compared with ordinary subjects of consciousness. The bubble suggests that a subject can have only one experience; the dead friend that he need have no bodily location. We can still maintain that an experience must have an owner even if the two poverties are superimposed. The subject in question will have as its only property the fact that it is the owner of the single experience. But there is nothing to distinguish the existence of such a subject from the occurrence of an unowned experience. So if the principle of ownership is to have any substantial content it must be understood to exclude this limiting, trivializing, case of ownership. It must be taken to say that there cannot be single, unlocated experiences. And to prove this we must show that the superimposition is illegitimate.

That there is something fishy about it is suggested by the difficulty, which I have so far evaded, of seeing just how the telepathic conviction of the existence of an unowned experience is to be formulated. 'George resents his wife's remarriage', said after George's death, rests on testable references to George's experiences while he was alive. But what can 'there is now a feeling of gloom' rest on? Existentially formulated telepathic convictions could only be checked against feelings of gloom found in the ordinary way in ordinary subjects.

What seems to show that the superimposition is illegitimate is that both the possibilities envisaged, and not merely the bubble case, presuppose the physical location at some time or other of the subject of the experiences in question. The dead friend must have been a physical thing with a real location in space in the past. Unless this is so my telepathic conviction fails to refer to anything. So every experience must belong to a subject which either has a position in space (and may be momentary) or used to have one (and thus cannot be momentary but must be continuous with some past existent). It does not seem necessary, as Ayer holds, that experiences can only occur if there are other experiences with which they are co-personal. But if they do not satisfy Ayer's condition they must have a current, physically located subject.

Experiences do, then, presuppose subjects, rather in the way that surfaces presuppose volumes. There cannot be a surface without there also being a volume whose surface it is. We may speak loosely of the skin of an orange as being the surface of the orange but it is, of course, a volume itself of a somewhat thin and irregular kind. Just as a true surface is not itself a physical thing but, one has to say, an aspect of a physical thing, so an experience is not itself a mental thing. For an experience to occur is for a subject to be active or affected in a certain way. But even if we should boggle at describing a true surface as a self-subsistent physical object we should not deny that the surface of a physical thing was physical. Similarly although we have reason for denying that an experience is a self-subsistent mental object we need not deny that it is mental. I conclude, therefore, that although there is something to be said for the view that the subjects of consciousness are pre-eminently mental it does not follow that they alone are mental. And it is worth noting that the view that conscious subjects are mental, far from excluding their being physical as well, entails that they either are or have been physical.

13

We may now turn to the other version of the active form of the consciousness criterion which says that what is mental is acts of consciousness, consciousnesses of something. On this view which is essentially Brentano's definition of the mental as the intentional, all and only acts of consciousness directed on to objects which need not literally exist, are mental. That every conscious act or consciousness of something is mental will not be disputed, subject to the qualifications introduced in the last section. It is the other half of Brentano's proposition that is questionable: the principle that everything mental is intentional in character or structure, is an act of consciousness directed on to an object.

Certainly many intuitively mental entities are intentional, as the unquestionable nature of the view that intentionality is a logically sufficient condition of being mental suggests. Beliefs, desires, hopes, fears and so forth are all consciousnesses by a subject of an object of the intentional kind. They do not imply, though they do not exclude, the existence of their objects, if these are individuals, or their truth, if they are propositions. But are all mental entities like this? Consider these three situations. (i) I am anxious about the refusal of my car to start. (ii) I am just anxious and, although aware of the fact, not disposed to pick out any particular thing as the object of my anxiety. (iii) I am anxious about nothing in particular and unaware of the fact. In case (i) the refusal of my car to start is the intentional object of my anxiety. It may well be 'inexistent' if I have forgotten to take the cotton wool out of my ears. But if this is the model for intentionality there is no object in case (ii) unless we rig up some large pseudo-object for my anxiety as Everything or Nothing. A defender of intentionality might argue, however, that my mood of anxiety in case (ii) is itself the object of my self-conscious awareness of what is going on within me. This escape is closed by case (iii), where there are objects in neither of the suggested senses. The state has no object and is not itself the object of self-conscious awareness. It is an irrelevant escape anyway since the mood is not itself shown to be intentional by pointing out that it is the intentional object of some other mental state of awareness which is intentional.

The distinction drawn in the last paragraph of section 2 could, however, be exploited to deal with these recalcitrant cases of seemingly objectless states of mind. It could be argued that intuitively mental states and conditions like objectless depression or the trait of generosity that are not straightforwardly intentional could be analysed as dispositions to perform intentional acts. A merely depressed person is one who is disposed, among other things, to regard all suggested activities with gloom. A generous person is one characteristically motivated by a desire for the happiness of others. The occurrent manifestations of these dispositions are clearly intentional. To view suggested activities without enthusiasm is to believe that they will not prove pleasing, a belief that may well be false. To desire the happiness of another person is to be concerned with an end that may not be actualized. If this sort of interpretation of apparently non-intentional mental states is accepted the intentionality criterion looks quite promising. It must simply be amended to say that every mental entity is, or is a construction out of, intentional states of affairs and that only mental entities are, or are constructions out of, such states of affairs.

14

Acts of consciousness are intentional and acts of consciousness are mental. But this does not entail that every intentional state of affairs is mental. Chisholm[12] has pointed out that we do use intentional constructions in talking about wholly non-mental subject-matter. As examples he gives 'the patient will be immune from the effects of any new epidemics' and 'it is probable that there is life on Venus'. These satisfy one or other of his three formal conditions of intentionality: (i) the accusative of the statement, if substantival, need not refer to anything; (ii) the accusative of the statement, if propositional, need not be true; (iii) the statement contains 'indirect reference' in the sense that it does not entail, together with a true identity-statement about one of its elements, the statement resulting from substitution within it in accordance with the identity-statement. Chisholm argues that any intentional statement about the non-mental can be analysed into a non-intentional statement ('if there are any new epidemics the patient will not be affected by them' or 'there is life in most Venus-like environments') or else it will turn out not to be non-mental after all (e.g. if the probability judgment is interpreted in terms of degree of belief). But statements about the mental, he maintains, are *irreducibly* intentional. This implies a threefold identity between the mental, acts of consciousness (or constructions from them) and what requires irreducibly intentional statements for its description.

There are strong arguments for the irreducibility of intentional

---

[12] *Proc. Arist. Soc.*, **56**, 125, 1955–6.

statements about the mental. Chisholm considers four attempts at the non-intentional rendering of statements about belief, the most discussed, and perhaps theoretically most central, of intentional mental concepts. 'A believes *p*' is interpreted by these theories as follows: (i) A's specific response to the fact stated by *p* has been activated. (Holt); (ii) A is disposed to act in a way which is appropriate to the truth of *p* (Braithwaite); (iii) A is disposed to assent to the utterance of *p* (Carnap, Ayer); (iv) A is in a bodily state which would be satisfied or fulfilled if and only if *p* is true (James). Chisholm has no difficulty in showing that each of these is inadequate as it stands and can only cover the facts of belief if it is hedged around with qualifications that are themselves intentional. Take the third interpretation in terms of verbal behaviour. 'A believes that Paris is the capital of France' does not mean the same as 'A is disposed to assent to the sentence "Paris is the capital of France" ' since A may not understand English. What it does mean is that A is disposed to assent to any utterance which he takes to mean that Paris is the capital of France. But 'takes to mean' is clearly an intentional notion.

15

What follows about the nature of the mental if irreducible intentionality is, as Chisholm contends with some force, an essential feature of it? Chisholm himself is reserved about the further philosophical significance of his argument. He confines himself to two points. First, he thinks it would be a mistake to suppose that the linguistic fact to which he has drawn attention 'indicates that there is a ghost in the machine'. He observes here that belief statements seem to be applicable to animals. But dualists do not have to follow Descartes all the way and hold that animals are automata. Many dualists would be happy to admit that animals have ghosts in their machines, that they have thoughts even if they cannot express them in words. His second point is that it is not helpful to try to escape by holding that intentional statements 'do not really say anything', that they are not really true descriptions of fact but have some quite different function. Quine, however, adopts a strategy of this sort.[13] He says 'one may accept the

[13] *Word and Object* (Wiley, 1960, sec. 45).

Brentano thesis either as showing the indispensability of intentional idioms and the importance of an autonomous science of intention or as showing the baselessness of intentional idioms and the emptiness of a science of intention.'[14] He would neither forswear the daily use of the idioms nor hold them to be practically dispensable. But 'if we are limning the true and ultimate structure of reality, the canonical scheme for us is the austere scheme that knows no quotation but direct quotation and no propositional attitudes but only the physical constitution and behaviour of organisms.' In Chisholm's favour it must be said that the capacity of intentional statements for objective, 'scientific', meaningfulness and truth is more solidly established than the requirements laid down *a priori* by Quine for discourse that it is truly objective and scientific.

Popper has been less restrained about the derivation of mentalistic conclusions from the Brentano thesis. He derives Cartesian dualism (the view that 'the body-mind problem arises in its classical Cartesian form') from the impossiblity of producing a causal and physicalistic theory of the descriptive use of language. Mental states exist in addition to behaviour. As well as the behaviour that manifests them there is belief, intention and understanding. Two empirically indistinguishable situations in which words are uttered may differ in that in only one of them is there the intention to describe or name which distinguishes the descriptive from the merely expressive or signalling use of language. To interpret a behaviour-sequence in which the sound 'Mike' is uttered in the presence of a cat of that name is to ascribe 'some kind of *knowledge that* 'Mike' is (by some convention) the name of the cat Mike, and some kind of *intention* to use it as a name.[15]

16

Does the Brentano thesis that irreducible intentionality is an essential attribute of the mental establish dualism in such a way as to rule out the identity theory? Its immediate victim is behaviourism. It aims to prove that there is more to thinking and meaning than verbal and other behaviour, that there are mental

[14] *Word and Object* (Wiley, 1960, p. 221).
[15] *Conjectures and Refutations* (Routledge & Kegan Paul, 1963), p. 298.

processes, accessible to introspection, over and above such behaviour. (And also, perhaps, that there are abstract intentional
objects such as propositions.) But the identity theory does not
deny that mental events and states are introspectible nor that they
are distinct from verbal and other behaviour. It takes them, after
all, to be causally related to such behaviour. What it does maintain is that every such introspectibly discriminable mental state
is also a discriminable brain state. Now if such brain states are not
irreducibly intentional does it follow that they cannot be identical
with mental states? It does not, because the identity theory does
not regard the physical and mental descriptions of states of mind
as *logically* equivalent. Only a contingent identity is claimed for
physical states of the brain and introspectible states of mind. The
theory is not undermined by the fact, if it is a fact, that no intentional description of a state of mind is logically equivalent to any
physical, and thus not irreducibly intentional, statement whatever.
It is wholly consistent with this possibility.

17

The idea that all and only acts of consciousness are mental seems
to rule out from the domain of the mental that class of entities
whose status in this respect is most controversial: sense-impressions and bodily sensations. I shall call these 'feelings'. This
conforms to a long-established philosophical practice although it
is at odds with ordinary speech. (We are not talking about them
when we refer to hurt or powerful or kindly feelings.) The expression has an obvious ambiguity which indicates, without beginning to resolve, a difficult problem. Is a feeling active or
passive? A consciousness of something or an object of consciousness? Or is it, perhaps, both, as the theory of self-intimating
experiences implies by making a logical identification of experiences with their owners' knowledge of them? For those who
distinguish the two, the thing felt and the feeling of it there
would seem to be three possibilities. (i) The thing felt is something non-physical and phenomenal. (ii) The thing felt is physical,
a state of the body or the external world. (iii) The thing felt is not
properly an object of the feeling at all, it is a mode or internal
accusative of it. If the phenomenal theory is adopted, it can be
said that things felt are mental, in which case some mental things

are not subjects of consciousness, or that they are not mental but neutral, in which case only acts of consciousness are mental. It might be objected against (ii), the physical theory of things felt, that one can have a sense-impression without there being any corresponding physical thing, or a bodily sensation without any corresponding injury or bodily disorder. This objection draws attention to an ambiguity in the word 'consciousness'. Understood as intentional act, as it occurs in the phrase 'acts of consciousness', it means, broadly, 'thinking of' and does not entail the existence of its object. But it can also mean 'knowledge' or, more properly perhaps, 'direct knowledge'. A defender of theory (ii) would say that to feel a sense-impression or bodily sensation is to think of a physical thing or bodily state but that it is not necessarily to know anything about one's physical environment or bodily condition.

These considerations prepare the way for the most popular account of the nature of the mental at the present time. It holds that all and only the objects of consciousness, in the second sense of direct awareness or knowledge, are mental. On this view it would seem that some mental things are not acts of consciousness and thus that the active form of the consciousness criterion is incorrect. For otherwise an infinite regress is set up. If everything mental is an act of consciousness and every object of consciousness is mental every object of consciousness is an act of consciousness. If I am conscious of x, x is mental. If x is mental it is an act of consciousness with an object y which is itself mental and so has an object z and so on. This regress can be halted in two ways: either by saying, with (iii) the modal theory, that some acts of consciousness have no objects, or, with the theory of self-intimation, that some acts of consciousness are their own objects.

18

There is also an infinite regress in the other direction, which leads up the hierarchy of consciousness to an impossibly sophisticated height rather than down it to an impossibly primordial object. It is obvious that all acts of consciousness are mental. If everything mental is an object of consciousness, as the criterion under discussion asserts, it follows that every act of consciousness is an object of consciousness, the reverse of the regressive proposition discussed in the last section. If x is an act of consciousness then it must be the object of a further act of consciousness y which itself is the object of z and so on. The falsity of this proposition, demonstrated by its regressiveness, can be shown in a more or less empirical way and so there is less disposition among philosophers to attempt to rescue it. It is empirically falsified, more or less, by the generally recognized existence of mental states whose owners are not conscious (i.e. directly aware) of them: repressed desires or aversions, unnoticed or subliminal perceptions and so forth. (These empirical terminators of the regress play the same part as physical things do in the opposite regress if, as I should contend, theory (ii) is correct.) It is clear, at any rate, that the active and passive versions of the consciousness criterion are incompatible.

Yet it seems obvious that at least one half of the active form of the criterion is correct: its assertion that all acts of consciousness are mental. How can the view that everything mental is an object of consciousness be reconciled with this, if, as seems clear, there are acts of consciousness whose performers are not aware of them? Some have tried to deal with this problem by distinguishing two kinds of mentality. If we say that all and only the objects of consciousness are *directly* mental, we can perhaps go on to define the mental in general in terms of this class of things. Pap, for example, says that the concept can be extended to include phenomena that are causally connected to what is mental in the direct or primary sense.[16] This proposal is inadequate since a blow on a man's knee and the cry he emits though causally connected to his feeling of pain are without doubt merely physical. We should rather define the derivatively mental as that which has similar effects to what is mental in the primary sense. My conscious hostility to a stranger who has injured me resembles my unconscious hostility to my brother since in both cases hostile behaviour is to be found. But only in the former case can admissions of hostility be elicited. Resemblance between causes can support the extension. The stranger and my brother may have treated me in a similar way. In what follows I shall consider only the version of the passive criterion that is not affected by this amendment: the proposition that every object of consciousness is mental.

[16] *Introduction to the Philosophy of Science*, Eyre and Spottiswoode, 1963, p. 382.

19

The claim to be discussed, though currently popular, is of ancient lineage. Descartes, explaining the nature of the thought or consciousness that is the essential attribute of the mental, defines it 'as all that which so takes place in us that we ourselves are immediately conscious of it'.[17] Locke's notorious definition of an idea as 'whatsoever is the object of the understanding when a man thinks'[18] has much the same purport.

It is clear that we cannot attribute mentality to all objects of consciousness in the most inclusive sense of the word. We are, in this sense, conscious of stones and numbers as well as of thoughts, sensations and emotions. The sort of consciousness involved must be rather narrowly specified if we are to hold with any plausibility that all objects of consciousness are mental. The simplest way of specifying the kind of awareness intended is to say that it is introspective. This would be splendid if only the concept of introspection did not already presuppose the concept of the mental. For introspection is simply the acquisition of knowledge or belief, without inference or reliance on testimony, about one's own mental states. This proposal is so good that it is no good at all.

Has introspection any distinguishing marks by which it could be picked out without such a circle-engendering dependence on the concept of the mental? It is characteristically direct or immediate. It is a non-inferential method of acquiring knowledge or beliefs, in which there is no reliance on statable grounds or evidence. We just know we are angry—or we just believe it. It is knowledge without observation—when it is knowledge. If called upon to report our current desires or emotions we do not have to assemble evidence though we may have to reflect, to focus our attention in the appropriate way. This kind of directness is not a guarantee against error. We can quite well say, with complete sincerity, that we are not in the least annoyed when we are palpably furious. Is everything of which we are directly aware in this way mental? Stout observed in *Mind and Matter* that what introspection discloses is not simply states of mind but also states of one's body. The object of direct awareness is not just the mind; it is the embodied self. More recently it has been claimed

[17] *Principles of Philosophy*, I, ix. [18] *Essay*, I, 1.8.

that our awareness of the position of our limbs is a case of know-ledge 'without observation', by which is presumably meant knowledge without evidence. Ayer has remarked, in another con-nection, of the kinaesthetic awareness we have of events in our own bodies. But this is only the beginning of the matter. Anyone who rejects the sense-datum theory of perception must agree that we sometimes have direct knowledge of physical existences other than our bodies and that to a great extent our beliefs about our physical environment are not the outcome of inference.

It may be objected that the sense attached to the term 'direct awareness' in this argument is an irrelevantly psychological one. The type of directness that characterizes our knowledge of our own mental states is logical. It is not the factual absence of in-ference that makes awareness direct but its logical superfluity. To be directly aware of something is to have certain and incorrigible knowledge of its existence and nature.[19]

20

With this we reach the most favoured current criterion of the mental, in its primary, restricted sense, as that which is the object of incorrigible awareness. There is at least a certain negative support for this proposition since nothing physical is the object of awareness of this kind. Though we often have knowledge of physical existences our beliefs about them are never incorrigible in the sense that they could not be false. Of course my true belief that there is a chair here cannot be corrected since it is already correct. It can be improved upon, no doubt, by the addition of more specific detail but if it is true there is no way in which it can be truer. To say that it is not incorrigible, however, is to say that its truth is not entailed by the fact that I believe it.

In most discussions of the subject the concept of incorrigibility is handled somewhat loosely and it may be useful to spend a little time examining it. In particular its relations to what Ryle has described as the supposed phosphorescent or self-intimating property of mental states should be considered. A statement p about some mental state of x is incorrigible when and only when 'x believes that p' (hereafter 'B') entails 'x knows that p' (here-after 'K'). To say it is self-intimating is to say that p entails K.

[19] Cf. Pap, *op. cit.*, p. 379.

Now I take it as obvious that knowledge entails belief (K entails B) and that knowledge entails truth (K entails p). Therefore B entails p where p is incorrigible and p entails B where p is self-intimating. But the definition of incorrigibility leaves open the logical possibility that not B and p, which is impossible if p is self-intimating, and the definition of self-intimation leaves open the logical possibility that not-p and B, which is impossible if p is incorrigible. Neither self-intimation nor incorrigibility, according to these definitions, entails the other. In practice, however, the two concepts are taken to be pretty much the same. There is a fairly reasonable assumption which, together with the premiss that p is self-intimating entails that it is incorrigible. Suppose the logical possibility left open by the fact that p is self-intimating is realized, that is that x believes p although it is false. If so he will be in the mental state correctly described as not-p. But in that case he knows, and therefore believes, that not-p. But he cannot believe that p and that not-p. Therefore the possibility mentioned cannot arise. The assumption involved is that we cannot believe that p and at the same time believe that not-p. This is not, perhaps, generally true but where both p and not-p are statements about one's current mental state it seems pretty reasonable. The other possibility is not so easily extinguishable. Suppose that it is realized: that p is true although x does not believe it. If it followed from x does not believe p that x believes not-p, it would then follow that not-p, contrary to the supposition that p. But it does not in the least follow that x believes that not-p from x does not believe that p. It will therefore be desirable to keep both concepts in mind when discussing this criterion.

21

The result of the discussion could have a crucial bearing on the identity theory. It can be argued that the theory must be mistaken if there are any mental things which are objects of incorrigible knowledge. Lewis[20] has maintained that the objects of direct acquaintance must be what they appear to be and must appear to be what they are. Since they do not generally and unreflectively appear to be states of the brain they cannot be identical

[20] Lewis in 'Some Logical Considerations Concerning the Mental', *Journal of Philosophy*, **38**, 225, 1941.

with states of the brain. As it stands this argument rules out *a priori* the possibility that a sense-impression is caused by a material object when it does not appear to be, and it entails that if a sense-impression appears to be caused by a material object it must actually be caused by it. But it could be argued that the properties of sense-impressions mentioned in these examples are not intrinsic to them. The statements involved mention things that are not objects of direct acquaintance. If this argument can be sustained the dualist's assertion that there is a causal connection between impressions and brain states is legitimate and intelligible but the identity theorist's view that impressions actually are brain-states stands condemned.

Discussions of incorrigibility are closely involved with the problem of the privacy of the mental about which something should be said. The connection between the two concepts is that if only one person can know that something exists nobody else can possibly be in a position to correct him. (Even so it is still possible that he may later correct himself.) I do not think any new principle is really involved here. What does it mean to say that all and only the mental is private? Following Ayer[21] we may distinguish four possibilities. (1) All and only the mental is necessarily owned or had by one person. Some things that are private in this sense are clearly not mental: my legs, my heart and my smile. On the other hand it is not necessary that everything mental has only one owner. Unless we lay it down that mental entities have a position in space it is not inconceivable that two people should share an experience. (2) The mental is what can only be known by one person. Ayer rightly observes that nothing at all satisfies this condition. Of course many things are in fact known only to one person, but they are not all mental and not all mental things are in fact known only to one person. (3) The mental is what can be known directly in the psychological sense to only one person. As things stand I think this is an adequate practical criterion of the mental, provided that the restriction to one person is contingent and not necessary. Telepathy, if it exists at all, is uncommon but it does not seem inconceivable that people should be in this sense directly aware of the experiences of others. If a thing is mental, then, it is, as things are, known directly to only one person. Equally if a thing is known directly to only one person it

[21] *The Concept of a Person,* Macmillan, 1963, ch. 3.

is mental, as things are. For the facts about one's bodily state and position which one can know directly can be known by others in a non-inferential way even if they are often not so known. (4) There remains only the interpretation that identifies the mental with what one person alone can know incorrigibly. If there is incorrigible knowledge it must, of course, be private. But this leads us back to the incorrigibility criterion itself.

22

The proposition we have to consider is that every object of incorrigible knowledge or every self-intimating object is mental. As we have seen this has the negative justification that nothing physical is the object of incorrigible knowledge. It is also the case that nothing physical is self-intimating. I believe that this support is of no real value since nothing whatever is either the object of incorrigible knowledge or self-intimating. I shall not rehearse the arguments for this position in detail since they have been very well set out in recent articles by Mackie[22] and Armstrong.[23] The following are arguments against incorrigibility as defined in section 20 above. (i) To believe something about an object is to ascribe a predicate to it and this involves a comparison with previous, remembered, objects of the same kind. But the memory involved may be mistaken. If it is objected that we do not *think* of these earlier objects now, it can still be said that the ascription of predicates is a learnt, skilled activity which we may not have mastered perfectly. (2) The formation of a belief about an experience takes time, during which the known fallibility of memory may operate. (3) I may believe that this experience is φ, that it is just like an experience I had a little while ago and remember that I believed that experience to have some property incompatible with φ. These three things cannot be consistently asserted together and it is not necessary to exempt the first of them from revision. The following arguments are directed against self-intimation. (4) We often have experiences about which we do not know what to believe, such as Ayer's lines which do not seem notably different or the same in length. (5) There must be a difference between having an experience and noticing or recog-

[22] *Australasian Journal of Philosophy*, **41**, 12, May 1963.
[23] *Philosophical Review*, **72**, 417, October 1963.

nizing it. Introspection suggests this. If my attention is momentarily distracted when I have a toothache it is more natural to say that I ceased to notice or be aware of it than that it ceased to exist. But even if it were contingently true that whenever I have a certain experience I know that I have it that experience would only be self-intimating if to have it were logically equivalent to knowing that one had it. But in that case an infinite regress would be generated. For what is it that one knows? That one knows that one knows that one knows. . . ?

If, as I believe, there are no incorrigible beliefs (which is not to say that there are no beliefs that are known to be true) and no self-intimating experiences (which is not to say that there are no experiences of whose existence and nature we are immediately conscious) it follows from the principle that all and only what is incorrigibly known or self-intimating (or, to take up some earlier points, is inferred by analogy from or constructed out of such things) is mental that nothing is mental, a *reductio ad absurdum* of the criterion. But what criterion can I offer in its place? As a supporter of the identity theory I must attach some sense to the assertion that mental states are identical with certain states of the brain. What I suggest is that the mental is not in fact very sharply marked off from the merely physical, that it consists of those states of affairs of which we can have direct awareness in the psychological sense, if we reflect or direct our attention appropriately, and which are private to the extent that there is no well-established way in which others, or I myself using other methods than attentive reflection or introspection, can check up on, except by inference. In the light of the identity theory this is, of course, only a provisional criterion. If that theory is accepted the criterion of the mental is the cerebral. But when it is accepted the provisional criterion ceases to apply since there is now a direct check on the findings of introspection in the form of observation of what is going on in the brain.

COMMENT BY C. J. DUCASSE

My criticism of Mr. Quinton's essay, as of so much of what philosophers write, is that the key terms of his arguments are not defined precisely and responsibly, or defined at all, and are therefore left ambiguous or metaphorical; and hence have no firm or far-reaching implications. So no conclusions having title to the name of know-ledge, as distinguished from merely opinion, can result. An example of this defect would be Quinton's speaking of 'experiences' without differ-entiating between the two senses of the term (distinguished in p. 95 of my own essay.)

Again, at various places, Quinton speaks of experiences as being 'owned' by a person (e.g. top of p. 212). This is but a vague metaphor. The statement made in the last lines of his Section 4 (page 207) is simply false; for it does not take account of the ultimate difference between telism and mechanism. A servo-mechanism, no matter how elaborate, is still a mechanism only. It may have been constructed by a *purposive being p* for the purpose of providing the eventual *users* of it with a mechanism that will enable them to achieve automatically certain of *their* purposes. But the servo-mechanism does not *itself entertain a purpose* in the sense in which its constructor did and its users do.[24]

Again, Quinton fails to make the crucial distinction between *states* of consciousness, and *objects* of consciousness. Some *objects* of con-sciousness may be certain *states* of consciousness (e.g. one's yesterday's feelings being remembered today) but a state of consciousness may occur without ever being an *object* of consciousness' i.e. without ever being *introspected*; i.e. without ever being *attended to*. (Cf. my own essay, where sadness is used as an illustration of this point.)

1. *Intentionality and the Identity Hypothesis.*

If Brentano is right in saying that all mental events have intentionality and that no physical events have it, this would seem to be a conclusive objection to the Identity Hypothesis. And if he were only right in maintaining that at least *some* mental events have intentionality, where-as no physical event can have it, this would still seem to be a conclusive objection against saying that *those* mental events are also physical ones.

Mr. Quinton's reply is that this is a misunderstanding of the Identity Hypothesis. 'It does not regard the physical and mental descriptions of states of mind as *logically equivalent*. Only a contingent identity is claimed' (Sn. 16, p. 225).

I am greatly puzzled about this contingent identity. Let us consider the relevant rock-bottom facts, and let us formulate them in terms of the instantiation of characteristics. Intentionality is a characteristic which is sometimes instantiated. Let us call it *I*. Being a neurological

[24] See my paper to the 1957 Interamerican Congress of Philosophy, published in *Philosophy and Phenomenological Research* for September 1959.

change of a particular sort is also a characteristic which is sometimes instantiated. Let us call it NC. We have a great deal of empirical evidence for the generalization 'whenever I is instantiated in the history of a particular human being, NC is also instantiated at or about the same time in the history of that human being'.

Now we have a choice between two ways of describing the empirical facts:

(a) On any such occasion there are *two* numerically different but closely correlated events, one of which is an instantiation of I and the other is an instantiation of NC.

(b) On any such occasion, there is a *single* event, which is an instantiation both of I and of NC.

The Identity Theory chooses alternative (b), as I suppose the Double Aspect Theory also does; whereas both Epiphenomenalism and Parallelism choose alternative (a).

But what difference does it make which alternative we choose? It seems to make no *empirical* difference at all. Our predictions, for example, or to put it more generally, our inferences from instantiations of I to instantiations of NC and *vice versa*, remain exactly the same in either case. We notice also that any empirical evidence there is *against* the Identity Hypothesis (e.g. from paranormal phenomena) is equally evidence against Epiphenomenalism and Parallelism. The difference between the two alternative formulations (a) and (b) looks like a purely metaphysical one—in the dyslogistic Positivist sense of the word 'metaphysics'.

Beloff of course rejects alternative (b), the 'single event' alternative. But he also maintains that is the one which is more consonant with the basic ideals of scientific explanation. I suggest, however, that this would only be true if the Identity Theory were proposing a conceptual scheme in which it was made a *matter of definition* that any event instantiating I must also instantiate NC. But that is just what the Identity Theory refuses to do, if Quinton is right.

2. *Disembodied minds and the spatial location of experiences*

The general principle laid down at the beginning of Section 8 is that 'unless experiences have a position in space they cannot be individuated'. If A and B have qualitatively indistinguishable experiences at the same time, why do we say that there are two experiences and not just one? Because they occur in different places. One occurs where Mr. A is and the other occurs where Mr. B is. But now let us suppose that both A and B are disembodied. In that case what ground could we have for saying that there are two qualitatively similar but numerically different experiences occurring at the same time? Should we not be committed to the absurd conclusion that one and the same experience can occur in the history of two distinct selves? Quinton presents this argument as a *reductio ad absurdum* of the Dualist Theory, since it follows from that theory that the existence of disembodied selves is at any rate logically possible.

Now let us imagine a discarnate Dualist philosopher who finds himself still existing after the death of his physical organism, and is wondering how he is to discriminate between the experiences of one discarnate person and the experiences of another. On Quinton's principles this Dualist would have no trouble if his fellow-discarnates (and himself too) were locatable in a non-physical space; and I see no ground for thinking that physical space is the only space there is or can be. It is true that this non-physical space would not serve the purpose we have in mind if it were a wholly private one. But it need not be wholly private, not even if we conceive of it as a 'space of images', as I myself did in the paper included in this volume. It is even conceivable that each person might have an image-body located in this image-space. That is, every discarnate person might have an 'image' body located in an 'image space' (as many believers in life after death have supposed). Again, on Quinton's principles, our discarnate Dualist would have no trouble, though the geometry of 'image space' might be different from the geometry of physical space, and it might take him a little while to get used to it.

Moreover, there might conceivably be other sorts of pluri-dimensional ordering which are *less* like physical space than an image-space or 'mental' space would be. Let us consider the relation of proximity. Swedenborg, I think, held that the equivalent for this in the Next World is an emotional relation. Being very near to someone would amount to liking him very much, and being less near to him would amount to liking him less. Again, it might be suggested that in the Next World the equivalent or analogue of 'being above' consists in being morally better or being at a more advanced stage of spiritual development. On some such lines, we might conceive of an ordered pluri-dimensional manifold in which the basic relations are quite different from ordinary spatial ones, and it might still be sufficient to ensure that each discarnate person could be unambiguously 'located'.

It is just worth while to point out that even in our familiar physical space there are several different ways of being located. Having a point of view is one. It is logically possible that a percipient might have a point of view P at a particular time without being himself in any way extended. He might also have what may be called a 'sphere of action', somewhat on the analogy of a magnetic field. The effects of A's volitions (or indeed of other mental events occurring in him) might be most intense in a certain small region R_1 and spread out from there with diminishing intensity; whereas the effects of B's volitions (or of other mental events in him) might be most intense in another small region R_2 and spread out from there. Yet neither of them need be himself an extended entity.

Moreover, we can think of cases where a person's body has been in a particular place at a particular time, and yet we should hesitate to say that *he* was there. 'Have you ever been in Wigan?' 'Well, I did once pass through it in the train, but I was fast asleep at the time.' In such a case you would certainly mislead your listener if you just answered 'Yes' to his question. On the other hand, suppose you had what psychical researchers call an 'out of the body experience',[25] in which you seemed to yourself to be visiting Wigan, to move about the streets and enter the Town Hall, while your body was asleep or in a coma in London; and suppose that you were able afterwards to give a good deal of correct information about the layout of the streets and the internal furnishings of the Town Hall, information which you had not acquired in any normal manner (e.g. from oral testimony, or from reading guide books). Then we might be inclined to say that you *had* been in Wigan, though in a very strange and paranormal manner. At any rate, an out-of-the-body experience of this kind would come much nearer to being in Wigan than passing through it in a merely bodily manner does, without having any experience of the place at all.

COMMENTS BY J. R. SMYTHIES

In section 7 Mr. Quinton argues that the spatiality of sensations and impressions is 'of a suspect, or at any rate, marginal kind'. His reasons for saying this are (i) the familiar puzzle: 'Where is the pain in my foot?' if I have in fact no foot—e.g. in the case of a phantom limb, and (ii) 'Impressions . . . can have shape but they have size and position only relative to one another.' The reply to (i) would be that the pain 'in' a phantom limb, the phantom limb itself and indeed all somatic sensations are all located in mental space and not physical space—*in* the 'body image' in consciousness and not *in* the physical body. As I have suggested before the basis of much of the confusion about the mind/body relationship lies not so much in 'mind' as in 'body'. So long as we unconsciously take the mass of somatic sensations present in our consciousness to *be* the physical body, it is impossible to make much sense out of the 2 space theory. You may read, for example, Quinton's sec-

[25] See also H. H. P.'s comments on Professor Ducasse's paper, p. 99.

tions 6 and 9 (and elsewhere) and ask if by 'body' he is trying to indicate
(*a*) the somatic sensory field (the 'body-image' of neurology) or (*b*)
the physical body. Also in the case of Flew's comments on Price—
what does 'incorporeal' mean if we wish to make a distinction between
the physical body and the somatic sensory field? The fact that the Ego
is located in the head of the somatic sensory field has led to the (mistaken) belief that the mind must be in the head. Quinton's second
objection can be met by distinguishing—as he does not—between the
various meanings of 'spatial'. We can conveniently distinguish three:
(i) the topological (ii) the 'rough' metrical and (iii) the 'precise' metrical.
To say that anything is spatial in sense (i) is to assert that it (or its
properties) satisfy at least some of the basic statements and theorems of
topology. Clearly sense-data and images (visual and somatic), satisfy
(or exemplify) certain topological concepts such as 'having a boundary',
'between', 'outside', etc. Secondly, it is also a fact that physical objects
themselves 'have size and position only relative to one another'. An
object is large or small only in relation to other objects. It is in the solar
system only in relation to the rest of the solar system and so on. To
say that an object is 1 metre long is only to say that it is the same
length as a certain piece of metal in Paris. Individual sense-data (e.g.
individual after-images) can also clearly be 'large' or 'small' in relation
to each other (and thus exemplify 'rough' metrical relations) and have
relative positions to each other. The *only* difference, in fact, between the
spatiality of sensations and images and the spatiality of objects is the
degree of refinement with which we can make metrical judgments
about them. In the case of sense-data the best we can say is, e.g. that
one is 'between 2 and 3' times longer than another. We can be *certain*
e.g. that, of two after-images compresent in our visual field, A is more
than twice as long, but less than three times as long, as B. But we cannot be sure of any more than that—we cannot say whether A is
'2·5 ×' or '2·7 ×' as long as B. In the case of physical objects we can
carry this degree of accuracy to great lengths but the difference is
purely quantitative and not qualitative.

It is a simple fact of observation that after-images, eidetic images,
mescaline hallucinations, hypnagogic images and indeed somatic
hallucinations are both topologically and metrically spatial. Visual
and somatic sense-data are, by definition, topologically (in my definition) and observably metrically spatial. Thus it makes good sense to
claim that sense-data and images are located in space and that this space
may well be a space of their own.

If this is allowed then we can distinguish between things 'mental' and
things 'physical' in the non-Cartesian manner of 'being in mental space'
in the one case, or 'being in physical space' in the other. My sense-data

and images together with a core of thoughts, emotions and feelings of various kinds are associated with my Ego to constitute my consciousness as 'I' (the observing, introspecting Ego) experience it, and these are all in mental space—my own private sensorium of consciousness—geographically *outside* the physical universe but closely linked thereto by the causal chains of perception and will. More complex states of the single unitary human organism constitute traits, wishes, hopes, the making of inferences, thinking, acts of consciousness, having intentions, etc. But these are all compound of momentary or continuing states of the brain-and-consciousness functional unity. In all respects non-Cartesian dualism is identical to the mechanistic and organic materialism except that it adds to the human organism an *extra* organ—the *sensorium*—compound as we have seen of sense-data, images, thoughts, feelings and the Ego, and located in a space of its own.

Thus Quinton's various possible criteria of the 'mental'—the qualitative, the purposive, the mnemic, the holistic and the emergent and any other such that one wishes to postulate—become merely additional denotations of the word 'mental' that we can adopt or reject as we see fit. The essential hard core distinction postulated by non-Cartesian dualism is that mental *things* are in one space and that physical things are in another.

THE REPRESENTATIVE
THEORY OF PERCEPTION
J. R. Smythies

IN this paper I intend to discuss the representative theory of perception. I think it is true to say that these days most philosophers reject this theory, whereas many neurologists and neurophysiologists accept some muddled version of it. However, in recent years a radically new form of the theory has been put forward and this seems to avoid many of the difficulties that beset previous versions. Most philosophers today are Direct Realists and believe that in perception we are immediately confronted with the physical world. That is, when we open our eyes and notice an expanse of coloured objects presenting themselves in our field of vision, they would say that these are literally the objects—the chairs, tables, trees, etc.—of the common physical world. This is, of course, the view currently taken by the man in the street. The alternative theory derives from Locke and was much in vogue among philosophers in the 1930s. This holds that this same expanse of coloured objects is not literally a direct view or prehension of the common physical world but is a copy or representation of it constructed in some way by our nervous system. Philosophers have given these coloured objects immediately present in our experience a technical name—'sense-data'. And here the first troubles of the representative theory arose. For the definitions of sense-data that were given by prominent sense-datum theorists such as Broad, Price and Russell were epistemological. Sense-data were defined in terms of knowledge, of what is indubitable about perception. As Price says in *Perception*:

> When I see a tomato there is much that I can doubt. (e.g. it may really be a piece of wax, or a reflection or even an hallucination) . . . one thing however I cannot doubt: that there exists a red patch of a round and somewhat bulgy shape, standing out from a background of other colour-patches, and having a certain visual depth, and that this whole field of colour is directly present to my consciousness. What the red patch is, whether a substance, or a state of a substance, or an event, whether it is physical or psychical or neither, are questions that we may doubt about. But that something is red and round then and there I cannot doubt.

This definition led to the criticism, made by G. A. Paul[1] for one, that sense-datum theorists make the mistake of reifying an abstraction, of giving object status to a mere appearance. To this it was replied that nevertheless the sense-datum language was at times useful—although it has appeared increasingly less so as time has gone by. Furthermore it tends to lead to phenomenalism—a theory which seems to make the worst of all possible worlds.

So I would suggest that it is better to use an ostensive definition of sense-data such as was first given by Moore and extended by myself.[2] This is based on the fact that we all have visual after-images and we can all observe directly their behaviour and relations in our visual field. Thus we can define a visual sense-datum as 'any x (that is not itself another after-image) that can be observed to have a spatial relation to a visual after-image: other sense-data (auditory, olfactory, etc.) are, or can be, compresent with x.' You can try this experiment for yourselves and you can decide for yourselves, once you have done so, if you then know what the term sense-datum means. As Quinton[3] says, '. . . my after-image is plainly a spatial thing, it occupies at any one moment a definite position in my visual field . . .' so, although we cannot point to sense-data with our fingers, as Paul would like us to do before we confer any genuine ontological status on them, we can use our own after-images as pointers instead. This ostensive definition leaves all other properties of sense-data, other than their spatial properties, indeterminate. This gives us a great advantage over the epistemological definition which soon ran into the following difficulty. It was based on what was supposed to be certain in perception and so it seemed that statements

---

[1] 'Is there a Problem about Sense-Data?' (*Proc. Aristot. Soc. Suppl.*, XV, 1936).

[2] *Analysis of Perception* (Routledge & Kegan Paul, London, 1956).

[3] 'Space and Times' (*Philosophy*, **37**, 130, 1962).

about sense-data should necessarily be themselves certain. It did not take long for ingenious philosophers to find questions that suggested that some statements about sense-data might not be certain[4] and this would undermine the whole theory. We also get led into difficult, unprofitable and Russellian questions such as whether there could be such things as unsensed sensibilia.

Very well—we now know what sense-data are. What can we say about them? The representative theory (R.T. for short) states that they are pictures, copies or representations of the physical world constructed by the nervous system. Philosophers have brought what they believe to be conclusive arguments against holding this view. But before I consider these I want to get our terminology straight. R.T. does not state that we cannot perceive or see physical objects, nor that we can never really know the nature of physical reality, nor that our ordinary knowledge of the physical world is inevitably inferential. Although these claims have all been put forward in the past, it seems clear that they are false.[5] Modern R.T. merely states that we see or perceive physical objects by means of the mechanisms of perception. These mechanisms include eyes, brain and finally the visual field in consciousness—that is the collection of visual sense-data that makes up a unitary visual field. The Ego can discriminate or observe or sense the properties of sense-data—including hallucinatory sense-data—by taking up what Quinton[6] has called the introspective frame of mind. Of course, we do not normally do this but merely use sense-data to perceive physical objects as unwittingly as we use our hands to deal cards or play cricket. We certainly do not sense sense-data and then make conscious inferences about the physical world that we suppose to lie behind the sense-data. We *can* do this if we are psychologists interested in such phenomena as constancy and the sort of phenomena studied by Ames, Michotte and Gibson.[7] If we ask how it is that sense-data can play this strange double role I would suggest that the answer lies in the singular logic of representative mechanisms. The logical

---

[4] See D. M. Armstrong, *Perception and the Physical World* (Routledge & Kegan Paul, 1961), pp. 37–47.

[5] A. M. Quinton, 'The Problem of Perception' (*Mind*, 64, 28, 1955).

[6] *Ibid.*

[7] See M. D. Vernon, *The Psychology of Perception* (Penguin Books, Harmondsworth, 1962).

relationship between sense-data and physical objects is the same, I suggest, as holds between the images on a television screen and the actual events being televised in the television studio. When we are watching television we normally *see*, and say afterwards that we have seen or watched, the cars racing, the politicians talking, the play enacted before our eyes. No *inference* of any kind is involved. Our vision is as direct as it would have been had we gone to the race track or to the theatre ourselves. This is so because the one is connected to the other by the appropriate mechanism. In contrast some representative mechanisms, such as morse or semaphore, do entail inference. Beloff[8] draws attention in his book to the important difference between mapping and coding mechanisms.

If we apply this model to perception itself—to the relation between sense-data and physical objects—several objections can be made. The first is quite familiar and states: 'If all that you know, or can observe directly, are sense-data, how could you ever find out that there are, in fact, any physical objects behind the impenetrable veil of sense-data that shrouds reality in this way?' As Aaron,[9] for example, says: granted epistemological dualism (i.e. R.T.) '. . . we cannot then prove beyond all doubt, even the existence of the world. . . . From our knowledge of *s* we cannot with certainty deduce the existence of *p*. There is a logical gap which makes the sceptic safe when he rejects our hypothesis. . . . But if any theory leads to so absurd a conclusion we feel we must reject it in the name of common sense.' Armstrong[10] puts the case thus: 'Now, if R.T. is correct, we have no evidence at all for passing from the immediate perception of sense-impressions to the mediate perception of physical objects. . . . This means that we have no good reasons for believing in the existence of physical objects' (p. 29). Note here the idea, that seems to be held by many philosophers, that the only way of finding out something about one set of events *b* by observing another set *a* is by inference: *a* or features of *a*, is *evidence* for *b*, or features of *b*. Their epistemological hero is clearly Sherlock Holmes. I shall make the point here that I have made before and that I shall make again, that representative mechanisms are designed to do just this task with-

---

[8] *The Existence of Mind* (MacGibbon and Kee, London, 1962).

[9] 'The Common-sense View of Sense Perception' (*Proc. Aristot. Soc.*, 50, 1, 1957–8). [10] *Op. cit.*, 1961.

out inference. The logic of evidence and inference do not apply to them.

Mundle[11] is another philosopher who supposes that R.T. states that 'knowledge about all material bodies is inferential, is a hypothesis'. He brings in the additional claim that an R.T. theorist, whatever else he may be, *is* a material body. 'If one's awareness of one's own body is not to be called "immediate", whatever possible use could we find for "immediate awareness"? Presumably defenders of R.T. are too high minded to remember their bodies. (Smythies is an exception, and his theory illustrates the extreme paradoxes which result from applying R.T. to knowledge of one's own body.)' He does not, however, go on to point out what these extreme paradoxes are. However, it is perfectly plain, as Mundle points out, that all sense-data must be treated equally, and, if visual sense-data are held to be representations of external physical objects, then somatic sense-data must be representations of the observer's own physical body and not parts of the physical body itself smuggled into immediate awareness. R.T. applies equally to all modes of perception. The idea that somatic sense-data are just as representative as visual sense-data is familiar to neurologists, who have even coined a word 'body image' to describe the representation in consciousness of the physical body.[12] Phenomena such as the so-called phantom limb offer no problem to R.T.. Mundle's claim however that a phantom limb is simply a compound of images and motor habits is phenomenologically untrue and particularly so, as Hirst points out, in the case of the pain in a phantom limb, which is often excruciating.

I have now presented three examples of this important argument against R.T. In order to reply to it we must surely distinguish certain principles and assumptions underlying it. Firstly the attack is made by a sceptic who demands a *logical proof* of the existence of the physical world. But it is impossible to give any such proof. Moreover, the sceptic is always quoted by the philosopher, but no philosopher ever puts forward these arguments as his own. Armstrong himself adopts a Realist theory in which

11 'Common Sense versus Mr. Hirst's Theory of Perception' (*Proc. Aristot. Soc.*, **60**, 61, 1959–60).

12 See J. R. Smythies, 'The Experience and Description of the Human Body' (*Brain*, **80**, 393, 1957).

perception is held to be *nothing* but the acquiring of knowledge of particular facts about the physical world by means of our senses. In visual illusions there are literally no odd shaped sense-data. There is only our belief—or inclination to believe—that the round penny is elliptical. In hallucination there are no actual sensations—there is literally nothing 'there' at all—there is just my mistaken belief that I am seeing something. He even tries to do without visual experience itself in veridical perception. If, for example, I press on my eye-ball, I would normally say that I could observe two visual fields. Armstrong would say that I had merely suddenly acquired the mistaken belief that everything I saw was double. I find it impossible to believe this theory but that is not the point I wish to make here. The point of all this is that even in this extreme attempt to get away from the Sceptic, Armstrong is in the end himself trapped. For, of course, the Sceptic can ask him 'How do you know which of your beliefs are true and which are false, since there is no intrinsic mark to distinguish true from false beliefs about the physical world? What is in fact true could have been false, what is in fact false could have been true. How then can we know which of our beliefs corresponds to reality? To say that we cannot know is to lapse into scepticism. To say that we just do know, is to lapse into dogmatism.'[13]

Armstrong himself says that proof must start somewhere and, in order to avoid an infinite regress, there must at least be some truths that we know without good reasons. He therefore feels justified in claiming that, 'since immediate [*sic*] perception is, avowedly, the court of last appeal when it comes to questions about physical reality, there is no objection, it seems, to saying that in immediate [*sic*] perception at least, we acquire knowledge of certain facts about the world without good reasons.' This statement is dogmatic and indeed tautological, since 'immediate perception' is *defined* as the acquiring of immediate knowledge (p. 191). It can be rephrased leaving out the legal metaphor: 'Since immediate perception gives us facts about physical reality, therefore we know certain facts about the world without good reasons.' By 'immediate' here Armstrong means 'not inferred from, or suggested by, any further knowledge, or any ground or basis for knowledge.' It should be noted that this meaning of 'immediate' can lead to confusion. For his meaning is epistemological whereas ours is ostensive, since it refers to the immediate contents of experience, and where 'immediate' means 'directly experienced'. The dangers of confusion can be emphasized by pointing out that, if we utilize his sense of 'immediately perceive', our theory becomes a Direct Realist one, since it postulates that we do immediately perceive the physical world: i.e. no inference is involved. Armstrong does make one last attempt to escape the Sceptic by adopting a criterion of coherence between beliefs to distinguish the true—which cohere with each other into some understandable system—and the false—which don't. But the Sceptic makes short work of this for 'if coherence is to be used as a test, we must have a way of discovering that coherence obtains. But what can we ever get except a *belief* that coherence obtains?' So we can see that Armstrong rejects R.T. on the grounds that it cannot cope with sceptical arguments about the existence of the physical world, whereas he himself is unable to deal with sceptical arguments against his own theory except by stating dogmatically: 'immediate perception gives us facts about the physical world'. However, there is another species of Sceptic who can make very short work of this dictum, if it is presented as a necessarily true sceptic-proof basic epistemological statement. The Solipsistic Sceptic is unable to find any evidence to suggest that anything exists outside his small circle of sense-data. No *proof* can possibly be offered to refute this position for anything—any ostensive communication with him from any other human being—carries with it no guarantee other than that particular part of his visual field has those particular characteristics at that particular time. These merely *purport* to be such communications. His private world is just very complex and there are certain clear-cut regularities in it. In his visual field there appear from time to time visual sense-data of the same general shape and type of behaviour as another visual sense-datum or family of sense-data that usually occupies the lower half of his visual field—his 'body'—his collection of somatic sense-data itself is merely correlated with these visual sense-data and also some auditory ones (the sound 'body') and thoughts (the thought 'body') in complex and regular ways. Nothing exists except these complex patterns of private sense-data. No logical argument can possibly overthrow this strange blend of Hume and Kafka. On the other hand, it is not reasonable to accept it as true. But at least we can say that the fact that such a position is *logically* unassailable makes it unlikely that the rival Realist Sceptic's position could be valid, for if it were, it is hard to see how the logically incompatible position of the Solipsistic Sceptic could also be valid since they are both based on the same logical principle. There is also the Historical Sceptic. He maintains that it is possible that the world suddenly came into existence in all its complexity, including human beings with just the right memory traces in their brains, just five seconds ago, or one minute, or one day, or any length of time he likes, ago. No *proof* can be advanced against this view, which makes nonsense of all history and most of science.

These considerations teach us to be more realistic and humble in our ambitions. The task is surely not to provide a logical proof of the existence of the external world nor to convince imaginary Sceptics who are amenable only to one type of conviction—that by rigorous logical proof. It is to present a comprehensive theory that explains all the phenomena of perception and mind and that avoids, as far as we can, all the paradoxes and confusion that beset previous theories. If we can do this in a way that anyone can easily grasp and understand, then surely our task is to convince reasonable men of the possibility and workability of the theory and not to argue with sea-green incorruptible logical Sceptics who demand rigorous proof for every statement, especially for those asserting the existence of anything—as though the existence of things was amenable to logical proof— and who cheat by asking *reasons* for basic statements. Armstrong himself says they are like children who never learn that it is sometimes proper to stop asking 'why?' As Quinton[14] says, 'It is not correct to say that a statement is certain only if there *can* be no reasonable doubt of its truth: a statement is certain, rather, if there *is* no reasonable doubt of its truth.' And if this is the case for 'certainty', how much more so for 'probability'! Armstrong is right in rejecting the Sceptic's argument, but he is wrong in doing so only in defence of his own theory, while allying himself treacherously with the Sceptic in criticism of any rival theory.

These considerations apply equally to Aaron's remarks. Commonsense does not in fact reject outright any theory that allows the sceptical 'possibility' that the external world does not exist.

[14] *Op. cit.,* 1955.

Commonsense has nothing whatever to say on the subject because ordinary people do not normally think of such things or in these terms. Mentally ill people, however, often do think in this way. They may be tortured by obsessional doubts as to whether the world really exists, or they may directly experience a shadowy, unreal, counterfeit world, as in the syndrome known as 'derealization' that follows some disorder, probably of temporal lobe function. Thus the average man's complacent belief in the comfortable solidarity of the commonplace world is merely contingent on the fact that he does not possess those minute alterations of brain function that lead to the painful syndromes described above. If these were very much commoner—imagine the possible fact that half the population developed derealization—commonsense might be much less dogmatic about the reality of the external world and about our means of perceiving it. I am not of course suggesting that the belief in the reality of the external world would disappear under such conditions—merely that a lot of people would have continually to be reassured about it. The anguish of the person with derealization derives from the fact that he can remember the time when the world *was* real. If everyone developed derealization, I suppose that the belief in the reality of the external world might die out with time, or the concept might cease to have meaning. The object of this speculation is really to point out that philosophers have not really paid sufficient attention to this phenomenon. Many normal people can experience this state by the aid of drugs such as mescaline. Therefore the 'commonsense' world would not seem to be a reliable guide in all cases for accepting or rejecting philosophical theories. For small changes in our brains could produce very large changes in so-called 'commonsense', to say nothing of the fact that 'commonsense' takes on a very different guise in different cultures. Furthermore, I think drugs like mescaline help us, by the unprecedented nature in the changes in perception that they produce, to grasp the idea of the logical possibility of solipsism. Once one has experienced a totally hallucinatory complete visual field it becomes easier to understand that one's own 'normal' visual field might logically lack any 'backing' in a similar way—as I said before it would merely last longer and be more complex. Happily we needed to introduce the Solipsistic Sceptic only to counterbalance the Realistic Sceptic. And if we recall the Historical

Sceptic as well, perhaps we can call a plague on all their houses and turn instead to argument with reasonable men who will base their beliefs on probability rather than on certainty, who demand only that an argument is intelligible and not merely immune to the virus of philosophical scepticism and who do not suffer from the misconception that nothing can even be possible unless something else is certain. In which case a sense-datum theorist is justified in claiming that he is reasonably certain of the existence of the external world—and of sense-data—(on opening his eyes there they all are). Armstrong's objection to this (p. 30) is a logical mistake. 'For,' he says, 'surely we are not prepared to degrade bodies into hypotheses.' The *body* is not the hypothesis: the hypothesis is the *statement* 'There are bodies'. Bodies remain just as they were—R.T. has no quarrel with commonsense about the nature of the world. As Hirst[15] says, 'I do not say that perceiving involves framing the hypothesis—only its justification against certain sceptical arguments requires this.'

Since the representative theory cannot be refuted on logical grounds, we have fair warrant to examine it again on its own merits. Direct realism has only one dogmatic statement, 'There are objects' (or perhaps 'We know that there are objects'), for which we have to pay the price of an account of perception riddled with confusion and paradox. R.T. has the disadvantage of having to make two dogmatic statements, 'There are sense-data' and 'There are objects', but from which we gain the advantage of a very simple account of perception free from shock and the sort of tortured linguistic gymnastics that Armstrong and others are forced to use to account for hallucination, illusion and particularly the famous time gap difficulty in Direct Realist theories.

Having dealt with these important logical points I will now present a very brief account of modern R.T. The definition of sense-data given above entails their most important property—extension or spatiality. Whatever relationship we posit between sense-data and physical objects must account satisfactorily for the intrinsic and extrinsic spatial properties and relations of sense-data and images. The direct realist would say that sense-data were literally parts of or the surfaces of, physical objects.

I find myself unable to accept Armstrong's claim that percep-

[15] 'A Reply to Professor Mundle' (*Proc. Aristot. Soc.*, **60**, 79, 1959–60).

tion consists of *nothing* but the acquisition of beliefs about the world and that there is no *content* to experience. The plain fact of the matter is that even in hallucination there is a genuine perceptual object in the visual field over and above what *beliefs* we may form about the matter. There is an absolute phenomenological distinction between an hallucination and a delusion sufficient to wreck Armstrong's theory beyond repair. Likewise—as Beloff[16] points out in his book—we do not get much help from Hirst's claim that illusions and hallucinations can be dealt with by an adverbial analysis of perception. In this, for example, when we press gently on one eye-ball, we do not say that we have two visual fields, but we say that we see one series of objects 'doubly'. But, as Tucker[17] says in his review of Hirst's book in *Mind*, 'It is clear that we can always perform such grammatical feats, but it is equally clear that nothing is gained by doing so.' There have been a variety of attempts to deal with these problems on purely linguistic grounds. However, the problem of perception is not a problem about language, nor is it primarily a problem about the relation of language to the world. It is a problem about the relation of our sensations and the world. It is a problem about what certain statements are *about*. There is a wide-spread confusion about the aims of theories of perception. *My* aim is not to give any logical *justification* for beliefs, or statements, about perception. It is to describe fully the events that constitute perceptual processes. As Quinton[18] says, 'The relationship between experiences and objects, then, neither is nor should be logical. On the contrary it is causal, a matter of psychological fact. Our beliefs about objects are based on experience in a way that requires not justification but explanation.'

A second theory that can correlate sense-data and physical objects is that form of R.T. which *identifies* sense-data with patterns of neuronal activity in our own brains. However I think this can be rejected on the grounds that the geometry of the sensory fields and their contents is non-congruous with any possible pattern of excitation of neurones in the brain and therefore they cannot possibly be identical. It is certainly true that all the *information* concerning the external world (necessary both to construct, from moment to moment, the various sensory fields

---

[16] *Op. cit.*, 1962.   [17] Review in *Mind*, **69**, 569, 1960.
[18] *Op. cit.*, 1955.

and also to direct the major portion of the behaviour of the organism) is coded in the form of various levels of neuronal organization. However, the geometrical properties of sense-data are *given* (in this analysis) and it is logically impossible for sense-data, as such, to be identical with their coded representations in the brain, any more than it is possible for the actual images on a television screen to be *identical* with the complex electronic events going on in the television transmitting station temporally juxtaposed between the studio events and the screen events.

So we come to the third theory. This states that sense-data and images form a spatio-temporal system of their own and bear close causal and temporal relations (but no spatial relations) to events in the physical world and in particular to events in that person's brain. This theory was first put forward by Broad in a slightly modified form in 1923[19] and independently by H. H. Price,[20] H. D. Lewis[21] and myself[22] in 1951–2. The man in the street believes, of course, that there is simply one space in the world and all that there is, is contained within it. However, this is simply an unwitting assumption and has no evidential or *a priori* basis. The assumption has been made because it *seems* self-evident, just as no one thought of denying for a long time the obvious 'fact' that the earth is flat or that the sun goes round the earth. The history of science surely makes it clear, however, that it is precisely those things that seem to be obvious that need the closest scrutiny. The concept that there is only one space in the world derives its support from three main sources. Cosmologists and physicists are usually neither particularly interested in theories of perception, and thus do not question very closely the Direct Realism by which they live their ordinary human lives; nor are they psychologists and thus they have never even considered the idea that *spatial* concepts could be applied to purely mental phenomena as well as to physical phenomena. Thirdly, the sense of our being immersed in one spatio-temporal world derives much from the confusion that most people make between their somatic sense-data (or the body-image) and their physical bodies.

[19] *Scientific Thought* (Routledge & Kegan Paul, London, 1923).

[20] 'Survival and the Idea of Another World' (*Proc. Soc. Psychical Research*, 50, 1, 1953). A Lecture given to the S.P.R. on July 16, 1952: see this volume.

[21] 'Private and Public Space' (*Proc. Aristot. Soc.*, 53, 1952–3).

[22] 'The Extension of Mind' (*J. Soc. Psychical Research*, 36, 477, 1951).

We can postulate that the Universe consists of a plurality of spaces—(or space-times with one temporal but many spatial parameters). It consists of one common physical world containing our physical bodies, stars, planets, trees, houses, etc. It also contains a number of private experiential spaces that each contains a person's sense-data (including his somatic sense-data), his images (including his dream images) and possibly a pure Ego. The theory states that there are no spatial relations between these systems but only causal and temporal ones. If you find it helpful to think of the physical universe as containing some kind of stuff or material, then clearly these experiential worlds also contain stuff or material—of a different sort of course—but which is both extended and capable of bearing causal relations—which is surely 'material' enough. This theory suggests that the visual field (and other sensory fields) of contiguous sense-data is literally part of, in fact the final step in, the visual mechanisms of perception. Its sense-data do not constitute the famous curtain between us and physical objects that opponents of R.T. depict. The proper model is not a pattern on a curtain *hiding* the real view out of the window but the images on a television screen that *reveal* what is going on elsewhere. The logic of perception is the logic of representative mechanisms. The only feature in this account that may seem strange to a physicist is the concept that events in space A may have causal relations with events in another space B. However, there is nothing in the logic of causality—as the logicians Price and Quinton have made plain—that states the causal relations must always obtain between events in the same space. Causality can be boiled down to some such statement as 'when *a* occurs then *b* usually does'. It has nothing to say about space.

A logical argument could be brought against this account based on the verification principle. It may be claimed that we can only say that *a* causes *b* if we can, or at least could in principle, observe *a* and then observe *b* and then note that *b* did follow *a* sufficiently frequently to satisfy our statistical criteria. And it may be claimed that we cannot do this if we claim that physical objects bear causal relations to sense-data, because we can never observe the former directly (under R.T.) but only their alleged effects (i.e. sense-data) and so we cannot fulfil the logical criterion of causality. However, we can reply to this criticism by pointing out that it fails to take into account the peculiar logic of representative mechanisms. If we are watching a game of billiards we can see that the cause of potting the red was the blow it received from white. We observe the contact between white and red and red moving off. We can also do this if we watch the game on television. We see white strike red and red moving off. How then do we establish that what we see on our screens corresponds to what goes on in the studio? We could, of course, go to the studio and the transmitting station and examine all the mechanisms minutely. But, as nobody ever does this, to claim that it would be *necessary* to do so, in order to validate what we see on our screens, would plainly constitute an obsessional defence against the sort of sceptical argument that we have already rejected. The possibility that I could not do this would not engender any suspicious attitude in me toward my television set. If the B.B.C. says that I am watching an International match between Scotland and Ireland I accept that I am doing so. And I do this because I have learned that the B.B.C. is usually trustworthy. Similarly I can regard my perceptual mechanisms as trustworthy because they usually do picture the physical world adequately. The Sceptic can ask how do I know this, to which only the coherence answer can be given. The world of my experience contains very great regularities most easily explained in this way. The Sceptic can, of course, complain about this, but, as even Armstrong's radical and extreme theory of Direct Realism has to refuse to argue with the incorrigible Sceptic at exactly this point, our theory appears to be as epistemologically sound as his.

It is natural to suppose that my perceptual mechanisms represent the external world faithfully enough. The Sceptic asserts that this cannot be proven. However, he has not explored the alternatives sufficiently. If my percepts do not represent the external world faithfully, what then? There are only four possible answers: (i) The solipsistic answer that there is *no* external world, with which we have already dealt. (ii) There is an external world but its nature is unknowable and bears no relation to our sensations. This leaves the great internal consistency of our sensible worlds quite unexplained—except along solipsistic lines—and thus it is no advancement on (i). (iii) That our sensations do bear some relation to the external world but that they systematically misrepresent the events of that world. We can note at once that they cannot misrepresent these events in any *unsystematic* way.

Square objects cannot at one time be represented by square (or squarish) sense-data and at others by round ones; red objects by red sense-data at one time and by blue at others (except under clearly specified conditions). For if I look steadfastly at a square object under standard conditions, it does not arbitrarily change its shape, colour, etc. But a *systematic* misrepresentation is at least conceivable. The perceptual mechanisms could, e.g. present all square objects as round sense-data and vice versa. However this aberration would soon be apparent following, for example, the advance of astronomy. The mathematical analysis of such circular motions as that of a moon round a planet or a piece of lead on a piece of string twirled round would indicate, soon enough, the nature of the peculiar defect in our vision. (iv) Lastly our sense-data could misrepresent objects in minor ways—which of course they do in the many ways discovered by experimental psychologists (constancy effect, contrast, etc.).[23]

R.T. would defend its statement that physical events bear causal relations to sense-data (or to our sensations) on the grounds that we observe the physical events *by means of* a representative mechanism and we observe the sense-data directly. But we certainly *observe* both. There is no logical difference between this problem and determining whether the events on our television screens really do portray events in a studio to which we are denied access. It is only to meet sceptical arguments that we are supposed to have to produce evidence of what went on in the studio by some independent means. For ordinary purposes the coherence of the events depicted by the representative mechanisms with our general body of knowledge is what counts. Imagine, for example, that we surround the head of a young child with a television apparatus cunningly contrived that the child would never find out that it was looking always at a television screen and not 'directly' at the world. The child would learn as much about the world as any other child. And if we removed the apparatus, say after 10 years, would we then say that all the knowledge that the child obtained was false, or had to be checked, or was unjustified, or suspect in any way? If this is true for one child it could be true for all. Thus we can see how sentient beings could acquire a body of knowledge about the physical world over a period of centuries under the mistaken impression that they were looking, as it were,

[23] See Vernon, *op. cit.,* 1962.

directly 'into' the physical world. If they then came to realize that their perceptual mechanisms might work like television rather than telescopes, this would surely in no way undermine their body of knowledge. Knowledge, in our sense of highly reliable information, of one set of events *a* can be obtained by observing another set of events *b* by three ways: (i) if *a* and *b* are identical, (ii) by inference, as when we find a trout in the milk, or (iii) when *a* is connected to *b* by a representative mechanism. Philosophers tend to see perception in terms of (i) and (ii) when it may be (iii) that really counts.

A similar kind of argument could be brought by a linguistic philosopher who could say that words like 'space', 'mechanism', 'representation' were learned with reference to events in the physical world and so cannot be used to describe other kinds of events such as the nature of our visual fields. This can be met by denying that the circumstances under which a word was learned necessarily limits thereafter its denotation to these or cognate circumstances. For example one can describe circumstances where all manner of words could be learned without reference to objects. If we inserted electrodes, for example, into select regions of the occipital and temporal lobes of the brain and stimulated the first to produce a red flash and the second to produce the sound or thought 'red', the person could learn the meaning of 'red' even if he had never seen any red or even any coloured objects. In which case no one would wish to say that thereafter he could only use 'red' with respect to hallucinations. So the linguistic argument would seem to be refuted.

In conclusion then Hirst's contention[24] that the epistemological basis of R.T. can rest securely enough on its claim to give us the best explanation of the world, would seem to be valid. It is admitted that we cannot give any proof to satisfy a sceptic of the existence of the external world. But scepticism relentlessly applied can demolish any theory of perception and, because of the paradoxical and (logically) irrefutable assertions of the Direct Realist Sceptic and the Solipsistic Sceptic, it can even demolish itself. So we have the best possible grounds for saying that R.T. allows us to make the most plausible hypothesis that there is an external world. The verification argument against the causal relations between physical objects and sense-data can be met by claiming

[24] *Op. cit.*, 1959.

that we *can* observe physical objects—by representative mechanism—and so we can observe the causes of their effects—our sensations. We do this by utilizing the principle of coherence for establishing causal relations rather than the principle of the necessity for independent verification. The logic of causality does imply that, in order to say that *a* causes *b*, we should be able to say, if we wish to be taken seriously, that we had observed *a* and had also observed *b*. But it does not imply that we are not to observe *a* by some representative mechanism and *b* 'directly'. Finally the sort of Universe that I have described is certainly a *possible* one. Therefore, any attempt to prove that an *empirically* possible Universe is *logically* impossible seems doomed to failure. As Quinton[25] says:

> My general conclusion, so far, then is that we do have reason for admitting the existence of a plurality of experiential spaces over and above the space of the common world. . . . There is no obvious contradiction in saying that there is such a plurality and, given the implausibility of strictly verbal accounts of private experience, better reason for saying that they do exist than that they do not.

COMMENTS BY LORD BRAIN

There is only one further question on which I want to comment, and that is the multiple space theory which comes into several chapters. I find myself in a difficulty, however, because (page 252) Smythies merely states the theory 'that sense-data and images form a spatio-temporal system of their own and bear close causal and temporal relations (but no spatial relations) to events in the physical world and in particular to events in that person's brain', without explaining why anyone should hold that view or what are the objections to what is described as 'our ordinary belief'. I assume that his reasons for believing that sense-data exist in a space of their own which is different from the space of physical objects are those which he has put forward before and therefore did not think it necessary to state them again. I used to be convinced by those reasons, but I am so no longer. Biologically, perception has been evolved in order to enable living organisms to deal with objects in their environment, to react to their food, their mates, and their enemies, all of which are physical objects. It seems to me that it would be inherently very odd indeed if this reaction were not a direct one to physical objects in some way directly perceived in the space in

[25] *Op. cit.,* 1962.

which they exist, but could only operate through the medium of innumerable private spaces consisting of perceptual objects with one
for each living creature from the insects up to man. I believe that the
difficulty which some philosophers feel in accepting this has arisen
from the fact that they have based their views on perception largely on
vision, and, having constructed a theory which they think necessary to
explain visual experiences, have felt compelled to extend it to other
sensory modalities. If on the other hand, we start from awareness of our
body and its parts, it seems quite unnecessary to suppose that when I
feel my arm in one position in space and move it into another, I am in
some mysterious way aware of it as being in a different space from
physical space. And I say aware of 'it' because it is my arm of which
I am aware and if, by a process of artificial abstraction, I say that I am
aware of it through certain somatic sense-data, I have still no reason to
regard those sense-data as existing in any other space than physical
space. In fact it is by a process of considerable sophistication involving
a knowledge of the functions of the brain and its disorders that I
arrive, if I do, at the idea of a separate space for sense-data. It is this
sophistication which, I think, has led us astray, and I plead guilty to
having been a victim of it myself. The argument which impressed me
was this. Percepts are in some way the product of the activities of the
brain. In many aspects they must differ, therefore, from the physical
objects they represent: colour, for example, is intimately related to the
activity of the visual areas of the brain, and is therefore not a part of
the physical object which is presented to consciousness as coloured.
Nevertheless, the argument continues, the visual objects of our experience are coloured, their coloured surfaces are extended in space, and
therefore sense-data exist in a space which is not that of physical objects. It would take too long to elaborate this view and to discuss in
detail the alternative which now seems to me preferable. Briefly it is
that what I may call the 'photographic film view' of perception, i.e.
that we can consider brain states as a basis of perception in static isolation, is a misleading abstraction. What the brain does is to provide us
with 'information', and I use the term 'information' here in the
technical sense in which it is used in information theory, and not as
Smythies[26] defines it, as 'a statement that something is, or is not, the
case'. To convey information about the spatial position of objects in
the physical world is one of brain's most important functions. This
information takes the form of sense-data. To heighten our powers of
visual discrimination, information relating to the different wavelengths
of light reflected by different objects is represented by differences of
sensory quality we call colour. Difficulties about the spatial localization of

[26] *Brit. J. Phil. Sci.,* 13, 163, 1962.

258

colour only arise when we artificially break up the whole process of perception into objective and subjective elements, which are in fact not self-subsistent. Smythies uses a television set as an illustration of what goes on in the process of perception according to the representative theory, and I could not wish for a better one to support the point of view I am putting forward. The electrical processes which intervene between the television camera and the viewer's screen are highly complex and for the most part quite unrecognizable as representing the objects they portray, and even on the screen the spatial relations of the objects are a complex transformation of those of their originals. But, and this seems to me the important point, they do not exist in a separate space from that of the objects they are portraying, and it does not now seem to me necessary to postulate personal spaces to accommodate phantom limbs or other hallucinations. The brain may be supplied with faulty information or its information-processing system may become disorganized. The result will be misinformation, as in dreams, but I do not think we need additional spaces to house our errors.

COMMENTS BY H. H. PRICE

1. *The logic of representative mechanisms*

Dr. Smythies' version of the Representative Theory differs very considerably from older versions, as he himself points out. He insists as firmly as any 'Direct Realist' that we do perceive physical objects themselves, though he also insists that we do it by means of a complex representative mechanism. Is he having it both ways? Of course we should all like to if we could. But can it be done without falling into inconsistency? Smythies claims that it can, if we pay attention to 'the logic of representative mechanisms'.

He does not formulate this logic in detail. But evidently the crucial point about it is that when we experience a representation of something we can justifiably claim to be non-inferentially aware of the thing represented. For instance, when we watch the Oxford and Cambridge Boat Race on television, it is the Boat Race itself that we see, not just a series of wavy lines on the television screen.

Now I do not think it would be at all plausible to say this if the representation were a static one. When you look at a photograph of someone you have never seen, you are certainly not entitled to say 'Now at last I see him'—not even if you add the qualifying phrase 'in a photograph' or 'by means of a photograph'. Nor would you be entitled to say that you had seen at any rate a bit of the Boat Race if you looked at a 'still' photograph in the *Illustrated London News*. The same applies to portraits and statues. A man might go round many museums and see statues and busts of Marcus Aurelius, and portrait-heads of him on coins; but this would not entitle him to say that he had seen the Emperor himself even once.

But it is a different matter if the representation takes the form of a series of occurrences. One does speak of hearing another person talking on the telephone (a telephone is quite a complicated representative mechanism). We notice however that we should not say this if the telephone were very thoroughly 'scrambled'. The essential requirement seems to be a fairly close correspondence in temporal order between the representing occurrences and the occurrences represented. This requirement is fulfilled by the television screen and the radar screen, but less completely by the cinema screen. The cinema producer may make cuts in his film, discarding some bits altogether, and sticking others together in a different spatial order. The result is that the temporal order in which the representations occur need not correspond very closely with the temporal order of the events represented. Events can be temporally juxtaposed in the representation which were not temporally juxtaposed in reality; and the representation of a later event may precede the representation of an earlier one. But Dr. Smythies could reply that rather similar temporal inaccuracies occur in our sensory representative mechanism too.

This emphasis on the logic of representative mechanisms is the most notable difference between Smythies' version of the Representative Theory and the classical version. Partly it is a difference of technological background. I would suggest that both the exponents and the critics of the classical Representative Theory thought in terms of static pictures. Their model, as it were, for a visual sense-datum was a portrait, and a visual field was something like a very short-lived Dutch landscape painting. In that case we do have to ask what evidence we have or could have that the picture resembles its original. Did it even have an original at all? Was it perhaps a work of pure imagination, like the pictures painted by Hieronymus Bosch? Here Sherlock Holmes really is the appropriate hero (cf. p. 244 of Smythies' paper).

Philosophers at that time were familiar with representations of this static kind, but not with the elaborate representative *mechanisms* which play such a large part in our daily lives in the second half of the twentieth century. These mechanisms provide us with representations of a much more 'life-like' sort, which reproduce a series of events or happenings spread over quite a long period of time, and the temporal order of the representations can correspond very closely with the temporal order of the events represented.

Hence we have acquired the habit of saying 'I saw the Boat Race on television', 'I saw the Derby at the cinema', 'I heard Mr. Harold Wilson speaking on the wireless'. We use these perceptual verbs 'see' and 'hear' because our cognitive state is quite clearly a non-inferential one. And we add the words 'on television', 'at the cinema', 'on the wireless', to refer to the particular sort of representative mechanism by which this non-inferential cognition came about.

In this common-sense way of speaking (for it is or is fast becoming part of the common-sense of industrial societies in the second half of the twentieth century) we do apparently succeed in 'having it both ways'. The television-viewer or cinema-spectator—indeed even the telephone user—is like a Direct Realist philosopher in claiming to have a non-inferential awareness of physical objects and events outside his own organism. And he is like a Representationist Philosopher in admitting that a complicated representative mechanism plays an essential part in the process.

2. *Perceiving and the using of sense-data*

So much for the logic of representative mechanisms. But certain other questions remain to be considered, and it is not very clear to me how Dr. Smythies would answer them. He distinguishes sharply between sensing and perceiving. But though he says a good deal about sensing and about sense-data, he says very little about perceiving. He does say that we 'use' our sense-data to perceive physical objects 'as we use our hands to deal cards and play cricket', and that in both cases this using is unwitting because we do not attend to the entities used. But I think he really tells us very little else about perceiving, as opposed to sensing.

What are we to make of this 'using' of sense-data, and how does it resemble the using our hands to deal cards or play cricket? Sense-data, on the face of it, are very unlike hands. They are not physical entities, for one thing; and if we use them we certainly do not do it by moving them about in physical space. Still, we might perhaps conceive of a sense-datum, or rather of a sense-field, as a kind of *organ*, and in that respect it might be like a hand. We might think of sense-data or sense-fields as a kind of pseudopods which the nervous system continually puts forth, to enable us to 'get in touch with' the world around us. The visual field in particular would be a highly complex and highly plastic kind of pseudopod, capable of changing its internal pattern from moment to moment. We should use it to 'grasp' distant objects.

I am sure that this 'pseudopod' picture is a caricature, but I wonder whether something a little like it was at the back of Smythies' mind when he spoke of using sense-data, and compared this with the using of a bodily organ such as the hand. And it is, I think, possible and perhaps helpful to conceive of sense-data or sense-fields as analogous to very short-lived organs.

But still, how are we supposed to use them? The expressions 'get in touch with' and 'grasp' are obviously metaphorical. What is the cash-value of these metaphors? Here we may remember a comment which some Representationist philosophers have made on the Naïve Realist philosophy. The Naïve Realist theory, they have held, is bad epistemology; but all the same, it is good or fairly good psychology. It is an epistemological error to identify sense-data with physical objects. But it is a psychological fact that the ordinary percipient does identify them, and this identification is precisely what his perceiving (as distinct from sensing) consists in. It is sometimes added that this mistaken identification is a *felix culpa*, so to speak—biologically useful, or even perhaps biologically indispensable, if we are to adapt ourselves rapidly and successfully to our physical environment.

I do not think that Smythies would accept this account of the using of our sense-data (though it is rather like what the television-viewer does with the changing patterns on the television screen). But I am not at all sure what he would propose to substitute for it. Nor am I sure what he would say about the connected problem concerning the status of secondary qualities. They are not explicitly mentioned in his paper, though there is perhaps an oblique reference to them on p. 255, where he asks whether sense-data might systematically misrepresent the physical world.

REPLY TO LORD BRAIN BY J. R. SMYTHIES

In reply to Lord Brain I would say that one's reasons for putting forward a sense-datum theory may be either epistemological or phenomenological. I would support the latter. In which case once one has given an unambiguous definition of 'sense-data' one can then discuss the problems of perception without merely assuming that naïve or direct realism *must* be true. I can see nothing odd in correlating the multiple space theory with the biological evolution of perception. Perception has certainly evolved so that organisms can communicate with their environment and with each other. But it seems to me that this in no way precludes the possibility that this communication system may not also subserve communication between minds, as minds and mind–brain interaction (as I have described them—see my comments on Brain's essay) themselves evolve. Whether there is only one space in the world, or many, must surely be a question of *fact*. If so, one can construct theories of perception and mind–brain relations taking this fact about the world into consideration. I do not see that we can simply assume that there can only be one space in the world nor that direct realism is the only possible theory of perception.

The Multiple space theory has certain advantages and disadvantages when compared with its rivals—but it is in essence a theory about the nature of the world and thus it is possible that the choice between them may eventually be made by experiment. It seems to me that the physics of causal intereactions in n-dimensional space needs working out—(Broad's version of the theory seems more fruitful here). To give one suggestion: the 'mind influences' (that Eccles supposed expressed mind–brain causal interaction) are hardly formulatable in any kind of physical terms under the Cartesian theory for the mind is held to be non-spatial. However, under this new theory they can be expressed in physical terms as follows. The physical events in the brain form a system with certain clear-cut biochemical and biophysical interactions in a 4-dimensional space–time system. A mind-influence could interact with this system and this interaction can be expressed (in the n-dimensional system where $n = 5$ or more) as a vector at right angles to *all* the vectors expressing biophysical interactions. Indeed, if the evidence for ESP and psychokinesis be accepted, these 'mind influences' may operate outside the brain. Once the possible physical properties of such vectors in an n-space are worked out it may be possible to detect their operation physically. Modern physics has by now successfully challenged just about every primitive preconceived notion we have about the nature of the world—except the one that space–time has only 4-dimensions. Perhaps this last assumption should now be seriously challenged.

There are also certain logical difficulties about Brain's arguments. The statement that the brain's main function is to convey information about the world is true for both non-Cartesian dualism and Brain's theory. The latter claims however that *all* important questions of mind-brain relation can be expressed in this form. This is linked with an epistemological concept of 'sense-data'. . . . 'This information takes the form of sense-data.' However, if we use an ostensive definition of sense-data, then it is certainly also true that they convey information about the external world but, and this is the whole point, this is not their *only* property or function. They also have observable *spatial* properties and relations in their own right and this follows inevitably from the ostensive definition employed. The validity of this definition can be called into question, of course, if we adopt some radically behaviourist position (such that there are no after images, but only beliefs that 'I'm seeing something', etc.). But once the validity of the ostensive definition of sense-data is admitted, then the problem of their spatial properties and relations appears as a *separate* problem to their un- doubted information content. And the multiple space theory arises out of the former consideration and not the latter. Both Brain's and my theory regard information as a cardinal concept, but in his case the 'physiology', as it were, takes precedence whereas I, accepting the validity of the sense-datum concept as defined, am more concerned with the spatial relations involved with its 'anatomy', so to speak. And I would argue that answers couched in purely 'physiological' terms cannot take care of all the 'anatomical' problems.

REPLY TO H. H. PRICE BY J. R. SMYTHIES

I think perhaps that my simile of 'using our hands to deal cards' for 'using sense-data in perception' is not a very good one. The only better one I can think of is to fall back on television again—we *use*—in a sense —the images on the television screen to *see* the Boat Race. 'Use' here entails 'make use of'. The simile of the nervous system putting forth pseudopods of sense-data recalls the old 'projection' theory of perception held by neurologists some time ago. A sense-field is certainly, I feel, an organ—not at all like a hand but very like the screen on a television set.

INDEX